CASA MORO

SAM AND SAM CLARK

PHOTOGRAPHS BY
SIMON WHEELER

EBURY PRESS
LONDON

NOTE:

All spoon measures are level unless otherwise specified.

---

5 7 9 10 8 6

Text © Sam and Sam Clark 2004
Photographs © Simon Wheeler 2004
except pages 228, 320 and endpapers © Toby Glanville, and pages 7, 8, 52, 58, 99, 142, 168, 192, 201, 223, 226, 227 and 288 © Sam Clark

First published in the United Kingdom in 2004 by
Ebury Press, 1 Stephen Street, London W1T 1AL

Random House Australia (Pty) Limited
20 Alfred Street, Milsons Point, Sydney, New South Wales 2061, Australia

Random House New Zealand Limited
18 Poland Road, Glenfield, Auckland 10, New Zealand

Random House (Pty) Limited
Endulini, 5A Jubilee Road, Parktown 2193, South Africa

Random House UK Limited Reg. No. 954009

www.randomhouse.co.uk

Design and Art Direction: Caz Hildebrand
Photography: Simon Wheeler simonwheeler@onetel.net.uk
Editorial: Lesley McOwan, Susan Fleming and Patricia Burgess

A CIP catalogue record for this book is available from the British Library.

Papers used by Ebury Press are natural, recyclable products made from wood grown in sustainable forests.

ISBN 13: 9780091894498

Printed and bound in Italy by Graphicom SRL

CONTENTS

CASA MORO   6

LAS ALPUJARRAS AND WILD FOOD   8

BREAD, FLATBREADS AND STUFFED BREADS   28

SOUPS   52

TAPAS AND MEZZE, STARTERS AND LIGHT MEALS   70

SALADS AND COOKED MOROCCAN SALADS   144

FISH MAIN COURSES   170

MEAT MAIN COURSES   192

VEGETABLES   228

GRAINS AND PULSES   248

HOME-MADE AND HOME-CURED   270

PUDDINGS AND CAKES   288

APPENDIX   312

INDEX   316

CASA MORO

The food of Moro has most of its roots in the home. Our main single influence in the last two years has been the fulfilment of our wish to have a house in Spain. It was quite by chance we found this place, and when we got out the map, we realised we must have passed through the Alpujarras, the foothills of the Sierra Nevada, in our camper-van eight years earlier. We took a small road that led to a pueblo (village) and, folding in the wing mirrors, squeezed the car through the narrow streets and parked. We walked up a lane until we came to a stone wall with a warped wooden door. After a couple of kicks it swung open to reveal a neglected garden overgrown with fig, jasmine, brambles and wild grasses, and at the end was a small dwelling. This became our foothold in Spain.

Unknown to us, the village is famous for just one thing. It was where the leader of Spain's last Moorish uprising, Aben Humeya, crowned himself king towards the end of the sixteenth century. How romantic, we thought! How perfect! A few weeks later, we got chatting with an old man in the village who asked where our house was. We told him; he nodded and said, 'Ah si, la casa moro.' We looked at each other and smiled, for our journey had taken us to Casa Moro.

This book has the same cultural culinary mix of Spain and the Muslim Mediterranean as our first. However, we have also included a chapter on the wild foods and traditional dishes we have come across in our Alpujarran village. We are always interested in a sense of place with our food, that place often being the street or home. This book therefore prefers to be at home, as there is no substitute for the love and care of the home cook.

SAM AND SAM CLARK

LAS ALPUJARRAS
AND WILD FOOD

After the Moors were expelled from Granada, they fled to the Alpujarras, where they lived for almost a hundred years. There is a ruin at the edge of the village that is reputed to be the palace of the famous Aben Humeya. In the 1950s, a mysterious man and his wife appeared. He claimed to be closely related to the Spanish royal family, and she a Moroccan princess. They bought the ruin and became obsessed with its excavation in the hope of uncovering Moorish treasure and revealing more of the palace's past. After a few months it is said that all that was found was a sword. The couple vanished, never to be seen again.

In trying to describe life in an Alpujarran village, it is nature that is the strongest image. It is all-encompassing, for physically it is never far away. Each villager cultivates the land; it provides their livelihood and their inspiration every waking day. To the locals we must seem very self-indulgent because we are here for the romance of the land: the mountains, wild flowers and river.

The food of the area is a combination of wild produce and crops introduced by the Moors. They opened up this previously uninhabitable land with acequias (irrigation channels), which allowed new crops and trees to be grown. Of these, the almond is probably the hardiest, and its produce the most versatile. Like country food throughout Spain, Alpujarran fare is uncomplicated and delicious because the ingredients are so good and the hand with which it is cooked so deft.

The following recipes are local dishes we have eaten. We have arranged them seasonally because the seasons are so clearly defined in the Alpujarras and largely dictate what is eaten when.

WINTER

To us the most evocative images of winter are the first settling of snow on the Mulhacén and surrounding peaks of the Sierra Nevada, the auburn spheres of kakis (persimmons) on their naked branches and the crimson seeds of wild pomegranates that have burst open. There is not much in the vegetable plots apart from cardoons, giant cabbages for potajes (stews) and broad bean shoots just emerging from underneath the trees. Only the laden orange trees in the lower valleys are at their peak. Their orange globes and shiny dark green leaves are so perfect they look almost un-real. As the nights and days grow colder, the sweet smell of almond wood fires fills the village. Winter has arrived.

ARROZ DE CONEJO
RABBIT RICE WITH ALMONDS AND ROSEMARY

After days of what seemed like interminable mist and drizzle, we awoke to a cloudless sky. As it was Samuel's birthday, we decided to cook a paella on the river bank. At the height of summer we always seek refuge from the hot sun under a large olive tree, but at this time of year we were able to sit out, and when the odd cloud passed by we had the warmth of the fire. Our children Eve and Luke had fallen asleep on the way, so we had an hour's peace to unpack and start the fire with nearby twigs and bark peelings, the perfect kindling. While the fire was establishing itself, we wandered up the hillside to gather rosemary, a fragrant and essential ingredient for this local rice dish. Paella is traditionally made outside, often at the weekends, when the whole family gathers together, and cooking paella outside has also become one of our favourite pastimes. You can use chicken instead of rabbit if you prefer.

Serves 6 as a starter, 4 as a main course

    1 large good-quality farmed rabbit, approx. 1.2kg in weight

    1 lemon, cut into wedges

    sea salt and black pepper

RABBIT STOCK

    1 onion, halved

    2 carrots, roughly chopped

    1 tomato, halved

    1 head garlic, halved

    3 bay leaves (preferably fresh)

    6 black peppercorns

    2 dried ñoras peppers, broken open, or 1 teaspoon sweet paprika

    75ml white wine

    a handful of parsley stalks

    1.5 litres water

RICE

    6 tablespoons olive oil

    1 large Spanish onion, finely chopped

    1 green pepper, seeded and finely chopped

    3 dried ñoras peppers, seeds and stalks discarded,
        broken up into small pieces, or 1 teaspoon sweet paprika

4 garlic cloves, finely chopped

1 tablespoon finely chopped fresh rosemary

2 tomatoes, cored and roughly chopped

100g whole almonds (skin on is preferable but not
   essential), lightly toasted and roughly ground

a small pinch of saffron (about 20 threads)

250g calasparra (paella) rice

75ml white wine or fino sherry

Get the butcher to remove the legs and shoulders of the rabbit, and to fillet the saddle. Cut the saddle meat into 2cm cubes. Keep the carcass, head and liver. Cut the liver in half.

To make the stock, place the rabbit carcass, including the head, legs and shoulders, in a large saucepan along with the onion, carrot, tomato, garlic, bay, peppercorns, dried peppers or paprika, white wine and parsley stalks. Cover with the water and place on a high heat. When it boils, turn down to a gentle simmer and cook for 1 hour, skimming the top occasionally when scum collects. Remove the stock from the heat, strain, then season with a little salt. Add the saffron and let it infuse for 10 minutes. Set aside. Save the legs and shoulders, but discard the rest. When they are cool enough to handle, pull away the meat from the bone and shred in medium pieces. Set aside.

When you are ready to cook the rice, heat 2 tablespoons of the olive oil in a 30–40cm paella pan or frying pan over a medium to high heat. When the oil is hot and just beginning to smoke, add the pieces of saddle and liver and stir-fry until sealed on all sides but fractionally undercooked in the centre. Pour the saddle and any of its juices into a bowl and put to one side. Wipe the pan clean with kitchen paper and put back on the heat. Add the remaining olive oil and, when it is hot, the onion and peppers, and cook for 15–20 minutes, stirring every so often. Turn down the heat to medium, add the chopped garlic and rosemary and cook for a further 5 minutes. Add the tomato and almonds, and cook until the garlic and onion have some colour and are sweet. Now add the rice to the pan and stir for 1 minute to coat with the vegetables and oil. (Up to now everything can be done in advance and you need only continue 20 minutes before you wish to eat.)

Put the heat to medium to high and add the white wine or fino to the pan, followed by 1 litre of the hot stock and season perfectly. Do not stir the rice after this as it affects the channels of stock, which allow the rice to cook evenly. Simmer for 10 minutes or until there is just a little liquid above the rice. Spread the shredded meat of the leg and shoulder and cubes of saddle evenly over the rice along with their juices. Push each piece of rabbit under the stock. Gently shake the pan to

prevent sticking and turn the heat down to low. Cook for 5 more minutes or until there is just a little liquid left at the bottom of the rice. Turn off the heat and cover the pan tightly with foil. Let the rice sit for 3–5 minutes before serving with wedges of lemon.

Note

If you are tempted to make a paella as part of a picnic, as in Spain, then our tips are as follows. Get to the moment where you have prepared your pan of the softened base of onion, peppers and garlic and mixed it with the rice in the comfort of your kitchen. Then cover it with foil (you can re-use the foil at the end of the cooking), take a bottle of white wine or sherry (which you can also drink with paella), a tub or Thermos of stock (preferably hot) and a parcel of the prepared meat. If you might struggle to find firewood in your picnic spot, it is possible to cook a paella for four on a large disposable barbecue. Just don't forget the matches!

WINTER LEAVES WITH FRISÉE, FRESH CHEESE, POMEGRANATES AND WALNUTS

Even in winter, there are wild leaves and greens to collect. Before the rains, the best place to find them is along the river. The abundance of snow on the mountains ensures plenty of meltwater in the rivers below. One of our favourite walks is along the river bank to the local town to do the shopping, and on the way we often forage for leaves. We collect vinagrera (sorrel), or cerrajas (leaves that look like those of dandelion but have a slight purple tinge at the base). We mix these leaves with frisée, and make a salad, a version of which we describe here.

Serves 4

300g Fresh Cheese (see pages 278–9)

$^1/_2$ garlic clove, crushed to a paste with salt

2 teaspoons fresh thyme leaves

150g frisée salad or a mix of frisée and escarole or mâche

a good handful each of sorrel leaves and watercress (50g each)

25g cerrajas or dandelion leaves (optional)

4 tablespoons extra virgin olive oil

$1^1/_2$ tablespoons red wine vinegar

seeds of 1 pomegranate

75g shelled walnuts, roughly chopped

sea salt and black pepper

Mix the cheese with the garlic and thyme and taste for seasoning. Place in the middle of a plate. Place the salad leaves in a bowl, pour over the olive oil and vinegar, season with salt and pepper and toss. Arrange the salad around the edge of the plate and sprinkle the pomegranate seeds and walnuts on top.

SPRING

One of the first signs of spring is the almond blossom. The steep slopes of the Alpujarras are terraced with a vast patchwork of the contorted black trunks of almond trees. The white blossom can be so delicate that it's barely noticeable at first, but then your eye catches the subtle veil. As you stand underneath the trees, the air vibrates with the gentle buzz of bees. At its height, spring is a mass of colours from the various wild flowers and shrubs, such as marguerites, poppies, sweet peas, roses, lavender and cistus.

Wanting to learn more about the local, edible wild greens, we recruited Josefa Castillo, who runs a health-food shop in town. As we walked through the countryside, she pointed out various leaves and herbs.

In the spring, there is an abundance of wild greens – espinaca de campo (wild spinach), borraja (borage), panerica (a furry leaf similar to a dandelion) – and these, along with perhaps the hinojo (wild fennel) and vinagrera (sorrel) are put in soups or stews, depending on what is available and which combination you like. Malva (mallow) grows everywhere, though the Spanish tend to make an infusion with it rather than eat it, whereas in Morocco one often sees piles of mallow in the market. There they cut up the tender leaves and stalks, blanch them and dress them in a charmoula dressing (see page 87). Mallow is quite common in Britain too.

SOPA DE HINOJO

FENNEL, POTATO AND WHITE BEAN SOUP

The pale green shoots of wild fennel are the first of the wild herbs to emerge along the roadsides. The locals pick these feathery fronds to make, among other things, their sopa de hinojo, a comforting soup of chopped fennel leaves, potatoes and white beans. Around this time, it is quite common to see people walking along the roads proudly clutching bunches of hinojo. It adds a wonderful flavour to fish or pork. In this recipe, we also use the cultivated bulbs of fennel because they are more readily available. Finely diced, they are slowly caramelised in olive oil, which gives the soup a sweet, subtle, aniseed flavour. If you have any fennel leaves, chop them up too and stir them in just before serving.

Serves 4

> 170g dried white beans
> 4 tablespoons olive oil, plus extra for drizzling
> 4–5 fennel bulbs, about 500g, outside layer removed, halved and
>   finely diced
> 2 garlic cloves, thinly sliced
> 1 teaspoon fennel seeds (optional)
> 3 medium waxy potatoes, about 350g, peeled, diced and lightly salted
> 1 litre bean liquor and/or water or Light Chicken Stock (see page 313)
> about 40 threads of saffron, infused in 2 tablespoons boiling water
> 2 tablespoons chopped fresh fennel leaves or flat–leaf parsley
> sea salt and black pepper

Soak the white beans overnight, then drain, cover generously with fresh water and bring to the boil. Simmer for about 1 hour, until soft, then drain, reserving the cooking liquor. In another large saucepan with a heavy bottom, heat the olive oil over a medium heat. Add the diced fennel with a pinch of salt and stir well. Lower the heat and continue to fry the fennel for 20–30 minutes, stirring occasionally, until the fennel begins to caramelise and become soft. Now add the garlic, fennel seeds (if using) and the potatoes, mix well and fry for another 5 minutes. Pour on the bean liquor and/or water or stock and the saffron–infused water. Stir well, scraping the bottom of the pan to release any caramelised bits, and bring to a gentle simmer. Cook for another 10–15 minutes or until the potatoes are soft, then add the drained beans. Season with salt and pepper and simmer for a few minutes before stirring in the chopped fennel tops or parsley, and serving with a little drizzle of extra virgin olive oil.

LENTEJAS CON HINOJO E ANDRAJOS
LENTILS WITH FENNEL AND NETTLES

Lentils cooked with chorizo (see page 267) are a hearty and much-loved Spanish institution. However, Amalia from the Hotel Berchules introduced us to this local and lighter version. The wild herbs she used were hinojo (wild fennel) and andrajo (a thistly type of plant, which has a slight purple tinge at the base). It is not bitter, and, when cooked, has a rather earthy flavour, similar to that of nettles.

Serves 4

> 4 tablespoons olive oil
>
> 1 large Spanish onion, roughly chopped
>
> 200g small brown lentils
>
> 1 head garlic, halved
>
> 1 small fennel bulb, finely chopped
>
> 1 green pepper, seeded and roughly chopped
>
> 1 tomato, halved
>
> 2 bay leaves (preferably fresh)
>
> 1.5 litres good stock (rabbit, chicken or vegetable, see pages 11 or 313)
>
> 50g hinojo (wild fennel), leaves roughly chopped, or $^1/_2$ fennel bulb and leaves, finely chopped
>
> 50g young nettle tops or andrajos, roughly chopped
>
> 2 carrots, roughly chopped
>
> 2 large potatoes, peeled and cut into small pieces
>
> 1 teaspoon sweet paprika
>
> $^1/_2$ teaspoon hot paprika
>
> sea salt and black pepper

Place a large saucepan over a medium heat and add the olive oil. When the oil is hot add the onion along with the lentils, garlic, fennel bulb, green pepper, tomato and bay leaves. Fry for a few minutes, then add the stock and bring to the boil. Lower the heat to a gentle simmer and cook for 5 minutes. Add the fennel and nettles (or substitutes) and the carrot. Cook for a further 10 minutes, then add the potatoes, salt, pepper and both paprikas. Simmer for 5–10 minutes until the lentils and potatoes are cooked, taste, then serve.

COLLEJAS
GREENS

Collejas is a local name for a wild variety of spring cabbage. The leaves look quite unlike cabbage leaves, although the flavour is similar. Josefa told us how to make a delicious local dish with these collejas, cooked, not surprisingly, with freshly ground almonds.

Serves 4

> 500g collejas, leaves picked and any tough stalks removed, or chopped young spring cabbage/greens
> 4 tablespoons olive oil
> 100g whole almonds, preferably with the skins on, lightly toasted
> 1 large Spanish onion, roughly chopped
> 1 leek, halved and thinly sliced
> 2 carrots, diced
> 2 garlic cloves
> sea salt and black pepper

Place a large saucepan of lightly salted water over a high heat and bring to the boil. Submerge the greens under the water and boil for 1 minute. Drain in a colander, keeping 100ml of the blanching water, cool and set aside. Place a large frying pan or saucepan over a medium heat and add the olive oil. When it is hot but not smoking, add the almonds and fry gently for 2–3 minutes until golden. Remove with a slotted spoon and set aside. Still with the pan over the heat, add the onion, leek and carrot with a pinch of salt and fry gently, stirring occasionally, for 10–15 minutes until soft and beginning to caramelise. While this is cooking, pound the almonds in a mortar or whizz in a food processor until roughly ground. Add the garlic to the pan, cook for a further 5 minutes, then add the greens and stir well. Add the almonds, a pinch of salt and pepper and the cooking liquor, and cook for another 2–3 minutes. Serve.

REVUELTO DE AJO PORRO Y ESPÁRRAGOS
SCRAMBLED EGG WITH WILD GARLIC AND ASPARAGUS

Ajo porro, or wild garlic, is quite prevalent in the Spanish countryside. The plants look like leek seedlings, but if you dig around the root with a penknife, you will un-cover the small white bulb that has the appearance of a fat spring onion, but the flavour of garlic. It is used in soups, stews or in revuelto (scrambled egg), which, mixed with the wild asparagus that also pops up in spring, makes a delicious light meal. If using wild asparagus stalks, it is better to blanch them in boiling water for 3 minutes before frying with the garlic as they can be quite bitter in taste. If you can't get hold of wild asparagus, then normal thin asparagus (sprue) will do. Britain has an abundance of wild garlic leaves, often found in bluebell woods from March onwards.

Serves 4

> 300–400g thin (or wild) asparagus stalks, trimmed and chopped into 2cm
>   pieces, tips intact, blanched until tender
> 100g wild garlic bulb or wild garlic leaves, or 2 garlic cloves, roughly
>   chopped
> 6 tablespoons olive oil
> 4 eggs
> toast, to serve
> sea salt and black pepper

Place a large frying pan over a medium heat and add the olive oil. When it is hot, add the chopped asparagus and wild garlic and a pinch of salt. Braise for about 7 minutes, stirring occasionally, or until sweet and tender. Crack the eggs into a bowl and whisk lightly. Season with a tiny bit of salt and pepper. Pour into the frying pan and turn with the asparagus and garlic until nearly set, or how you like your eggs to be cooked. Season and serve immediately with toast.

SUMMER

As the hot summer sun bakes the ground, the warm air is scented with wild rosemary, lavender, thyme and other fragrant plants. The swallows cling to holes in the cracked plaster of the house to keep out of the sun. The long, once green grass has turned golden and sways in the gentle breeze. The contraviesa, the hills opposite our valley, are bleached out in the midday sun. A walk to the agua agria, the local natural spring of slightly fizzy water, gives some relief as it is damp and shaded by giant willows and walnut trees.

Wild herbs are at their best in early summer: wild oregano and marjoram del río (from the river valley), wild thyme and rosemary on the hills.

ENSALADA DE PATATAS CON OREGANO
POTATO SALAD WITH OREGANO

Our neighbour Adoración told us about this salad made with oregano that she picks near the river in June. Everyone in the village has little pots of dried local oregano, thyme and rosemary that they willingly share out.

Serves 4

1 kg firm, waxy salad potatoes (Cyprus, Linzer, Charlotte or Ratte),
    scrubbed and halved
1 small red onion, finely chopped
2 tablespoons roughly chopped fresh oregano or marjoram
sea salt and black pepper

DRESSING

$^1/_2$ garlic clove, crushed to a paste with salt
6–8 tablespoons olive oil
2 tablespoons lemon juice

Bring a large saucepan of salted water to the boil over a medium to high heat. Add the potatoes, making sure the halves are more or less the same size so that they cook in the same time, and put on the lid. Turn down the heat and simmer for approximately 15 minutes or until tender. Drain in a colander. Meanwhile, place the onion in a large salad bowl and mix the dressing ingredients together. Add the potatoes and oregano to the onion, and pour over the dressing. Season with salt and black pepper. Toss well, check for seasoning once more, then serve immediately or at room temperature.

CORDERO AL HORNO CON TOMILLO
ROAST LAMB WITH TOMATOES, POTATOES AND THYME

In the early summer we often drive up into the Sierra Nevada. The journey takes a slow and bumpy 45 minutes, and friends we have taken up there think we are mad. But when you turn the final corner, you come face to face with the snowy peak of the great Mulhacén at over 3,000 metres. Walking along the ridge, we step between the flowering bushes of thyme and lemon thyme, which, grown at this altitude, are particularly pungent. One would expect it to be quite windy, but often there is an extraordinary eerie silence and the feeling of nature is very strong.

Serves 4–6
  1 leg of lamb, about 1.6–1.8kg in weight, trimmed of excess fat and ready
    for roasting
  sea salt and black pepper

MARINADE
  3 garlic cloves
  2 tablespoons fresh thyme leaves
  $^1/_2$ teaspoon black peppercorns
  150ml white wine or fino sherry
  2 tablespoons olive oil

POTATOES
  1.5kg waxy potatoes, peeled and thinly sliced about 5mm thick
  2 garlic cloves, sliced
  1 large Spanish onion, finely sliced
  2 ripe tomatoes, cored and roughly chopped
  rind of 1 lemon, removed with a potato peeler
  1 tablespoon fresh thyme leaves
  5 tablespoons olive oil

For the marinade, pound the garlic with the thyme and peppercorns in a mortar. Add the wine or fino and olive oil, and pour over the lamb. Rub the marinade into the meat, pushing it into any cracks or crevices, and then leave it to marinate for anything between 2 and 24 hours, turning the leg every so often.

A couple of hours before you are ready to eat, mix all the potato ingredients together in a large bowl. Season well with salt and pepper and spread them out in a large roasting tray. The tray should be big enough to accommodate all the potatoes in a layer about 3 or 4 slices deep around the edges and with a dip in the centre where the lamb will sit. About 20 minutes before you want to start cooking, preheat the oven to 230°C/450°F/Gas 8.

Season the lamb well with salt and place in the middle of the potatoes, pouring any extra marinade on top. Follow the instructions for roasting a leg of lamb on page 194. Baste the meat a few times as it is cooking and stir the potatoes so they become evenly golden. Remove, transfer the lamb to a board and let it rest for 10 minutes loosely covered with foil before slicing and serving with the hot potatoes.

AUTUMN

The poplars are beginning to turn bright yellow and one's eye naturally follows the trees up the valley. Now is harvest time. It is the end of October, and the almonds are being gathered in the fields. There are piles of cracked husks in the countryside and outside the cooperative in the local town. Ripe red peppers from the huerto (allotment) are strung up to dry against the whitewashed walls of the terrazas (verandas); tomatoes and figs are spread out on azoteas (rooftops). The only vegetables that are still growing are the calabaza (pumpkin), acelgas (chard) and col (cabbage). Later the grapes and olives will follow, along with chestnuts and kakis (persimmons). It is time to prepare for the winter months, preserving the fruits that have been grown during the summer. The finale is usually the slaughter of a fattened pig. Over a couple of days the beast is turned into myriad salcichón (salami), chorizo and morcilla (blood sausage), jamón and paletillas (cured ham and shoulder), as well as tocino (pig fat) and panceta (cured pork belly) to last the whole year. Autumn is also the hunting season. It is common to spot hunters in camouflage clothing with their dogs around the mountains. They are after most wild things: perdiz (partridge), jabalí (wild boar), ciervo (venison) or cabra montés (the ibex or wild mountain goat). These are often stewed al ajillo, with garlic and wine (see page 207).

TASCABURRAS

SALT COD, TOMATO AND OLIVE SALAD

The red peppers and tomatoes that are dried on the terraces and rooftops are often made into a salad called tasca burra. We have tasted a couple of versions, a simple one made with chopped dried tomato and red pepper, thyme and cured black olives, served with Fresh Cheese (see pages 278–9) flavoured with thyme, or a more traditional version with bacalao (salt cod).

Serves 4

    100g sun-blushed or half-dried tomatoes

    1 garlic clove

    1 teaspoon fresh thyme leaves

    75g black olives, halved and pitted

    $1/2$ teaspoon ground cumin

    2 dried ñoras peppers, broken open and covered with boiling water, or

      $1/2$ teaspoon sweet paprika

    $1/2$ small red onion, finely chopped

    100g salt cod, soaked for 12–24 hours, then skinned and shredded (optional)

    2 tablespoons extra virgin olive oil

    1 tablespoon roughly chopped fresh flat-leaf parsley

    sea salt and black pepper

Coarsely chop the tomatoes. Pound the garlic and thyme together in a mortar. Put all these together in a bowl, along with the olives, cumin, peppers, onion and shredded salt cod. Pour over the olive oil, toss and season with a little salt and pepper. Serve with the chopped parsley on top.

CARNE EN SALSA DE ALMENDRAS
PORK IN ALMOND SAUCE

Carne en salsa is found throughout Spain and is eaten as a tapa or main course. What makes this recipe particular to the Alpujarras area is the way the sauce is thickened with almonds.

Serves 4

>6 tablespoons olive oil
>
>50g whole almonds, preferably with skins on
>
>50g white bread, without crusts, roughly diced
>
>1 head garlic, plus 4 garlic cloves
>
>1kg free-range pork shoulder, trimmed and cut into
>approx. 2cm cubes
>
>1 teaspoon sweet paprika
>
>2 small mild onions, halved
>
>1 large tomato, halved
>
>2 bay leaves (preferably fresh)
>
>1 dried ñoras pepper, seeds removed and torn in pieces,
>or $1/2$ teaspoon extra paprika
>
>400ml white wine
>
>sea salt and black pepper

In a large saucepan, heat the olive oil over a medium heat and add the almonds and bread. Fry for a couple of minutes until golden, remove with a slotted spoon and set aside on a plate with the 4 garlic cloves. Still with the saucepan on the heat, salt the pork and add to the pan, along with the whole head of garlic (sliced in half widthways so as to release its flavour), the paprika, onion, tomato, bay leaves, dried pepper and white wine. Simmer for 50-60 minutes, covered. Remove from the heat. With a spoon, take out the onion and tomato and transfer to a food processor along with the almonds, bread, the 4 garlic cloves and 4 tablespoons of the cooking liquid, and whizz until almost smooth. Add this sauce to the meat, replace on the heat and continue to simmer for another 20–30 minutes, uncovered, or until the meat is soft and tender and the juice as thick as double cream (add water if too thick). Check the seasoning once more. Traditionally served with fried potatoes, but mashed would be just as delicious.

PASTEL DE ALMENDRAS
ALMOND CAKE

We find many Spanish puddings very sweet, but we could not finish this chapter without some kind of almond cake. This one is very simple, but delicious and is made by Hilde, a friend of Josefa, who lives above our village. She prepares her almonds by soaking them in boiling water until the skins loosen and can easily be popped off. Almonds prepared this way do have a better flavour, which is preferable for this cake, though not essential.

Serves 6–8

150ml extra virgin olive oil, plus extra for oiling the tin

165g light brown sugar

4 medium eggs

200g blanched almonds, ground (some fine, some medium, some coarse, for bite and texture)

100g plain flour, sifted

Preheat the oven to 180°C/350°F/Gas 4.

In a processor or with an electric whisk (or, indeed, by hand), whisk the olive oil, sugar and eggs together until pale and fluffy (about 10–15 minutes on a medium-high speed). This whisking is important as it beats air into the mixture and makes it light. Now gently fold in all but 2 handfuls of the almonds and all the sifted flour until evenly mixed, taking care not to knock out any air. Pour into a 26cm flan or pastry tin, sprinkle the remaining ground almonds on top, and place in the oven. Cook for 20 minutes or until the cake is firm and golden brown. Remove and cool on a rack.

We ate this accompanied by an infusion made from local wild rosemary, thyme and rosebuds from the hills. Nectar!

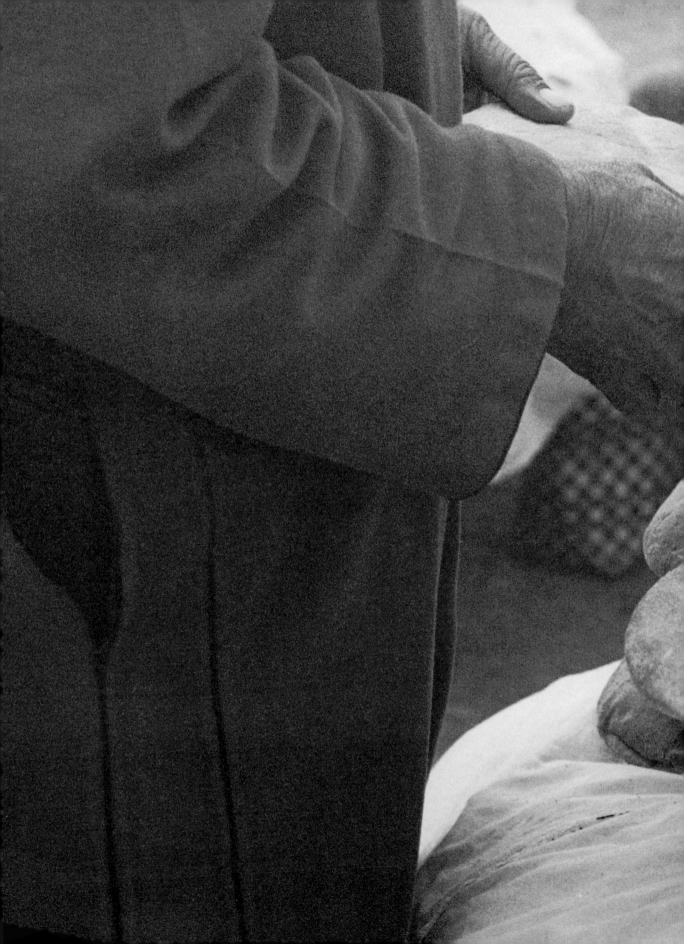

BREADS, FLATBREADS
AND STUFFED BREADS

Some bread recipes are so complicated that they can take away much of the fun and double the preparation time. The inertia towards baking bread at home in the UK has arisen because many of our grandparents stopped making it, so the technique has not been passed on. In addition, trying to introduce oneself effortlessly to bread-making through a book can be difficult. At Moro we are not frightened of baking bread and treat it with a healthy degree of disrespect (and respect too, of course). We are its masters, for scared bakers never make good bakers. Our advice is to try to take on the persona of a brisk matron, occasionally slapping the dough and proclaiming: 'You'll live!' Bread dough is resilient and, if given the time, wants nothing more than to rise and make beautiful bread.

MAKING BREAD IN A MIXER

Although our dough recipes are straightforward enough to mix by hand, they can also be made in a kitchen mixer if you have a dough hook (apart from the small quantity for Quick Flatbread). Measure out and prepare everything as the recipe dictates. Add the water to the mixing bowl along with the yeast. Turn on the mixer to a medium setting. Add the flour to the bowl a third at a time, pausing briefly before adding each third. When all the flour is added and the dough is formed, turn down the mixer to a low speed and continue mixing for 3–4minutes. If your recipe has additional ingredients, pour them in and mix for a further minute. Now go back to the original recipe for how to prove and bake the bread.

WET BREAD

Here is a very simple recipe that any beginner can successfully make. We believe that anybody can make a delicious loaf in 10 minutes (excluding proving and baking), with little mess. So what is our big secret? Our dough is wet enough to make, knead and prove in one large bowl. Think of it as whisking water (with your fingertips) into flour to make a very thick batter. This is not a light and fluffy bread, but a dense loaf, with crust and character.

Makes 1 x 1kg loaf

600g unbleached strong white bread flour (Doves Farm or Shipton Mill)

1 heaped teaspoon fine sea salt

1 level teaspoon dried yeast, dissolved in 1 tablespoon warm water

450ml warm water

semolina flour, for dusting

Place the flour and salt in a large bowl. Pour the yeast on to the flour at one side of the bowl where you intend to start working in the water. Add a little water, incorporate a bit of the flour with your fingers until smooth, add more water, mix in, incorporate more flour and knead in. As the dough increases in size, larger amounts of both flour and water can be added. Use a beating action with your fingertips, breaking up the lumps that appear; this also kneads the dough at the same time. When all the water is mixed in, beat for a further minute with your fingertips. Cover the bowl with a cloth or oiled clingfilm and leave the dough to rise in a warm place at roughly 20°C/68°F for 4–6 hours.

About 20 minutes before you are ready to bake, preheat the oven to 220°C/425°F/Gas 7. Place a large baking sheet or roasting tray (approx. 30 x 30cm) on the middle shelf. When hot, sprinkle a liberal handful or two of semolina flour over the tray to prevent the bread sticking. Now gently pour the dough on to the tray and dust the top surface with a little more semolina. Return to the oven, and after 15 minutes, reduce the heat to 200°C/400°F/Gas 6 and bake for a further half-hour.

Lift the bread off the tray, loosening it with a large knife if stuck, then place directly on the middle rack, right side up. Bake for another 15 minutes to crisp up the base. Now turn off the heat and leave the oven door open for the bread to cool completely. Don't be tempted to slice the loaf while it is still hot or it will become stodgy.

SEED BREAD

This bread has originated more from our love of baking bread than from a specific country. Once we had mastered making white bread, we put our minds to this seed bread for the family and home. For this recipe you will need two 500g rectangular bread tins approximately 22cm long, 11cm wide and 6.5cm high.

Makes 2 x 500g loaves

> 650g wholemeal flour (Doves Farm or Shipton Mill)
>
> 250g unbleached strong white bread flour (Doves Farm or Shipton Mill)
>
> 750ml warm water
>
> 1 heaped teaspoon dried yeast, dissolved in 125ml tepid water
>
> 2 level teaspoons fine sea salt, to taste
>
> 75g pumpkin seeds
>
> 100g sunflower seeds
>
> 35g poppy seeds
>
> 50g sesame seeds

FOR THE TINS

> 2 tablespoons sunflower or olive oil
>
> 2 tablespoons sunflower seeds
>
> 1 tablespoon sesame seeds
>
> 1 tablespoon poppy seeds

Place the flours, water and dissolved yeast in a large bowl. Mix together by hand or with a spoon for about 5 minutes until more or less smooth. Leave to rest for 15–20 minutes covered by a cloth or oiled clingfilm. The dough is meant to be wet, so don't be alarmed when it doesn't form into a ball. Now add the salt and seeds and mix for another 3–5 minutes so that all the ingredients are evenly incorporated. Taste a little bit of the dough to check there is sufficient salt, remembering that once the bread is cooked, you will taste the salt ever so slightly less. Quickly prepare the bread tins: oil the insides well (like greasing a cake tin). Mix the extra seeds for the tins together in a bowl, then sprinkle two-thirds of them on to the bottom and sides of both tins so that they stick as much as possible. Now divide the dough between the tins, sprinkle over the remaining seeds and leave to rise in a warm, draught-free place, covered once more by a cloth or oiled clingfilm for 2–3 hours or until the dough has risen level with (or a tiny bit over) the top of the tin.

About 20 minutes before you are ready to bake the bread, preheat the oven to 220°C/425°F/Gas 7. When the oven is up to temperature and you are satisfied that the dough has risen sufficiently, is light to the touch and a little springy, place the bread tins on the middle shelf, making sure they do not touch. Bake for 25 minutes, then remove from the oven and let the bread sit for a couple of minutes before you carefully prise each loaf out of its tin. You may need to slide a knife around the sides and corners especially. Turn down the heat to 180°C/350°F/Gas 4 and bake the loaves upside down for a further 15–20 minutes. When each loaf has formed a hard crust and is golden brown all over, give it a tap on the bottom. If it sounds hollow, it should be ready. Transfer to a cooling rack and leave until completely cool before cutting.

RUSTIC MOROCCAN BREAD

In Moroccan towns and cities, the community bakery is still a thriving and essential part of daily life. In the morning, once Mum has made the dough, the children carry the moulded loaves to their local baker on wooden trays covered with a cloth. These trays are then lined up on the tiled floor of the bakery as they await their turn in the large wood oven. At midday the children return and, recognising their cloth, claim their bread in time for lunch. In Morocco, these breads are used like utensils to eat food. They are the cutlery for soups, Moroccan salads and tagines (stews).

Makes 2 breads, approx. 15cm wide (enough for 4)

$^3/_4$ teaspoon dried yeast

4 tablespoons warm water

1 level tablespoon runny honey

200g wholemeal flour (Doves Farm or Shipton Mill)

100g unbleached strong white bread flour (Doves Farm or
   Shipton Mill), plus extra for dusting

$^1/_2$ tablespoon whole anise seeds or fennel seeds

$^1/_2$ teaspoon fine sea salt

180ml warm milk

4 tablespoons coarse semolina for dusting

Place the dried yeast in a cup and add the water. Let the yeast dissolve for a couple of minutes, then add the honey and stir. Place the two flours, anise and salt in a large bowl. Make a well in the centre of the flour and add the yeasty mixture, and then the warm milk, a bit at a time while mixing, preferably with your hand (or a wooden spoon) so you can smooth out any lumps as they appear. When all the milk is added, transfer the dough to a surface lightly floured with extra white flour and knead well for 2–3 minutes until the dough is no longer sticky, but soft, smooth and elastic. Taste for salt, adding more if necessary. Now divide the dough in two and roll into balls. On a surface now dusted with 1 tablespoon of the coarse semolina, gently roll each ball into a circle approximately 2cm thick and about 12–14cm in diameter. Place on an oiled baking tray dusted with 1 more tablespoon of semolina, and sprinkle the top of the breads with another tablespoon of semolina. Cover with oiled clingfilm or a cloth and set aside in a warm place to rest for 2–4 hours, depending on the outside temperature. The bread is ready to bake when it has almost doubled in bulk and the dough has only a slight spring when pressed gently.

About 20 minutes before you are ready to bake, preheat the oven to 220°C/425°F/Gas 7. Sprinkle the remaining semolina all over just before the tray goes in the oven. Bake for about 20–25 minutes or until the dough has risen slightly, is light brown in colour and sounds hollow when tapped on the bottom. Remove and cool on a rack before eating.

ANISE BREAD

This yellowy bread has a light, crumbly texture and is flavoured with anise. Sometimes we dry it out in the oven at a low temperature until almost hard, which is delicious with the feta and tomato salad we make on page 136.

Makes 1 x 1kg loaf

> 300g fine polenta, yellow corn semolina, or coarse yellow cornmeal such as Dunn's River corn polenta, plus extra for dusting
> 300g unbleached strong white bread flour (Doves Farm or Shipton Mill), plus extra for dusting
> $1^1/_2$ tablespoons anise seeds or fennel seeds
> $1^1/_2$ teaspoons fine sea salt
> 1 teaspoon dried yeast
> 380ml warm water (or more, as different kinds of cornmeal absorb different amounts of water)
> 2 tablespoons olive oil

Place the flours, anise seeds and salt in a large mixing bowl. Dissolve the yeast in the water and then pour the oil into the water. Now pour the yeast mix into the flour a bit at a time while mixing with your fingertips or a wooden spoon. When all has been added, transfer to a surface floured with extra white bread flour and knead well. You should get a soft, slightly sticky dough. If it is very sticky, add a little more flour; if it is still crumbly, add more water. Continue kneading for about 5 minutes until the dough is soft, elastic and smooth. Taste a little bit of the dough to check there is sufficient salt, then form into an oval loaf. Oil a baking sheet well, then sprinkle a little extra polenta (or semolina) over. Place the dough in the middle and leave to rise in a warm, draught-free place covered by a cloth for approximately 2–3 hours.

Some 20 minutes before you are ready to bake, preheat the oven to 220°C/425°F/Gas 7. When the oven is up to temperature and the dough has risen sufficiently, is light to touch and a little springy, dust the top of the dough with more polenta. Bake for approximately 25–30 minutes until it has formed a hard crust and is slightly golden in colour. Slide a knife along the bottom of the loaf if it is a little stuck, and finally give it a tap on the bottom. If it sounds hollow, it should be ready. Transfer to a cooling rack and leave until completely cool before eating.

FLATBREADS

One of the secrets to rolling successful flatbread is an even sprinkling of flour on every centimetre of dough, work-top, rolling pin and hands at every stage. You never want a sticky patch to appear on anything and if it does, scrape off the offending area and re-flour.

BASIC FLATBREAD

Makes 4 thin breads, enough for 2–4 people

450g unbleached strong white bread flour (Doves Farm or Shipton Mill),
  plus extra for dusting
$3/_4$ teaspoon fine sea salt
$1/_2$ teaspoon dried yeast
300ml warm water
2 tablespoons olive oil

Place the flour and salt in a large mixing bowl. Dissolve the yeast in the water and pour into the flour a bit at a time while mixing. We like to do this by hand, squelching out the lumps as they appear. When all the water has been incorporated, add the olive oil and knead it in. Now transfer the dough to a floured surface and continue to knead well for about 5 minutes until the dough is no longer tacky, but soft, elastic and smooth. Add more flour a little at a time if it is too sticky. Set aside, covered by a cloth, to rest for an hour on the floured surface.

About 20 minutes before you are ready to bake, preheat the oven to 230°C/450°F/Gas 8. Divide the dough into four and, on a very well floured surface, roll out each piece into a rough circle 3mm thick. Transfer to two large baking sheets that have been lightly floured. Put in the oven immediately and bake for 5–10 minutes until the bread is cooked. Each bread should partially bubble up and colour slightly, yet not be totally crisp.

QUICK FLATBREAD

Our line is that it is easier to make flatbread for two people than go to the local shop and buy some pitta bread. This bread is rolled almost as thin as lavash (an Arabic bread), and will improve if you allow it to prove for 20 minutes. But if you are hungry and impatient, just cook it without proving. It tastes good.

Makes 4 thin breads, enough for 2 people

100ml warm water

$^1/_4$ teaspoon dried yeast

130g unbleached strong white bread flour (Doves Farm or
    Shipton Mill), plus extra for dusting

$^1/_4$ teaspoon fine sea salt

1 tablespoon olive oil

Measure out your water precisely. (If your measuring jug does not register 100ml, weigh it instead: 100g = 100ml.) Stir the yeast into the water. Put the flour into a medium bowl along with the salt. Give the yeast and water another stir and begin to add to the flour. Start at the side of the bowl, pouring in a little water, incorporating some flour, and so on, all the time working out the lumps with your fingertips and kneading with a slapping motion. When all the flour and water have been incorporated, beat in the olive oil (with your fingertips). Let the dough sit for 20 minutes. Give it another quick beat to make it more elastic. Clean and dry your hands. Now flour your hands and the dough and lift out of the bowl on to a floured surface. Make into a rough sausage shape and slice into four equal pieces.

Heat up a large frying pan (minimum 25cm in diameter) over a medium to high heat. With floured hands, shape one piece of dough into a circle. To make it fit your frying pan, roll it a little bit with a rolling pin, turn the bread by a third, roll it a little again and turn and roll one more time. The bread should be pretty thin and circular. Supporting the bread with a spread-out hand, place in the pan. When the bread starts to bubble, turn it over with a spatula. Cook until the underside has brown spots. The bread should be cooked but still pliable. Keep warm, covered with a tea-towel. Now do the same with the other three pieces of dough.

FLATBREAD BAKED IN ASHES

When in Marrakech, we took a day trip to the High Atlas. We wanted to re-create a memorable experience Samuel had had, aged six, whilst on holiday in Morocco in 1973: to eat frogs' legs at the hotel Le Sanglier Qui Fume. Sam had seen a man come down from the hills tightly clutching a rough sack. Inside were green frogs jiggling and jumping in an attempt to escape. We arrived not expecting much at all. But frogs' legs were on the menu, and when we asked for them, the waiter just nodded his head. Some 15 minutes later, a large earthenware plate of tender frogs' legs arrived. They had been dipped in seasoned flour, quickly deep-fried, and sprinkled with chopped raw garlic and parsley, and were served with lemon on the side. They were delicious. It was very touching to see our son Luke, of a similar age, tucking into them.

'What has this to do with flatbread?' you might ask. Not much, except while we were there we watched the cook baking bread in the dying embers of the fire. This is a common technique among the Berber people of the Atlas Mountains, and it is fun to cook flatbread in this way.

Serves 4

1 quantity Basic Flatbread dough (see page 36)

Follow the ingredients and method on page 36 to make and prove the dough.

When you are ready to bake, divide the dough into four and roll out each piece into a circle roughly 1cm thick.

Now prepare your embers. These can be from a wood fire at home, a campfire or a barbecue with sufficient ash. Flatten the embers and, if necessary, place a thin layer of old ash on them to insulate the bread from any coals that are red hot. Now place a flatbread on top of the ash. When the bread begins to bubble or rise, wait for 1 more minute, then turn over to cook the other side. All this does slightly depend on how hot the embers are, so you may have to peek underneath to see the bread's progress. Repeat with the remaining breads. Don't worry if there is any ash on the bread, it will just brush off – it all adds to the flavour! You can always use a metal grill rack to form a barrier between the ash and the bread if you prefer. This bread is delicious with argan oil (see page 60) and honey.

LAHMACUN

TURKISH PIZZA WITH TOMATO, LAMB AND ALLSPICE

We often go to the Turkish Food Centre in Ridley Road, Dalston, near where we live in London, as it has such a wonderful selection of herbs, vegetables and spices that come direct from Turkey and Cyprus. If we get our timing right, we grab a couple of Turkish pizzas from a pile that are produced around lunchtime, still hot from the oven. There is a bowl of chopped parsley and onion that you can sprinkle on top of your pizza as well as a squeeze of lemon. Roll it up and away you go.

Makes 4 pizzas

    1 quantity Basic Flatbread dough (see page 36)

STEWED LAMB

    300g boneless shoulder or neck of lamb, cut into
       approx. 1cm cubes
    $1/2$ small onion, grated
    $1/4$ teaspoon ground allspice
    100–150ml water
    sea salt and black pepper

TOMATO SAUCE

    600g ripe tomatoes
    4 tablespoons olive oil
    4 garlic cloves, sliced
    $1/2$ teaspoon caster sugar

TO COOK AND SERVE

    2 tablespoons roughly chopped fresh flat-leaf parsley
    2 tablespoons sliced red onion (optional)
    $1/2$ tablespoon Turkish chilli flakes (kirmizi biber) or
       pickled chillies (optional)
    1 lemon, quartered

Put the lamb, onion and allspice into a medium saucepan and stir well. Just cover with cold water (100–150ml should do it), add a pinch of salt and pepper and place a piece of baking parchment on top. Simmer over a low flame for about 1–1$1/2$ hours or until tender. Uncover the pot, increase the heat and reduce until the cooking juices run thick. Remove from the heat to cool, and keep aside.

While the lamb is simmering, follow the ingredients and method on page 36 to make and prove the dough. While the dough is resting, cook the tomato sauce.

Start the sauce by preparing the tomatoes. Remove the stalks, then lower the tomatoes into a saucepan of boiling water and count to 20. Lift the tomatoes into a bowl or sink of cold water. When cool, peel, quarter and seed them. If the quarters are large, cut them in half. Pour the olive oil into a medium frying pan and fry the garlic over a medium heat until golden brown. Now add the tomatoes and a pinch of salt and pepper. If you are not cooking this dish in the late spring to late summer, you might find it necessary to add the sugar because the tomatoes may not be so sweet. Simmer for 15 minutes or until the tomatoes are cooked but not totally broken up and the excess liquid has more or less evaporated.

About 20 minutes before you are ready to bake the pizzas, preheat the oven to 220°C/425°F/Gas 7. Divide the dough into four and roll out each piece into roughly an oval shape no more than 3-4mm thick. Flour everything well. Transfer to two large, lightly floured baking sheets or tins. Now spread on the tomato sauce, using a quarter of the sauce for each flatbread, hardly leaving a border of dough. Then add the lamb. Put in the oven immediately and bake for 10-15 minutes until the bread is cooked. Remove from the oven, transfer to a plate and sprinkle over the chopped parsley, onion (if using) and chilli flakes and serve with the lemon. Eat immediately – as if you want to wait anyway! Delicious with ayran, the chilled yoghurt drink, which we love lightly sprinkled with ground cumin.

FLATBREAD WITH LAMB, PINE NUTS AND POMEGRANATES

This is a Lebanese recipe inspired by film-maker Robert Golden, who sent us some short films he had made around Spain, Morocco, Syria and the Lebanon. In one film we watched a woman making pomegranate molasses and then a flatbread with lamb, pine nuts and the molasses. Both recipes are so wonderful that we had to include them in this book.

Makes 12 small round breads
    1 quantity Basic Flatbread dough (see page 36)

LAMB
    2 tablespoons olive oil
    1 medium onion, finely chopped

500g minced lamb

1 teaspoon ground cinnamon

4 tablespoons Pomegranate Molasses (see page 284)

5 tablespoons water

12 teaspoons pine nuts

4 tablespoons pomegranate seeds (Iranian or Turkish variety if possible)

sea salt and black pepper

Follow the ingredients and method on page 36 to make and prove the dough, using 1 teaspoon salt instead of $^3/_4$ because of the sweet–sour pomegranate molasses.

For the lamb, place a frying pan over a medium heat. Add the olive oil, and when it is hot, the onion and a pinch of salt. Fry, stirring occasionally until the onion is golden, then add the minced lamb and the cinnamon. Brown the meat, breaking it up with a spoon. When the meat is cooked and lightly caramelised, season well with salt and pepper. Mix the pomegranate molasses with the water and add to the lamb. Warm through briefly, check for seasoning, then remove from the heat and set aside.

Some 20 minutes before you are ready to bake, preheat the oven to 230°C/450°F/Gas 8. Divide the dough into 12, and roll out each piece on a lightly floured surface until it measures 11cm in diameter and is 5mm thick. Flour every-thing well. Transfer the circles of dough to two large, lightly floured baking sheets or tins. (You could also bake them in two batches if easier.) Spread 2 tablespoons of lamb mixture on each circle, leaving a 5mm border of dough around the edge. Sprinkle 1 teaspoon of pine nuts over the top of each, and bake in the preheated oven for 10–15 minutes until the bread is cooked. Remove, transfer to a plate and sprinkle over the pomegranate seeds.

STUFFED BREADS

We like stuffed breads, for when you break them open they reveal their goodies. When cooked, the ingredients inside steam, retaining their juices and oils. As a rule, we prefer to eat these recipes warm. They can be cooked in advance and reheated.

GÖZLEME
ANATOLIAN STUFFED FLATBREAD

A short walk from the Blue Mosque in Istanbul is a restaurant called Cennet. It specialises in making exquisite Anatolian stuffed breads called gözleme. In the centre of the room are three women kneeling on the floor. One rolls out a small ball of dough as thinly as possible before resting it on a padded cushion. The second woman then transfers the bread from the cushion on to a metal dome inverted over a low gas flame. She proceeds to cook one side, then flips it over to cook the other, dabbing the surface with melted butter from time to time. Once the bread is off the heat, the third woman then stuffs it with a variety of things – spinach, potato, meat or cheese – and it is then folded up into a neat little parcel and returned to the dome for a few more seconds to warm through before being swiftly served piping hot to your table. We were so inspired by this spectacle that we immediately went to the bazaar and bought one of these domes, known as a saj, along with a selection of bread paddles for our wood oven. We have since made gözleme a number of times at the restaurant. It is not essential for you to procure one of these domes; a large frying pan will suffice, so you can try making gözleme at home.

Serves 4 (makes 8 breads, enough for a main course)

    250g unbleached strong white bread flour (Doves Farm or
      Shipton Mill), plus extra for dusting

    $^1/_2$ teaspoon fine sea salt

    185ml warm water

    $^1/_4$ teaspoon dried yeast

    1 tablespoon olive oil

TO FILL AND COOK

    120g butter, cut into 16 pieces

    gözleme stuffing of choice (see page 46)

For the dough, place the flour and salt in a large mixing bowl. Pour the water on to the dried yeast, let it dissolve for a couple of minutes, then stir. Now pour the yeast mixture into the flour a bit at a time while mixing. We like to do this by hand, squelching out the lumps as they appear. When all the yeast mixture has been added and the dough is fairly smooth, add the olive oil by drizzling it down the side of the bowl and kneading it in. Transfer to a lightly floured work surface and continue kneading for about 3 minutes until the dough is no longer tacky, but soft, elastic and smooth. Place in a bowl covered with oiled clingfilm and set aside in a warm place to rest for 20 minutes to 1 hour. While the dough is resting, make the stuffings (our favourites are overleaf).

When the dough has proved, divide it into eight pieces and knead into balls. On a generously floured surface with a floured rolling pin, gently roll out each ball, turning the bread a quarter turn each time you roll, as this keeps the shape round. The dough should be very elastic, so will spring back on itself once you have got it to about 5mm thick. At this point, lift it off the board and stretch it by hand, rotating as you go for an even thickness. You should be able to achieve a 20cm round of almost paper thinness, nearly transparent at its centre, a little thicker around the edge. (You can roll out all the gözleme breads at the same time if you like, but to do this you will need to stack each one between squares of greaseproof paper lightly dusted with flour to prevent sticking. Place a large frying pan over a medium to high heat, add a knob of butter and when it begins to foam, gently ease one sheet of dough into the pan. Fry one side, allowing it to blister and brown in places before turning it (lower the heat if it burns too quickly). Add another knob of butter to the pan and cook the other side. Transfer the bread to a plate and place a quarter of either spinach or potato filling on the centre. Spread it out a bit and then fold the edges of the gözleme over like an envelope to enclose the filling. Return to the pan over a low heat to warm the stuffing through, and eat straight away, or keep warm in a dish in a low oven while making the other gözleme. Alternatively, for drinks or an informal meal, share out each gözleme as it becomes ready.

At Cennet they place small bowls of Turkish chilli flakes, dried oregano and sumac (a ground spice made from tart red berries) on each table for sprinkling on top of the gözleme. We also do this at Moro, as well as serving some yoghurt seasoned with garlic, a rocket salad and a wedge of lemon.

GÖZLEME SPINACH STUFFING

Fills 4 gözleme

>   4 tablespoons olive oil
>
> $1/2$ medium onion, very finely chopped
>
>   250g spinach, washed and drained well
>
>   a good pinch of ground allspice
>
>   1 tablespoon sumac
>
>   sea salt and black pepper

Heat the oil in a frying pan over a low to medium heat. When the oil is hot, add the onion and a pinch of salt. Fry the onion for a good 10 minutes, stirring occasionally, until golden and sweet. Add the spinach and allspice and cook until just wilted. Remove from the heat and if a little wet, leave to drain for a moment in a colander, then transfer to a board and chop coarsely. Add the sumac before tasting for seasoning.

GÖZLEME POTATO STUFFING

Fills 4 gözleme

>   300g firm potatoes, such as Desirée or Cyprus, cut in half
>   lengthways and sliced about 3mm thick
>
>   4 tablespoons olive oil
>
>   6 spring onions, thinly sliced
>
>   2 teaspoons caraway seeds
>
> $1/4$ teaspoon Turkish chilli flakes (kirmizi biber), or a pinch of
>   crushed chilli flakes
>
>   3 tablespoons roughly chopped fresh dill
>
>   sea salt and black pepper

Salt the potatoes 5 minutes before cooking as this helps bring out their flavour. In a large saucepan or frying pan heat the oil over a medium heat. When the oil is hot, add the potatoes, onions and caraway seeds, and stir around until they are mixed evenly. Reduce the heat slightly and put a lid on the pan so the potatoes cook but do not colour. Stir from time to time, and scrape up the bits of potato that stick to the bottom of the pan. When the potatoes are soft, remove from the heat, and place in a bowl. Now add the chilli flakes and the dill and check for seasoning, adding a tablespoon or two of water if the mixture seems a little dry.

CHORIZO ROLLS

We once ate bread similar to this in Avila. One day in the restaurant we had some left-over flatbread dough and, wanting to replicate this bread, we decided to experiment. We impulsively fried some chorizo with fennel seeds, then briefly kneaded it and its oil into the dough, put it on a baking tray and straight into the oven. The result was magic, just a nice thing to eat whenever. Warmed is preferable. In the recipe, you could use slicing chorizo cut into strips, with no need to cook beforehand. A tablespoon of chopped rosemary instead of fennel seeds is also a good alternative.

Makes 8 rolls

> 200g cooking chorizo, in 1cm rounds
>
> 1 tablespoon olive oil
>
> $1-1^1/_2$ teaspoons fennel seeds
>
> $^1/_2$ teaspoon dried yeast
>
> 230ml warm water
>
> 350g unbleached strong white bread flour (Doves Farm or
>
>   Shipton Mill), plus extra for dusting
>
> $^3/_4$ teaspoon fine sea salt

Fry the chorizo in the oil over a high heat until browned and crisp, then add the fennel seeds and fry for half a minute more. Drain off the oil and reserve, and leave the chorizo and seeds to cool.

Combine the yeast and water, and once dissolved, work it into the bowl of flour and salt. Knead for 4–5 minutes, then slowly work in the chorizo's cooking oil (now cool) and knead for 5 minutes more. Now divide the dough into eight pieces. Roll each piece into a little ball on a floured surface. Then take a ball in your hand and stuff two to three pieces of chorizo and some fennel seeds into the centre of it. Close the dough up around them and roll once more until the hole has closed up. Place on an oiled baking tray. Lightly oil the surface of the rolls and leave the dough in a warm place, covered with oiled clingfilm, to rise until at least doubled in bulk and soft to the touch.

About 20 minutes before you are ready to bake, preheat the oven to 220°C/425°F/Gas 7. Uncover the breads and bake for 20 minutes. Best when still warm from the oven.

EMPANADILLAS

Empanadillas are petite empanadas, the famous Galician pies, and their size makes them perfect for tapas or a starter. The dough is half bread dough, half pastry, so it should be rich and flaky, but elastic.

Makes approx. 28–30 empanadillas

> 400g unbleached strong white bread flour (Doves Farm or Shipton Mill)
>
> 100g coarse or instant polenta, plus 2 extra tablespoons for dusting
>
> 4 tablespoons olive oil
>
> 50g butter, melted
>
> 75ml white wine
>
> $1/2$ teaspoon salt
>
> $1/2$ teaspoon caster sugar
>
> 3 tablespoons warm water

TO FILL

> 1 quantity of each stuffing overleaf

For the dough, combine all the ingredients together except the water and blend in a food processor or rub together with your fingers as you would pastry. Transfer the mixture to a board, knead in the warm water, then cover with a cloth or oiled cling-film and allow to rest for 1 hour.

About 20 minutes before you are ready to bake, preheat the oven to 220°C/425°F/Gas 7.

To make the empanadillas, pinch off walnut-sized pieces of pastry and roll them into rough balls (you should get 28–30). Dust your work surface with polenta and roll out the balls until they are nice and thin. They should be fairly round in shape. Place a dessertspoon of stuffing mixture just off-centre on each round. Fold over the pastry to make a semi-circle (like a mini Cornish pasty). Push down the edges with a fork to seal, and trim off the excess pastry. Sprinkle a baking tray with polenta flour to put your empanadillas on. (You can glaze them with beaten egg if you like, but this is not essential.) Bake for 10–15 minutes until light brown. Dust with extra polenta before serving if you wish.

EMPANADILLA PORK STUFFING

Fills 14 empanadillas

     5 tablespoons olive oil

     250g minced pork, or pork fillet or loin, sliced and finely chopped in a food processor

     1 large onion, finely chopped

     1 red pepper, seeded and finely chopped

     3 garlic cloves, finely chopped

     2 tablespoons roughly chopped fresh flat-leaf parsley

     1 teaspoon fennel seeds, ground

     1 dessertspoon tomato purée

     $1/2$ teaspoon hot smoked paprika

     1 teaspoon sweet smoked paprika

     sea salt and black pepper

Place a large frying pan over a medium to high heat and add 2 tablespoons of the olive oil. When the oil is hot, add the pork and brown quickly. Put the pork to one side. In the same pan, heat the remaining oil and add the onion and pepper. Soften until they are no longer watery and are beginning to caramelise. Add the garlic, parsley and fennel seeds and cook for a further 10 minutes. Stir in the tomato purée, paprikas and pork and cook for 5 more minutes. Season.

EMPANADILLA SARDINE STUFFING

Fills 14 empanadillas

     4 tablespoons olive oil

     1 large onion, finely chopped

     1 green and 1 red pepper, seeded and finely chopped

     3 garlic cloves, finely chopped

     1 dessertspoon finely chopped fresh rosemary

     $1^1/2$ dessertspoons tomato purée

     250g canned sardines, mashed with a fork

     sea salt and black pepper

Place a large frying pan over a medium to high heat and add the olive oil. When hot, add the onion and peppers. Soften until they are no longer watery and are beginning to caramelise. Add the garlic and rosemary and cook for a further 15 minutes. Stir in the tomato purée and sardines. Cook for 5 minutes more. Season.

SOUPS

Being the sort of restaurant that we are, with our love of ancient culinary utensils, such as the mortar and pestle and wood-burning oven, it seems unlikely that we would be keen on an electric gizmo for soups. However, Spanish households and restaurants have taken to hand-held blenders, and so have we. They do not destroy the texture, allowing the cook to blend with some sort of sensitivity.

SALMOREJO

THICK GAZPACHO

Salmorejo, from Córdoba, is a thicker, richer version of gazpacho, and, like gazpacho, is served chilled with bits of jamón serrano (cured ham) and chopped egg on top. Last year, whilst driving to see a friend in Seville, we stopped for lunch in a venta (roadside café) and ordered salmorejo. To our surprise and delight, there were segments of orange in the soup, as well as the usual jamón and egg. The sweet, juicy orange cut through the soup and was quite refreshing. As we are familiar with Spanish food now, one of our great pleasures is sampling local twists on dishes, even on something like salmorejo that is already fairly regional.

Serves 4

> 2 garlic cloves
>
> 1 kg sweet, ripe tomatoes, halved
>
> 100g white bread, crusts removed, roughly crumbled
>
> 10 tablespoons extra virgin olive oil
>
> 2 tablespoons good-quality sweet red wine vinegar or
> sherry vinegar (see page 287)
>
> a pinch of caster sugar (optional)
>
> sea salt and black pepper

TO SERVE

> 1 hard-boiled egg, finely chopped
>
> 3 tablespoons finely chopped jamón serrano

Crush the garlic in a mortar with a good pinch of salt until you have a smooth paste. Using an electric hand-held blender or food processor, purée the tomatoes and bread until completely smooth. If there are many seeds, strain through a sieve. Then, with the machine still running, add the garlic and slowly pour in the olive oil. When the oil has combined, transfer the mixture to a large bowl and add the vinegar, salt and pepper to taste, and also a pinch of sugar if the tomatoes are not particularly sweet. The consistency of the soup should be like apple purée. Add some water if necessary. Place the bowl in the fridge for 2 hours to chill. Just before serving, check the seasoning once more, then ladle the soup into four bowls and sprinkle the chopped egg and ham on top.

Variation

Salmorejo is often used as a sauce with fish or chicken or deep-fried aubergines.

SOPA DE HABICHUELAS

WHITE BEAN, CHORIZO AND PARSLEY SOUP

In the Sierra de Avila between Madrid and Portugal, an array of wonderful pulses are grown. Grocers in local towns proudly display their harvest of jet-black frijoles negros, white planchada, speckled brown pinto or judiones, the luxuriously plump butter beans. We devised this soup to make the most of one of these wonderful beans. The soup should be velvety, with spicy bits of chorizo and fresh parsley. If you can't get hold of these white beans, then tins or jars of good-quality cooked white beans are a suitable alternative.

Serves 4

> 750g soft, cooked, drained white beans (375g dried, see page 17), such as
>   planchada, judiones or cannellini
> 800ml bean liquor or, if not enough, a mixture of liquor and water
> 6 tablespoons olive oil
> 5 garlic cloves, finely chopped
> $^1/_2$ teaspoon hot paprika
> 6 tablespoons finely chopped fresh flat-leaf parsley
> 180–200g chorizo, preferably cooking type, diced into 1cm cubes
> sea salt and black pepper

Purée the white beans with the bean liquor or water until quite smooth using a food processor or electric hand-held blender. If necessary, thin the beans with more water to get the desired consistency of double cream. In a large saucepan, heat 5 tablespoons of the olive oil over a medium heat. When the oil is hot, add the garlic and quickly fry until it begins to colour. Add 4 tablespoons of the parsley. Stir around until the garlic is golden brown and the parsley a translucent dark green. Stir in the paprika and then add the bean purée. Bring to a gentle simmer and season with salt and pepper.

Meanwhile, in a frying pan over a high heat, heat the remaining olive oil and fry the chorizo until slightly crisp. Remove the soup from the heat, stir in the remaining parsley and ladle into bowls. Spoon the chorizo and its paprika-red oil on top.

CALDO DE PESCADO

GALICIAN FISH SOUP WITH CLAMS AND PRAWNS

This recipe was given to us by one of our chefs, David Loureiro Martínez, who is from Galicia. When chefs demonstrate something cooked by their mother or from their home region, one can see their chest literally puff up. Quite right too! The soup is a relatively simple, yet wonderfully flavoursome, broth.

Serves 4-6

> 300g North Atlantic prawns, preferably in their shells
>
> 8 tablespoons olive oil
>
> 1 large tomato, quartered
>
> 2 sprigs fresh thyme
>
> 2 litres water
>
> 500g small to medium clams, such as palourdes or venus, or mussels
>
> 2 medium onions, finely chopped
>
> 3 garlic cloves, thinly sliced
>
> $1/2$ teaspoon fennel seeds (optional)
>
> 3 bay leaves (preferably fresh)
>
> 3 teaspoons sweet smoked paprika, preferably Spanish, such as La Chinata
>
> $1/2$ teaspoon hot smoked paprika
>
> 40 threads saffron, infused in 6 tablespoons boiling water
>
> 100g basmati rice
>
> 2 tablespoons roughly chopped fresh flat-leaf parsley
>
> sea salt and black pepper

Shell the prawns as described on page 141, keeping the shells aside, then cut the prawns in half and put in the fridge. In a saucepan heat 4 tablespoons of the olive oil over a high heat. When it is hot, add the shells and fry until they change colour and give off a nutty seafood smell, about 3–5 minutes, stirring occasionally. Then add the tomato, thyme and water and simmer for 20 minutes. Remove from the heat, strain the prawn stock through a fine-mesh sieve and set aside.

Meanwhile, rinse the clams well in a colander under cold water, discarding any that are broken or open, and leave to drain. In a large, heavy saucepan, heat the remaining olive oil over a medium heat until hot. Add the onion and a pinch of salt and cook for about 15 minutes, stirring occasionally until the onion becomes golden in colour. Now add the garlic, fennel seeds and bay leaves and continue to fry, stirring once or twice, for a further 3–5 minutes, being careful not to burn the garlic. Add the two paprikas, saffron infusion, rice, half the parsley and the prawn stock. Bring to the

boil and simmer until the rice is cooked, about 10–15 minutes. Add the clams. When
the clams have opened (after a few minutes), remove from the heat and stir in the
prawns to heat through, and the rest of the parsley. If using raw prawns, make sure
they are cooked (you may need to pop the pan back on the heat for 1 more minute).
Check the seasoning and serve.

SOPA DE GARBANZOS

MOORISH CHICKPEA AND SPINACH SOUP

This is a surprisingly rich and complex soup that is a delight. A thicker version of it is a classic tapa from Seville.

Serves 4

450g home-cooked chickpeas (see below) or 2 x 400g cans chickpeas, rinsed and drained

150ml olive oil

300g spinach, washed and drained well

75g white bread, crusts removed, cut into 2cm cubes

3 garlic cloves, thinly sliced

$^3/_4$ teaspoon cumin seeds

2 heaped tablespoons roughly chopped fresh oregano

1 small dried red chilli, crumbled

1 tablespoon red wine vinegar

700-800ml water or chickpea liquor, or a mixture of the two

60 threads saffron, infused in 4 tablespoons boiling water

$^1/_2$ teaspoon sweet Spanish paprika

sea salt and black pepper

If using dried chickpeas, place them in a bowl with plenty of cold water and a pinch of bicarbonate of soda and leave to soak overnight. Drain in a colander, rinse well, then place in a large saucepan with half an onion or 1 head garlic. Cover with 2 litres cold water and bring to the boil. Reduce the heat and simmer, skimming off any scum, for 1-2 hours or until soft and tender.

Place a large saucepan over a medium heat and add $2^1/_2$ tablespoons of the oil. When hot, add the spinach with a pinch of salt and stir well. Remove when the leaves are just tender, cool then chop quite finely and set aside. Heat the remaining oil in a frying pan over a medium heat. Fry the bread for about 5 minutes until golden brown all over, then add the garlic and cumin. When the garlic begins to colour, add the oregano and chilli, and continue to cook until the garlic is brown. Transfer to a mortar or food processor along with the vinegar, and mash to a paste. Now put the bread mixture in a saucepan, add the drained chickpeas, water, saffron infusion and paprika, and simmer for 10 minutes. Whizz the chickpeas until almost smooth (we prefer a little bit of texture to the soup). Return to the pan if necessary, and season with salt and pepper. If the consistency is too thick (a bit thicker than double cream), add some more water. Stir in the spinach until it too is hot. Check the seasoning and serve.

BESSARA

DRIED PEA SOUP WITH CUMIN AND ARGAN OIL

Of the great choice of street food to eat in Morocco, two soups are almost always on offer. The first is the famous harira, of which we have a summer version on page 63, and the other is bessara. It is made from either split green peas or dried shelled fava (broad) beans and flavoured delicately with cumin, and both versions are magical considering their simplicity. Fava beans are available from Middle Eastern shops, especially Lebanese or Turkish shops, and the split green peas from supermarkets and Moroccan shops. We like to finish this soup with a drizzle of argan oil (made from the nuts of the argan tree, which is indigenous to Morocco, and available here in Middle Eastern food shops) to give it a more complex, nutty flavour.

Serves 4

> 300g split dried green peas (such as Batchelors quick-cook dried peas, not
> marrowfat peas) or dried shelled fava beans, rinsed well
>
> 1.75 litres cold water
>
> 4 tablespoons olive oil
>
> $^1/_2$ large onion, chopped
>
> 4 garlic cloves, chopped
>
> 2 teaspoons cumin seeds, lightly pan-roasted and roughly ground
>
> $^1/_4$–$^1/_2$ teaspoon crumbled dried red chilli
>
> 2 tablespoons roughly chopped fresh coriander
>
> $1^1/_2$ tablespoons argan oil mixed with $^1/_2$ tablespoon olive oil,
>   or 2 tablespoons olive oil
>
> sea salt and black pepper

Bring the peas or fava beans to the boil with the water and skim off any scum that appears. Simmer for between 40 minutes and 1 hour. In a large saucepan, heat the olive oil over a medium heat. Add the onion with a pinch of salt and cook for about 15 minutes, stirring occasionally, until sweet and golden. Now add the garlic and cumin and fry for another 2 minutes until brown. Remove from the heat and add the dried chilli. When your beans are cooked they should be soft. Mix in the onion mixture and simmer for another 5 minutes. If you like a very smooth-textured soup, whizz with a hand-held blender or in a food processor. Season with salt and pepper and stir in the fresh coriander. If the soup is too thick, simply add more water and adjust the seasoning (it should be the consistency of double cream). Ladle into bowls and drizzle the argan/olive oil mix on top.

TURKISH VILLAGE SOUP WITH
BREAD AND CARAWAY

The inclusion of bread and caraway in this Turkish recipe gives a humble vegetable soup an original texture and flavour, and is a great way to use up old bread. As much as possible, the pieces of bread and vegetables should retain their shape and not be mushed up in the soup.

Serves 6

> 8 tablespoons olive oil
>
> 1 large onion, roughly chopped
>
> 3 large carrots, roughly chopped
>
> 4 celery sticks, roughly chopped
>
> 4 garlic cloves, thinly sliced
>
> 3 level teaspoons caraway seeds
>
> 3 tablespoons roughly chopped fresh flat-leaf parsley
>
> 1 x 400g can whole plum tomatoes, drained of juice and broken up
>
> 1 litre water, or 750ml water/250ml bean liquor if using home-cooked beans
>
> 500g white cabbage, sliced and then roughly chopped
>
> 400g home-cooked borlotti or pinto beans (200g dried weight, see page 17),
>   or 2 x 400g cans beans, drained
>
> 200g day-old ciabatta or white rustic bread, half the crusts removed,
>   roughly torn or sliced into bite-sized pieces
>
> 2 tablespoons extra virgin olive oil
>
> sea salt and black pepper

Heat the olive oil in a large saucepan over a medium flame. (Make sure the saucepan is big enough to accommodate all the vegetables.) When the oil is hot, add the onion, carrot, celery and a pinch of salt and gently fry, stirring occasionally, until the vegetables begin to turn golden, about 15 minutes. Now add the garlic, caraway and half the parsley and fry for another minute or two, followed by the tomatoes. Cook for 10 more minutes, add the water or water/bean liquor and cabbage, bring to the boil, check for seasoning, and simmer for 20 minutes or until the cabbage is almost cooked. Add the beans and cook for a further 10 minutes, stirring frequently, until the cabbage is tender. Remove from the heat, stir in the bread and the rest of the parsley and let it sit for 5 minutes so that the bread absorbs the liquid. Serve this soup with the extra virgin olive oil drizzled on top. If you have to reheat this soup, do so gently, with minimal stirring and an extra splash of water.

HARIRA WITH CHARD, TOMATOES AND OREGANO

Traditional harira is a thick lamb soup from Morocco. This version, with fewer pulses and more vegetables, is lighter and fresher – good for summer.

Serves 8 as a starter, 4 as a main course

    2.75 litres cold water

    1 neck of lamb (1–1.5kg), in 3–4 pieces

    1 large onion, finely chopped

    3 garlic cloves, finely chopped

    3 celery sticks, finely chopped

    a pinch of saffron (40 threads)

    $1/2$ teaspoon each of ground cinnamon, turmeric and ginger

    2 ground cloves

    nutmeg (5 grates on a fine grater)

    1 large bunch fresh coriander, stalks and leaves separated, washed and
      chopped

    100g small green lentils

    120g chana dhal (small, split and skinned chickpeas)

    500g small to medium ripe, sweet tomatoes, quartered

    2 tablespoons roughly chopped fresh oregano

    150–200g chard, leaves roughly chopped, stalks finely chopped

    3 tablespoons plain flour mixed with 3 tablespoons extra virgin olive oil

    a squeeze of lemon

    sea salt and black pepper

Put the water and lamb into a large saucepan. (Make sure the saucepan is big enough to accommodate all the ingredients.) Bring to the boil and simmer for 5 minutes, skimming any scum or fat off the surface. Now add the onion, garlic, celery, saffron, spices and some salt and pepper, as well as the stalky half of the coriander. Cook for 1 hour before adding the lentils and chana dhal, then simmer for another half-hour. Take out the pieces of lamb, which should now be soft enough to be pulled off the bone and flaked a little. Return the lamb meat to the pot, season with salt and pepper, then add the tomatoes and oregano. Cook for another 10 minutes, then add the chopped chard and simmer for a further 5 minutes. Finally, add the flour mixed with the oil and stir briskly. Season the soup with salt, the coriander leaves and lemon juice. Continue to cook the soup for another 10 minutes, or until the pulses are soft. Check the seasoning and serve.

CHICKEN DUMPLING BROTH

This is a soup to make with the bones of a Sunday roast chicken. Dried limes are a speciality of Iran, not strictly Moro's domain, yet they provide such an interesting eastern flavour that we felt we should include them. If you cannot source Iranian dried limes, you can dry your own (see page 286). However, the soup is also very fine with the zest and juice of $1^1/_2$ fresh limes added at the end.

Serves 4

BROTH

> 1.5 litres flavoursome home-made Chicken Stock (see page 313)
>
> 3 dried limes (see page 286), crushed finely in a coffee grinder or food processor
>
> 2 tablespoons roughly chopped fresh flat-leaf parsley
>
> 2 teaspoons lime juice
>
> sea salt and black pepper

CHICKEN AND CARDAMOM DUMPLINGS

> 200g raw organic or free-range chicken breast, skinned
>
> 3 level tablespoons chickpea (gram) flour
>
> 10 green cardamom pods, black seeds inside only, finely ground in a mortar
>
> $^1/_2$ garlic clove, crushed with a good pinch of salt
>
> 1 egg, lightly beaten

To make the dumplings, place the chicken breast, half the chickpea flour, the cardamom, garlic, egg and a pinch of salt and pepper in a food processor and whizz until fine. Now drop teaspoon-sized lumps into the remaining flour and roll into little balls each the size of a marble or a hazelnut with the shell on. Set aside on baking parchment for later.

Bring the chicken stock to a gentle simmer and add the crushed dried limes. Once the limes have infused for 15–20 minutes, strain off, return the stock to the heat and taste for seasoning. Now add the dumplings, simmer for a minute, then add the chopped parsley and fresh lime juice to taste. You may need to adjust the seasoning. Serve at once.

THREE YOGHURT SOUPS

We make yoghurt on a daily basis in the restaurant and leave it round the back of the wood-burning oven to set (see our recipe on page 279). The miracle of the yoghurt is that at the same time as giving a soup freshness, it also imparts richness. These three variations are very distinct, inspired by the famous yoghurt soups of Turkey.

PEA SOUP WITH YOGHURT AND MINT

This refreshing soup can be made in minutes. We like to serve it with toast rubbed with garlic and drizzled with olive oil. It is also delicious chilled or served at room temperature on a warm day.

Serves 4-6

> 1 egg yolk
>
> $^1/_2$ tablespoon cornflour or plain flour
>
> 400g Greek yoghurt
>
> 750ml Light Chicken or Vegetable Stock (see page 313)
>
> 50g butter
>
> 1 tablespoon olive oil
>
> 2 garlic cloves, thinly sliced
>
> 3 tablespoons roughly chopped fresh mint
>
> 750g peas or petits pois, fresh or frozen (petits pois are usually more tender)
>
> sea salt and black pepper

TO SERVE

> 100g Greek yoghurt, mixed with $^1/_2$ garlic clove, crushed
>
> extra virgin olive oil

In a large bowl, stir the egg with the cornflour until smooth. Now whisk in the yoghurt, thin with half the stock and set aside. (The flour and egg will stabilise the yoghurt so it will not split when heated.) Place a large saucepan over a low heat and add the butter and olive oil. When the butter begins to foam, add the garlic and half the mint and fry until the garlic turns golden. Add the peas, and cook for 5 minutes, stirring occasionally, before adding the remaining stock. Bring to a gentle simmer and cook for about 2 minutes or until the peas are tender. With an electric hand-held blender, liquidiser or food processor, blend the peas very well, making sure that the texture is as smooth as possible. Return to the saucepan and stir in the thinned yoghurt. Put the saucepan back on the heat and season with salt and pepper. Do not allow the soup to boil, but remove from the heat just before it bubbles. Stir in the remaining mint, check for seasoning and serve with a swirl of seasoned garlic yoghurt on top and a drizzle of extra virgin olive oil.

CAULIFLOWER AND CORIANDER SOUP

The mustiness of cauliflower, the earthiness of fresh coriander and the citrus quality of coriander seed combine to make a wow of a soup. It is then finished with nutty caramelised butter, a traditional Turkish accompaniment to yoghurt.

Serves 4–6

> 60g butter
>
> 3 tablespoons olive oil
>
> 1 medium onion, finely chopped
>
> 3 garlic cloves, finely sliced
>
> 1–1$^1/_2$ tablespoons coriander seeds, roughly ground
>
> 1 x 1 kg (or 2 small) cauliflower, leaves discarded, washed and sliced roughly 1cm thick
>
> 750ml Vegetable Stock (see page 313) or water
>
> 1 egg yolk
>
> $^1/_2$ tablespoon cornflour or plain flour
>
> 400g Greek yoghurt
>
> 2 tablespoons roughly chopped fresh coriander
>
> 2 teaspoons Turkish chilli flakes (kirmizi biber, optional)
>
> sea salt and black pepper

CARAMELISED BUTTER

> 75g unsalted butter

In a large saucepan, melt the 60g butter with the olive oil over a medium heat. Stir in the onion, garlic and coriander seeds and cook for 10–15 minutes or until light brown, stirring once in a while. Add the cauliflower and 300ml of the stock to the pan, then cover and simmer over a medium heat for 20–30 minutes. Every now and then mash the soup (with a potato masher) instead of stirring it. When the cauliflower is soft and smooth, add the rest of the stock and bring to a simmer. This soup does have a slightly granular texture due to the cauliflower, which we like. (If it is not to your liking, give it a whizz in a blender.) In a large bowl, stir the egg with the cornflour until a smooth paste is formed (this will stabilise the yoghurt when it is heated). Now stir in the yoghurt and whisk the mixture into the soup. Bring to the boil, season with salt and pepper and stir in the fresh coriander.

To serve the soup, melt the 75g butter over the lowest heat. The pale whey will separate, turn golden brown and develop a nutty, caramelised aroma (but take care as it can burn easily). Sprinkle some on each bowl of soup and top with chilli flakes.

SAFFRON, TAHINI AND YOGHURT SOUP

This subtle and intriguing velvety soup is unique. Perhaps not for unadventurous palates, but we feel it is very special and deserves to be tried. The rich, nutty flavours of the tahini and saffron need to be carefully balanced by the sharpness of the yoghurt and lemon.

Serves 4

1 egg yolk

$^1/_2$ tablespoon cornflour

500g Greek yoghurt

3 tablespoons tahini

2 tablespoons extra virgin olive oil

1 garlic clove, crushed to a very smooth paste with 1 teaspoon salt

juice and finely grated zest of about $^1/_2$ lemon

sea salt and black pepper

750ml Light Chicken or Vegetable Stock (see page 313)

40 threads saffron, infused in 2 tablespoons boiling water

3 tablespoons roughly chopped fresh flat-leaf parsley

$1^1/_2$ tablespoons roughly chopped fresh mint

2 tablespoons roughly chopped fresh dill

Although this is a very simple soup to prepare, there is a particular way of combining the ingredients to ensure it is successful. In a large mixing bowl, gradually stir the egg yolk into the flour, avoiding lumps, and then whisk in the yoghurt (this stabilises the yoghurt when it is heated). Add the tahini, olive oil, garlic, lemon zest and juice, some salt and the chicken stock, and stir with a balloon whisk until all the ingredients are combined. Transfer to a saucepan and gently heat the soup over a low to medium heat, stirring every now and then. Never allow the soup to boil but remove from the heat just before it bubbles.

Stir in half the saffron infusion and all the herbs, and check the seasoning – you need to achieve a fine balance of salt and lemon flavours. Serve with a swirl of the remaining saffron on top.

TAPAS AND MEZZE, STARTERS AND LIGHT MEALS

The following recipes are starters at Moro, but that is because we are a restaurant. Most of these dishes actually originate from tapas and mezze we have enjoyed throughout Spain and the Muslim Mediterranean, but they are infinitely flexible and can equally be used as starters or light meals. As part of a selection of tapas or mezze, the quantities we give will be enough for six to eight people. For a starter or light meal, they are sufficient for four. There is a huge amount of choice in this chapter, so we have divided the recipes into fish, meat, vegetables and eggs to make things easy.

FISH AND SHELLFISH

Gambas y setas (Prawns and oyster mushrooms with manzanilla sherry)

Salpicón de marisco (Seafood salad)

Gambas al ajillo (Garlic prawns with white wine and chilli)

Cigalas con oloroso (Langoustines with oloroso sherry)

Prawns marinated in yoghurt and spices with wheat berries

Mussels with harissa

Almejas con habichuelas (Clams with white beans and saffron)

Chocos con habas (Cuttlefish with broad beans and mint)

Calamar a la parrilla (Grilled squid)

Pan-fried squid and prawns with harissa

Grilled sardines wrapped in vine leaves with tahini sauce

Cured mullet roe with avocado and dill

Pimientos de piquillo rellenos con bacalao (Piquillo peppers
stuffed with salt cod)

Remojón (Salt cod, orange and potato salad)

Ensalada de anchoas (Grilled red pepper and anchovy salad)

Bacalao frito (Deep-fried salt cod in saffron batter)

One of the joys of visiting the Mediterranean is the quality and variety of shellfish and fish so readily available. In the UK it's necessary to make a bit more effort, by finding out what your area has to offer. Know the state of your local market or fishmonger, and once you get there, use your eyes. Is the squid white? Are the scales of the fish bright? Shopping has always been one of the skills of a good cook, and for seafood especially. Good luck!

GAMBAS Y SETAS

PRAWNS AND OYSTER MUSHROOMS WITH
MANZANILLA SHERRY

On arriving back in the Alpujarras one February, we discovered our basement had flooded due to particularly heavy rains. It wasn't long before our neighbour Antonio was inviting us to witness the peeling paint in his cellar. Antonio's cellar had boxes of vegetables in store, crates of lethal local wine and bales of hay. Each bale was cascading with oyster mushrooms. (Mushroom spores are widely sold in Spain as mushroom growing is a popular pastime.) On seeing our eyes light up, he cut off a clump, and we made the following recipe for supper that evening. We recommend drinking a glass of ice-cold manzanilla or fino sherry with this dish, as well as cooking with it.

Serves 6–8 as a tapa, 4 for a starter or light meal

> 500g oyster mushrooms
>
> 3–4 tablespoons olive oil
>
> 2 garlic cloves, finely chopped
>
> 150ml manzanilla or fino sherry
>
> 500g North Atlantic prawns in their shells, peeled (see page 141)
>
> 2 tablespoons roughly chopped fresh flat-leaf parsley
>
> sea salt and black pepper

Trim the tough stalks off the mushrooms and discard. Place a very large frying pan (or a smaller one, and cook in two batches) over a high heat and add the olive oil. When a light haze appears, add the mushrooms, gill-side down. Fry for 30–60 seconds until slightly golden, salt lightly, then turn and cook for 30 more seconds. Now add the garlic in the spaces between the mushrooms, and fry for a few more seconds, taking care the garlic does not burn, then pour on the sherry, and add a tiny bit more salt and black pepper. Seconds before serving, add the prawns (if already cooked) just to warm through. If using uncooked prawns, add them earlier, when you add the sherry. Stir in the parsley and serve immediately. Good with toast.

Variation
The combination of prawns and oyster mushrooms is also delicious in Revueltos (see pages 141–2).

SALPICÓN DE MARISCO

SEAFOOD SALAD

Although this dish is served throughout Andalucía, it tastes especially good at the classic Jerez restaurant La Mesa Redonda. Chunks of crunchy green pepper, ripe tomatoes and mild onion are mixed with prawns, squid and mussels and tossed with olive oil and vinegar. It is easy to make and a delight to eat.

Serves 6–8 as a tapa, 4 as a starter or light meal

- 16 cherry tomatoes, quartered
- $^1/_2$ medium red onion or mild salad onion, thinly sliced
- 2 green peppers, halved lengthways, seeded and cut into thin strips 3cm long
- 2 medium squid, the size of your hand, cleaned (see page 84)
- 12 large or 20 small mussels, rinsed well and cleaned of beard
- 3 tablespoons white wine or fino sherry
- 2 tablespoons water
- 24 North Atlantic prawns, preferably in their shells, peeled (see page 141)
- 3 tablespoons roughly chopped fresh flat-leaf parsley
- sea salt and black pepper

DRESSING

- 1 small garlic clove, crushed to a paste with salt
- 3 tablespoons good-quality red wine vinegar (see page 287)
- $^1/_4$ teaspoon caster sugar
- 6 tablespoons extra virgin olive oil

Place the tomatoes, onions and peppers in a large bowl. Then make the dressing. Mix the garlic with the vinegar and sugar, whisk in the olive oil and season with salt and pepper. Set both the vegetables and dressing aside.

Cut the bodies of the cleaned squid into small strips or rounds no bigger than 1cm wide and the tentacles in half or quarters, depending on size. Heat the white wine or sherry and water in a large saucepan and when it begins to simmer, add the mussels. Steam, lid on, for roughly 2–3 minutes or until the shells have opened fully (discard any that are still closed). Remove from the pan with a slotted spoon and set aside to cool. Now add the squid and prawns (if raw) to the saucepan and replace the lid. Give the saucepan a little shake and steam for a couple of minutes, stirring once, or until the squid is tender and the prawns are pink all over. If your prawns are already cooked, they do not need to be heated through.

Remove from the heat and transfer the squid, prawns and half the mussels to the bowl of chopped vegetables. Take the meat out of the other mussels, discarding the shells, and add to the bowl along with 4–5 tablespoons of the steaming juice from the pan (strained through a small sieve just in case it is gritty). Pour over the dressing, add the parsley, toss well and season with salt and pepper. Place in the fridge (making sure the seafood is only just warm) for 30 minutes to 1 hour for the flavours to mingle. Before serving, give the salad another good toss and serve with lemon, if you wish, and bread.

GAMBAS AL AJILLO

GARLIC PRAWNS WITH WHITE WINE AND CHILLI

At Moro we recently bought some pale pink prawns from Barcelona and served them, briefly boiled, with alioli (garlic mayonnaise) and lemon. They were delicious but not quite as sweet as we had expected, so we served the rest al ajillo – sautéed with garlic, white wine and chilli. Once you taste these prawns, you will want to suck the heads, gnaw the legs and crunch the shell until not a drop of the sweet garlicky juice is left.

Serves 6–8 as a tapa, 4 for a starter or light meal

      4 tablespoons olive oil

      500g prawns in their shells (raw tiger prawns or cooked North Atlantic prawns), or brown shrimps (see page 141)

      sea salt

      4 garlic cloves, thinly sliced

      $1/2$ Spanish dried guindilla chilli, seeds removed, sliced into rounds, or 1–2 small dried bird's-eye red chillies, seeds removed and crumbled, depending how picante (hot) you like the sauce

      100–150ml white wine

      2 tablespoons roughly chopped fresh flat-leaf parsley (optional)

In a large frying pan or wide saucepan, heat the olive oil over a high heat. When the oil is hot and just beginning to smoke, add the prawns (only if using large raw tiger prawns) and a pinch of salt, and fry for a minute until they smell sweet and the shells begin to blister. Now turn over, adding the garlic and chilli. Fry for 30 seconds or until the garlic turns golden. (If using cooked North Atlantic prawns or brown shrimps, add the garlic and chilli to the pan first.) Add the wine and cook for another minute or two to burn off the alcohol. There will be a fair amount of sizzling and spluttering from the pan, so beware! Finish with the parsley (if using) and taste for seasoning. Serve immediately with some bread to mop up the juices. Finger bowls are a good idea too!

CIGALAS CON OLOROSO
LANGOUSTINES WITH OLOROSO SHERRY

One doesn't often see langoustines, what the Spanish call cigalas, in the small fish market in our local town, but when it is a bank holiday, local fiesta, Christmas or Easter, the fishmongers get in special things. We were in a shop opposite our fishmonger's when we spotted the langoustines, and because there were only a few left, we quickly dashed over and asked for them to be saved for us. When we came to buy them, the woman next to us was most amused: 'Tu sabes cuanto cuestan?' (Do you know how much they are?) We knew they were going to be expensive, but when the fishmonger said 40 euros a kilo, we were a bit stunned. We felt embarrassed at having brashly ordered them without asking the price, but couldn't back down now. Luckily, there weren't many, so we ended up handing over 10 euros for some very fresh cigalas from Adra and that evening steamed them with nutty oloroso sherry. It was worth it. If you cannot get hold of langoustines, then large prawns are a good alternative.

Serves 6–8 as a tapa, 4 for a starter or light meal

> 6 tablespoons olive oil
>
> $^1/_2$ large onion, finely chopped
>
> 24 medium langoustines
>
> 150ml medium oloroso sherry (if you can only get hold of sweet oloroso, reduce the amount to 100ml and add a squeeze of lemon)
>
> 2 tablespoons roughly chopped fresh flat-leaf parsley (optional)
>
> sea salt and black pepper

In a small saucepan, heat half the olive oil over a low heat. Add the onion and a tiny pinch of salt and fry for about 10–15 minutes, stirring occasionally, until it turns golden brown, caramelises and is sweet in flavour. Remove from the heat, drain off any excess oil and set aside. (This can be done in advance.) About 10 minutes before you are ready to eat, put a large saucepan (big enough to accommodate the langoustines) over a high heat. Add the remaining olive oil and, when it is hot, add the langoustines and cover with a lid. Give the pan a good shake and cook for half a minute. Remove the lid, add the softened onion, oloroso sherry and a splash of water. Gently simmer for 3–4 minutes or until cooked, stirring once or twice. Season with salt and pepper, and add the parsley (if using) just before serving. Serve with bread and a finger bowl.

PRAWNS MARINATED IN YOGHURT AND SPICES WITH WHEAT BERRIES

As well as making an unusual flavour combination, the textural contrast between the soft grilled green pepper and the chewy wheat berries is delicious. Yoghurt marinades are a brilliant vehicle for most meat or fish. This is an adaptation of a recipe from a book called 'The Arabian Delights Cookbook' by Anne Marie Weiss-Armush (Lowell House).

Serves 6–8 as a mezze, 4 for a starter or light meal

    600g North Atlantic prawns, shell on, peeled (see page 141),

      (250g peeled weight)

    50g wheat berries or pearl barley

    4 tablespoons extra virgin olive oil

    2 squeezes lemon

    2 green peppers

    6 tablespoons fresh coriander leaves

    sea salt and black pepper

YOGHURT MARINADE

    200g Greek yoghurt

    1 garlic clove, crushed to a smooth paste with salt

    $1^1/_2$ teaspoons cumin seeds, freshly ground

Place the marinade ingredients in a mixing bowl, stir together, then add the peeled prawns. Leave in the fridge for 30 minutes to 2 hours.

While the prawns are marinating, cook the wheat berries (or pearl barley). Put in a small saucepan, cover with 1 litre water and simmer over a medium heat for about 45 minutes or until tender. Drain in a colander, transfer to a bowl and season with a little salt and pepper, 2 tablespoons of the olive oil and a squeeze of lemon juice. Set aside.

To char the peppers for peeling, there are four ways: one is over charcoal on a barbecue, the second under a hot grill, the third on a heat diffuser over gas and the fourth in a very hot oven (220°C/425°F/Gas 7). Blacken the skin of each pepper on all sides (the oven will make the peppers soft but not black). Put in a bowl and cover with clingfilm. When cool enough to handle, take out the stalk and central core, remove the seeds and peel off the charred skin. To retain the flavour, all this is best done without using water to peel the peppers; wash your hands from time to time instead. Tear the flesh into strips, transfer to a small mixing bowl, add the remaining olive oil and lemon juice and season with some salt and pepper. Set aside.

When you are ready to assemble the salad, mix the coriander with the green peppers and put on a plate. Now warm the wheat berries in a saucepan with the prawns and any extra marinade over a medium heat until just hot. It is important not to cook the prawns for too long as they will toughen. Nor must you bring it to a simmer as the yoghurt might split – just steaming hot is fine. Spoon the warm prawns, wheat berries and any extra sauce on top of the peppers and serve immediately.

MUSSELS WITH HARISSA

Serves 6–8 as a mezze, 4 for a starter or light meal

1 kg mussels or small to medium clams

4 tablespoons olive oil

2 cloves garlic, finely chopped

100g Harissa (see page 282)

3 tablespoons roughly chopped fresh coriander

extra virgin olive oil for drizzling

sea salt and black pepper

Wash the mussels under cold water, discarding any that are open or broken. Clean well and pull off any beards. Drain. In a large saucepan, heat the oil over a medium heat. When hot but not smoking, add the garlic and fry for a few seconds until it just begins to colour. Add the mussels, the harissa and half the coriander, and cook, covered for the first 30 seconds to a minute until the mussels begin to open and release their juices, shaking the pan as you go. Then cook uncovered for a further minute or two until the shells have opened fully. (Throw away any that are still closed.) Taste for seasoning; the mussels may need a little salt, but not much. Serve immediately with the remaining coriander, an extra drizzle of olive oil over the top and bread.

ALMEJAS CON HABICHUELAS

CLAMS WITH WHITE BEANS AND SAFFRON

Clams are adored by the Spanish, and when you visit a fish market in Spain (our favourite is in Jerez), there tend to be a few sizes on offer, according to what is available locally. Whether it is the tiny coquinas (wedge shells) with a purple blush, or almejas finas (carpet-shell/palourdes) or chirlas (striped venus) or the larger (and often chewier or grittier) almejones brillantes (smooth venus, which are light brown in colour), or indeed berberechos (cockles), all are delicious. With so many different varieties (and often local names) come many recipes. If you have tried the classic way of steaming them open with garlic, parsley and white wine or sherry, then try this clam dish we have enjoyed.

We use the Spanish planchada beans, which are like flat cannellini beans, or butter beans, but any white bean will do.

Serves 6–8 as a tapa, 4 for a starter or light meal

    1 kg small-medium clams, such as venus or palourdes (or mussels)

    4 tablespoons olive oil

    2 garlic cloves, finely chopped

    150ml manzanilla sherry or white wine

    2 tablespoons roughly chopped fresh flat-leaf parsley

    300g cooked, drained white beans (see page 17)

    30 threads saffron, infused in 3 tablespoons boiling water

    extra virgin olive oil

    sea salt and black pepper

Wash the clams under cold water and drain thoroughly, discarding any that are open or broken. In a large saucepan, heat the oil over a medium heat. When hot but not smoking, add the garlic and fry for a few seconds until it just begins to colour. Add the manzanilla or white wine and reduce by two-thirds. Then add the clams and half the parsley, the beans and the saffron-infused water, shaking the pan as you go. Simmer for about 2–3 minutes or until the clams are fully opened. (Throw away any that are still closed.) Taste for seasoning (the clams may well not need any salt), and serve immediately with the remaining parsley, a drizzle of extra virgin olive oil over the top, bread and a spoon.

CHOCOS CON HABAS
CUTTLEFISH WITH BROAD BEANS AND MINT

This is an Andalucían tapa that is typical of Cádiz, especially around the beginning of spring when broad beans come into season, which in Spain is roughly the end of February or early March. Choco is the colloquial name for cuttlefish (other names include sepia or jibia). Cuttlefish is a close relation of squid, although the tube tends to be thicker and it has a slightly creamier taste. Substitute squid for cuttlefish if need be.

Serves 6–8 as a tapa, 4 for a starter or light meal

3 small cuttlefish or 3 medium squid, roughly the size of your hand, cleaned (see page 84)

4 tablespoons olive oil

$^1/_2$ large onion, roughly chopped

sea salt and black pepper

2 garlic cloves, thinly sliced

$^1/_4$ teaspoon fennel seeds (optional)

1 bay leaf (preferably fresh)

$^1/_2$ teaspoon sweet paprika

150ml white wine or fino sherry

200ml water

1 kg small, young broad beans in pods, shelled, or 280g fresh (or frozen) shelled broad beans

3 level tablespoons roughly chopped fresh mint

2 tablespoons extra virgin olive oil

Cut the bodies and wings of the cuttlefish or squid into small strips no wider than 1cm or longer than 4cm, and the tentacles in halves or quarters, depending on size.

In a medium pan with a lid, heat the olive oil over a medium heat. Add the onion and a pinch of salt and fry gently for 5–10 minutes, stirring occasionally. When the onion begins to turn golden and caramelise, add the garlic, fennel seeds and bay leaf, and fry for 2 more minutes. Now add the cuttlefish or squid and paprika, stir well, then pour on the wine and water. Cover, bring to a simmer and turn the heat down low. Depending on the thickness of the cuttlefish or squid pieces, cook for 30–50 minutes, stirring occasionally, or until they begin to tenderise. Add the broad beans and cook uncovered over a higher heat for 10–15 minutes more, until the beans are tender and the juices run thick. Stir in the mint and the extra virgin olive oil, and serve straight away with a glass of chilled sherry.

CALAMAR A LA PARRILLA
GRILLED SQUID

At Moro, we are lucky enough to be able to grill squid over charcoal, but cooking it at home under a grill or on a barbecue also works well. We serve it with a number of sauces, though not at the same time, and there are five to choose from on pages 86-8.

Serves 6-8 as a tapa or mezze, 4 for a starter or light meal

> 4 medium squid, roughly the size of your hand
> 2-3 tablespoons olive oil
> sea salt and black pepper

TO SERVE

> sauce of choice (see pages 86-8)
> 150g rocket leaves, dressed with a little olive oil, lemon and salt
> 1 lemon, cut into wedges

To clean the squid, first pull the head away from the body, then empty out the body cavity, discarding the gut, ink sac and transparent quill. Gently pull the wings free from the sides, being careful not to puncture the body, and remove any pinkish membrane. Rinse clean under running water and drain. Keep the tentacles intact but remove the eyes and mouth by cutting just above where the tentacles join.

To prepare the squid, run a small sharp knife along the seam of the cleaned body so you can open it into a rough triangle. Placing the outside of the body face down on a chopping board, use a blunt serrated table knife to score the flesh in a criss-cross fashion trying to go at least halfway through the flesh without cutting a hole.

If serving the squid with charmoula (see page 87), rub the mixture in as described and let it sit in the fridge for between 20 minutes and 2 hours.

If you are grilling over charcoal, light it 20 minutes before you wish to cook. If you have a griddle pan, get it very hot (no oil) before putting on the squid. If you are grilling under a domestic grill (a griddle pan is preferable), turn it to a high heat 5 minutes before you are ready to cook. Season the squid all over with a little salt and black pepper and drizzle with olive oil. Grill for about 2-3 minutes on the scored side, then turn over for another 2 minutes or until cooked but tender and a little coloured. The squid bodies should curl into a cigar shape when you turn them. If you prefer to roast the squid, preheat the oven to 220°C/425°F/Gas 7, and cook for 5-10 minutes until cooked, but still tender. Alternatively, you can pan-fry it.

If serving as a tapa, cut each squid in half; otherwise, serve whole with one of the following sauces, and the rocket salad and lemon.

BLACK INK SAUCE

4 tablespoons olive oil

1 medium onion, finely chopped

1 green pepper, seeded and finely chopped

3 garlic cloves, finely chopped

150ml white wine

1 tablespoon tomato purée

6 x 4g sachets squid/cuttlefish ink (from fishmonger or good delicatessen),
   or $1^1/_2$ tablespoons

2 piquillo peppers, cut into strips, to decorate (optional)

sea salt and black pepper

Place a medium saucepan over a medium heat and add the olive oil. When it is hot, but not smoking, add the onion, pepper and a pinch of salt and soften for 15–20 minutes, stirring occasionally, until golden. Turn down the heat if necessary. Now add the garlic and continue cooking for another 5 minutes. Pour in the wine, bring to a gentle simmer and reduce by half. Stir in the tomato purée and squid ink. Taste for seasoning and add a little water if your sauce is thicker than pouring consistency. Serve warm, spooned over the grilled squid, and decorate with strips of piquillo peppers.

SAFFRON ALIOLI

Alioli is the Spanish garlicky mayonnaise, delicious with fish, rice or chicken. This one has a little bit of saffron, which makes it particularly good with grilled squid.

2 garlic cloves

sea salt

a squeeze of lemon

2 egg yolks

250ml each of extra virgin olive oil and sunflower oil

30 strands saffron, infused in $^1/_2$ tablespoon boiling water for 10 minutes

Crush the garlic cloves in a mortar with a pinch of salt. When as smooth as possible, add the squeeze of lemon juice. At this point, you can transfer the garlic and egg yolks to a mixing bowl and whisk in the oils drop by drop with a balloon whisk (especially if your mortar is small), otherwise, continue in the mortar. Add the egg yolks and stir to break the membrane. Continue stirring whilst you add the oils, almost painfully

slowly at first, drop by drop, then with more confidence when a thick emulsion has formed. When all the oil has been incorporated, stir in the saffron–infused water carefully, and season to taste with more salt and lemon juice if necessary. When the squid is ready, serve immediately with the saffron alioli on the side.

CHARMOULA

This is the classic Moroccan marinade (actually more of a paste) used to flavour meat, fish and vegetables.

> 2 garlic cloves
> 2 teaspoons cumin seeds, freshly ground
> juice of 1 lemon
> $^1/_2$ tablespoon red wine vinegar
> $^3/_4$ teaspoon sweet paprika (preferably Moroccan)
> 8 tablespoons roughly chopped fresh coriander
> 2 tablespoons extra virgin olive oil
> sea salt and black pepper

We make charmoula in a mortar. Pound the garlic with 1 level teaspoon salt until a smooth paste is formed, then add the cumin followed by the lemon juice, vinegar, paprika, coriander and olive oil. Check the seasoning. Rub two-thirds of the mixture on to the prepared squid and let it stand in the fridge for between 20 minutes and 2 hours. Grill the squid as described on page 84 and serve the rest of the charmoula drizzled over the top.

POMEGRANATE SAUCE

2 tablespoons Pomegranate Molasses (see page 284)
2 tablespoons extra virgin olive oil
2 tablespoons pomegranate seeds (preferably Iranian or Turkish)

Grill the squid as described on page 84 and serve with the molasses and olive oil drizzled all over and pomegranate seeds scattered on top.

ZHOUG

Zhoug is a green chilli paste. It is refreshing and different from harissa (see page 282) because it contains fresh coriander and ground cardamom. Harissa, though, is also wonderful with grilled or pan-fried squid (see opposite).

250g long green chillies, about 5-6cm long
$^1/_2$ teaspoon green cardamom seeds, green husks removed, finely ground
$^1/_3$ teaspoon coriander seeds, ground
$^1/_2$ teaspoon cumin seeds, ground
4 tablespoons very roughly chopped fresh coriander
$1^1/_2$ garlic cloves
juice of $^1/_4$ lemon
2-3 tablespoons extra virgin olive oil
sea salt and black pepper

It is advisable to wear rubber gloves when preparing the chillies. Remove the tops of the chillies, then slice in half lengthways. Lay each chilli on a chopping board, cut-side up, and gently scrape away the seeds with a teaspoon and discard. Roughly chop the chillies and place in a food processor with a sharp blade. Blend the chillies with a pinch of salt, the cardamom, coriander, cumin, fresh coriander and garlic until smooth. It is important that the paste is as smooth as possible. Transfer to a mixing bowl. Now add the lemon juice and olive oil, with salt and pepper to taste. When the squid is cooked, serve immediately with the zhoug on the side.

PAN-FRIED SQUID AND PRAWNS WITH HARISSA

If you like the combination of squid and chilli, then try this. The squid and prawns are pan–fried, so it is really quick to cook, provided you already have the harissa.

Serves 6–8 as a mezze, 4 for a starter or light meal

>   3 medium squid, about the size of your hand, cleaned (see page 84)
>   (300g prepared weight)
>   3–4 tablespoons olive oil
>   sea salt and black pepper
>   60g Harissa (see page 282)
>   500g North Atlantic prawns, shell on, peeled (see page 141).
>   (200g peeled weight)
>   3 tablespoons roughly chopped fresh coriander

Clean the squid as described on page 84, then cut the bodies into small strips or rounds no bigger than 1cm wide, and the tentacles in halves or quarters, depending on size.

In a large frying pan, heat the olive oil over a high heat. When the oil just begins to smoke, add the squid, taking care as it might spit a bit. Add a pinch of salt and pepper and sizzle the squid for roughly a minute, stirring a couple of times. Then add the harissa, and stir once more until evenly distributed. Finally, add the prawns and coriander, and taste for seasoning. (If using raw prawns, add at the same time as the squid, using 4 tablespoons of olive oil instead of 3.) Serve immediately with bread and a little salad dressed with olive oil and lemon.

GRILLED SARDINES WRAPPED IN VINE LEAVES WITH TAHINI SAUCE

Whenever we say 'grilled', we ideally mean over charcoal, but this dish will still taste fantastic if cooked under a domestic grill (not in a griddle pan) or in a hot oven (200°C/400°F/Gas 6). The gum mastic, a resin from a tree native to Greece and Turkey, brings a 'can't put my finger on it' exoticism to the dish, but is by no means essential.

Serves 6–8 as a mezze, 4 for a starter or light meal

    8 large or 12 small fresh sardines, scaled and gutted

    24 vine leaves in brine or fresh, blanched (2–3 vine leaves per sardine)

    2 good pinches of gum mastic, pounded in a mortar with a teaspoon of
       sea salt (optional)

TO SERVE

    1 quantity Tahini Sauce (see page 242)

    1 lemon, cut in half

    Flatbread (see page 36, optional)

Scaling sardines is easy: just place each fish under running water and rub as you would a bar of soap. The scales will fall away and any left behind will be easily visible. To gut the fish, make a slit up the length of the belly with a sharp knife or scissors. Wash out the interior of the belly under running water and cut off the fins with scissors (a fishmonger could easily do all of this in a couple of minutes). Pat the sardines dry with kitchen paper. In a large bowl toss the sardines with the gum mastic/sea salt mixture, cover and chill for about half an hour.

Rinse the vine leaves in cold water to get rid of any excess brine, then dry and pinch off the stalks. It is only necessary to wrap the main part of the sardine body in the vine leaves, not its head or tail. First cover the belly of the sardine with one vine leaf, then cover the back with another leaf. Repeat this with all the sardines.

If you are grilling over charcoal, light it 20–30 minutes before you wish to cook. If you are grilling under a domestic grill, turn it to a high heat 5 minutes before you are ready. Grill for about 2–3 minutes on either side. The vine leaves should be slightly charred and the flesh cooked through to the bone (when it comes away easily), but still juicy inside. Serve with the tahini sauce on the side, lemon and warm flatbread. The vine leaves are edible as long as they are not too charred!

CURED MULLET ROE WITH AVOCADO AND DILL

We really have Engin Akyn to thank for teaching us about Turkish food, from the classic manti (see page 106) to this more unusual mullet roe and avocado salad. To the trained foodie's eye, the market near the famous spice bazaar has some of the great speciality foods of the world, one being bottarga (cured grey mullet roe). Bottarga is found all along the Mediterranean/Adriatic, known as bottargue in France and bottarga in Italy. The roe of the grey mullet is first salted, then pressed to extract the moisture. Sometimes sealed in a yellowy wax, this roe can be used in the same way as salted anchovies. Sliced thinly or grated, its delicious salty flavour and waxy texture is wonderful with scrambled eggs, on warm beans (borlotti with lemon and olive oil), on blanched sprouting broccoli, or, indeed, in this recipe (one of our favourite starters), with creamy avocado and dill. We adore Turkey and will find any excuse to go back, one being we need some more bread paddles for our wood-burning oven.

Serves 6–8 as a mezze, 4 for a starter or light meal

> 3 ripe Hass avocados
>
> $1/2$ small red onion, finely chopped
>
> 50g block bottarga, sliced across very thinly, or salted anchovies
>
> 3 tablespoons small sprigs fresh dill
>
> 1 bunch wild rocket leaves, about 100g (optional)

DRESSING

> $1^1/2$ tablespoons lemon juice
>
> 3 tablespoons extra virgin olive oil
>
> sea salt and black pepper

For the dressing, whisk the lemon juice and olive oil together in a small bowl until emulsified. Season with salt and pepper and taste. Just before dressing the salad, whisk again.

Cut each avocado in half lengthways. Take out the stone and remove the skin. Slice each half lengthways to within 1cm of the narrow end so the slices are still attached. Each slice should be about 4–5mm thick. Fan out each half and arrange on a large plate. Spoon over the lemon dressing. Sprinkle over the chopped onion, followed by the slices of mullet roe and finally sprigs of dill. Season with a little salt and pepper and serve with the extra rocket if you want a bit more salad.

PIMIENTOS DE PIQUILLO RELLENOS CON BACALAO

PIQUILLO PEPPERS STUFFED WITH SALT COD

Just after leaving cooking school, I (Samuel) drove with my friend Johnny to San Sebastian, where I had this exciting dish. I thought to myself, 'No one ever told me Spanish food could be like this.' When I got home determined to re-create it, I was puzzled where the smoked flavour came from. Unfamiliar with all things Spanish at that time, I could only think it must be the fish. Smoked haddock is what I used, which is a good substitute for salt cod, but the grilled Dutch peppers I used instead of piquillos were disastrous! Good piquillo peppers (from Navarra in northeast Spain) are grilled over beechwood, and that was the smokiness I was tasting. The concentration of flavour and the slight piquancy are also what make piquillo peppers unique.

Serves 6–8 as a tapa, 4 for a starter or light meal

110g salt cod, soaked for 24 hours in cold water in the fridge, changing
the water 2 or 3 times

400ml milk

$1/4$ medium onion, peeled

5 black peppercorns

2 bay leaves (preferably fresh)

175g potatoes, peeled and quartered

2 garlic cloves, thinly sliced

2 tablespoons olive oil, plus extra for drizzling

$1^1/2$ tablespoons finely chopped fresh flat-leaf parsley

8 piquillo peppers for stuffing

sea salt and black pepper

PIQUILLO SAUCE

4 piquillo peppers

$1/2$ garlic clove, crushed with a good pinch of salt

2 teaspoons good-quality red wine vinegar (see page 287)

2 tablespoons extra virgin olive oil

2 tablespoons water

1 teaspoon chopped fresh oregano or thyme leaves

a pinch of caster sugar (optional)

TO SERVE

> 1 bunch watercress or rocket (about 100g)
>
> a squeeze of lemon
>
> 2 tablespoons extra virgin olive oil
>
> wedges of lemon (optional)

Place a large saucepan over a medium to high heat and add the milk, onion, peppercorns and bay. Bring to a simmer, then add the salt cod and cook gently for 4–5 minutes or until the fish is just cooked and flakes easily (salt cod will stay more juicy and tender if cooked this way). With a slotted spoon, carefully lift out the fish and set aside to cool on a large plate. Now add the potatoes and garlic to the same saucepan of simmering milk and boil gently for 20 minutes or until soft. When the salt cod is cool enough to handle, go through the flesh, discarding any skin or bones. Now mash or shred the cod, either between your fingers or with a potato masher. At this point the cod should have no large or hard bits, but just be soft fibre. All of this is best done when the cod is warm, if not hot, as it will become stubborn and gluey when cold. When the potatoes are cooked, drain them (keeping 3 tablespoons of the liquor), and discard the onion, peppercorns and bay. Mash the potatoes well, then add the fish and continue to mash (still warm) until there are no lumps. Now transfer to a bowl, add the 2 tablespoons of olive oil and 2–3 tablespoons of the cooking milk and mix until smooth and soft. Stir in the parsley and taste for seasoning. With a dessertspoon, stuff the piquillo peppers with this creamy mixture.

Now make the piquillo sauce. In a food processor or with a hand-held blender purée all the ingredients together and taste for seasoning. If a little vinegary, add some sugar to balance it, and salt if necessary. Line the stuffed peppers in an oiled baking dish just large enough to hold them. This can be done in advance.

About 40 minutes before you are ready to serve the peppers, preheat the oven to 200°C/400°F/Gas 6. Cover the baking dish with foil, place on the middle shelf and heat for 10 minutes. Take off the foil, drizzle on a little olive oil and return to the oven for another 10 minutes or until the peppers are hot in the middle. Heat the sauce, transfer the peppers to a plate and spoon the hot sauce on top. Serve with the watercress dressed with a squeeze of lemon juice, the olive oil and salt and pepper, and the lemon wedges (if using).

REMOJÓN

SALT COD, ORANGE AND POTATO SALAD

Remojón is a refreshing salt cod and orange salad. We first tried it in Granada and have since had many variations. Traditionally, it is made with the sour Seville oranges that come into season in late December, early January. If you can't source these, then a good-quality eating orange is a more than adequate alternative. Some people recommend that the salad sit overnight for the flavours to infuse.

Serves 6–8 as a tapa, 4 for a starter or light meal

- 300g thick fillet of salt cod (dried weight), washed and soaked in the fridge for 48 hours, changing the water 4 times
- 250g small waxy salad potatoes (Anya, Charlotte, Pink Fir, Ratte or Cyprus), washed
- 2 Seville or eating oranges, peeled, all zest and pith removed, then sliced
- a large handful of fresh flat-leaf parsley leaves (roughly chopped, if coarse)
- $1/2$ small salad or red onion, thinly sliced
- 100g purple or black olives
- sea salt and black pepper

DRESSING

- $1/2$ garlic clove, crushed to a paste with salt
- 1 tablespoon good-quality red wine vinegar (see page 287)
- 3–4 tablespoons extra virgin olive oil
- a pinch of caster sugar (optional)

Drain the salt cod and remove any skin or bones. Shred the cod between your fingers into soft, fibrous flakes or short strips. Set aside.

Boil the potatoes for 10–25 minutes or until tender. While the potatoes are cooking, make the dressing. In a small bowl, mix the crushed garlic with the vinegar. Pour on the olive oil, then add a little salt and pepper. Taste for seasoning. If the vinegar is quite acidic, or if you are using the sharp Seville oranges, add a pinch of sugar and taste again.

When the potatoes are tender, drain in a colander and allow to cool a little until you are able to cut them into 5mm rounds. Place in a mixing bowl, pour on half the dressing and mix well. Season with a little salt and pepper. Now add the slices of orange, parsley leaves, onion, salt cod, the remaining dressing and olives, and toss. Taste for seasoning (if the salt cod is still quite salty, you may not need any extra). Let it sit in the fridge for at least an hour before serving lightly chilled.

ENSALADA DE ANCHOAS
GRILLED RED PEPPER AND ANCHOVY SALAD

If we were asked to name a dish that represented some of the finest hallmarks of Spanish ingredients, we would perhaps think of this salad. It is so simple; the only complicated bit is hard-boiling the egg. However, as so often with simple dishes, sourcing good ingredients is the challenge. We are now lucky enough to have a few suppliers who offer excellent Spanish ingredients (see pages 314–15). Brindisa supply us with the wonderful Ortiz salted anchovies, the wood-roasted piquillo peppers from Navarra, and a sweet red wine vinegar called Forum. This is a great starter for a dinner party or for a lunch dish; it is colourful and quick to make.

Serves 6–8 as a tapa, 4 for a starter or light meal

    2 medium eggs, hard-boiled and peeled whilst still warm

    12 piquillo peppers, kept whole

    12 salted anchovy fillets

    2 tablespoons roughly chopped fresh flat-leaf parsley

DRESSING

    $\frac{1}{2}$ garlic clove, crushed to a paste with salt

    1 tablespoon good-quality red wine vinegar (see page 287)

    4 tablespoons extra virgin olive oil

    a pinch of caster sugar (optional)

    sea salt and black pepper

For the dressing, mix the crushed garlic with the vinegar in a small bowl. Whisk in the olive oil and add a little salt and pepper. Taste for seasoning. If your vinegar is quite acidic, add the pinch of sugar and taste again.

When you are ready to assemble the salad, chop the eggs finely and set aside. Place the piquillo peppers in a bowl and pour over half the dressing. Leave for 5–10 minutes, or longer if you prefer. Then lay the peppers on a large plate or individual ones, and sprinkle over the chopped egg, followed by the anchovies in a criss-cross fashion. Finish with the chopped parsley and remaining dressing drizzled over, and a tiny pinch of salt and pepper.

BACALAO FRITO

DEEP-FRIED SALT COD IN SAFFRON BATTER

We distinctly remember this tapa, for we tasted it on our first visit to Seville. We parked the camper-van outside the city in a nearby campsite and cycled in on our bicycles. To call them rickety was a compliment, and the 6km journey into the city centre proved too much, for suddenly one of our front tyres blew up like a balloon, then burst with an almighty bang that made passers-by stare at us even more than they were already. It so happened we had stopped outside a rather good tapas bar, and, feeling in need of comfort and refreshment (the Andalucían sun was pretty hot by now), we sat down for an ice-cold caña (beer) while we contemplated our next move. Whenever we go into a bar or restaurant we are always very nosy about what other customers order. We craned our necks to follow the waiter as he carried a golden parcel on a small white plate round the corner. Intrigued, and noticing several others were eating the same, we beckoned the waiter on his return and ordered one. Soon we were crunching into a succulent piece of salt cod that had been dipped in a light batter tinted golden with flecks of saffron. The cod had been perfectly soaked; it was not very salty but dense and juicy, and the batter was delicate, as was the saffron, which was perhaps more for colour than taste.

Serves 6–8 as a tapa, 4 for a starter or light meal

>   3 thick fillets salt cod (about 200g each, dried weight), washed and soaked in
>   the fridge for 48 hours, changing the water 4 times, or Home-salted Cod
>   (see page 272), or any fresh, firm white fish, such as cod, halibut, monkfish
>   or huss
>   750ml sunflower oil, for deep-frying

BATTER

>   100g plain flour
>   175ml soda water
>   60 threads saffron, infused in 1 tablespoon boiling water
>   2 medium eggs, separated
>   sea salt

TO SERVE

>   1 quantity Alioli (without the saffron, see page 86)
>   1 lemon, cut into wedges

Slice the fish fillets into strips as wide as two fingers, about 2–3cm thick.

To make the batter, sift the flour into a bowl and slowly add the soda water, mixing it in with your fingertips or a wooden spoon and trying to avoid lumps forming. Mix together the saffron infusion and the egg yolks, and add to the batter, which should have the consistency of something between single and double cream. Salt to taste. Chill the batter, covered, for at least 40 minutes.

When you are ready to fry the fish, heat the oil in a large saucepan or fryer until hot but not smoking, about 180°C/350°F (never fill the pan more than half-full). Just before you start frying, whisk up the egg whites until quite stiff and fold into the batter. Dry the fillets on kitchen paper, and dip each one in the batter, coating it all over. Transfer straight into the hot oil. Fry for 2–3 minutes or until golden. You will probably need to do this in two batches. Drain on kitchen paper and serve straight away with the alioli and lemon.

MEAT

Ensalada de chorizo (Hot chorizo salad with fino sherry)

Guisantes con jamón (Peas with ham)

Morcilla con manzana (Morcilla with caramelised apple)

Spiced beef salad with fenugreek and hummus

Manti (Turkish ravioli with spiced lamb and yoghurt)

Khlii with green bean salad

Potato cakes stuffed with minced lamb and pine nuts

Higado con oloroso (Calf's liver with oloroso sherry, pine nuts and raisins)

Sweetbreads with artichokes, cardamom and preserved lemon

ENSALADA DE CHORIZO
HOT CHORIZO SALAD WITH FINO SHERRY

Chorizo, the Spanish paprika sausage, combines well with sweet piquillo peppers, bitter salad and musty fino sherry. You could also use morcilla (Spanish blood sausage) instead of chorizo.

Serves 6–8 as a tapa, 4 for a starter or light meal

150g prepared escarole or frisée salad, mostly pale leaves

a drizzle of olive oil

200g chorizo, preferably cooking type, mild or spicy, cut into bite-sized
   pieces

8 piquillo peppers, torn into strips

100ml fino sherry

2 tablespoons roughly chopped fresh flat-leaf parsley

DRESSING

$^1/_2$ garlic clove, crushed to a paste with salt

4 tablespoons extra virgin olive oil

1 tablespoon good-quality red wine vinegar or sherry vinegar
   (see page 287)

sea salt and black pepper

For the dressing, whisk all the ingredients together in a bowl and check for seasoning.

Dress the salad leaves well and arrange on a large plate. Set a frying pan over a medium to high heat and, when hot, add a drizzle of olive oil. Now add the bits of chorizo and fry until slightly crispy on both sides. Turn down the heat to medium, add the piquillo peppers and stir briefly with the chorizo before adding the fino. Take care when adding the sherry as it might spit. After about 30 seconds, when the alcohol has burnt off, add the parsley and check for seasoning. Spoon the chorizo, piquillo peppers and juice over the dressed leaves. Serve immediately.

GUISANTES CON JAMÓN

PEAS WITH HAM

A classic tapa that is delicious with broad beans too.

Serves 6–8 as a tapa, 4 for a starter or light meal

    4 tablespoons olive oil
    100g jamón serrano, thinly sliced, cut into short matchsticks (the fat is
        good for flavour)
    2 garlic cloves, thinly sliced
    1.2kg peas in pods, podded (about 340g podded weight), or frozen peas
    250ml Light Chicken or Vegetable Stock (see page 313) or water
    3 tablespoons roughly chopped fresh mint
    sea salt and black pepper

TO SERVE

    toast rubbed with garlic and drizzled with olive oil

In a frying pan, heat the olive oil over a medium to high heat and add half the jamón. Fry for a minute or two to release its flavour into the oil, and then add the garlic. Continue to cook until the garlic begins to colour. Add the peas and the stock or water and cook until tender and sweet, about 7–10 minutes. Stir in the mint and the remaining jamón and season with salt and pepper. Serve with the toast.

MORCILLA CON MANZANA
MORCILLA WITH CARAMELISED APPLE

This is a variation of a dish we once ate in Asturias – chorizo with apples and cider. Asturias is real apple country, and the combination of either morcilla or chorizo with apples and cider is wonderful. At Moro we often serve this dish with roast chicken, guinea fowl or partridge, deglazing the roasting juices with the cider.

Serves 6–8 as a tapa, 4 for a starter or light meal

> 50g clarified butter or ghee (from Indian shops)
> 2 Golden Delicious apples, peeled, quartered and then cored
> 2 tablespoons olive oil
> 200g morcilla (Spanish blood sausage), cut into rounds about 1–2cm thick
> 2 tablespoons roughly chopped fresh flat-leaf parsley
> 75ml medium-dry cider
> sea salt and black pepper

TO SERVE

> 150g watercress, dressed with 2 tablespoons extra virgin olive oil, a squeeze of lemon, salt and pepper
> 2 tablespoons pine nuts, lightly toasted (optional)

Set a large frying pan over a medium heat and add the butter or ghee. When it is hot, add the apple and gently fry until golden brown on one side, then turn over to caramelise the other side. Continue to cook until the apple is a nice golden colour all over and soft. Remove from the pan and set aside.

When you are ready to serve the dish, place the cleaned frying pan over a medium to high heat and add the olive oil. When it is hot, add the morcilla and fry for a minute on each side until slightly crisped, turning carefully so as not to break the sausage up too much. Now return the apple to the pan and add the parsley, then the cider, taking care as it might spit. Continue to fry for another 30 seconds to burn off the alcohol, then taste for seasoning. Transfer to a bed of dressed watercress, sprinkle on the pine nuts (if using), and serve immediately.

SPICED BEEF SALAD WITH FENUGREEK AND HUMMUS

The marinade for this salad is inspired by the Turkish spiced cured beef, pastirma.

Serves 6–8 as a mezze, 4 for a starter or light meal
>   1 big thick sirloin steak, approx. 2.5cm thick, total weight about 400g
>   olive oil
>   sea salt and black pepper

MARINADE
> $3/4$ teaspoon fenugreek seeds, pounded in a mortar to a fine powder
> $1^1/2$ teaspoons black onion or nigella seeds
>   2 teaspoons coriander seeds, roughly ground
> $1/2$ teaspoon sweet paprika
> $1/4$ teaspoon Turkish chilli flakes (kirmizi biber, optional)

TO SERVE
>   1 quantity Hummus (see opposite)
>   1 large handful fresh flat-leaf parsley leaves
>   a drizzle of extra virgin olive oil
>   1 teaspoon black onion or nigella seeds
>   8–12 pickled chillies (optional)
>   Flatbread (see page 36)

Mix all the marinade ingredients together, adding 1 teaspoon fine sea salt and a pinch of ground black pepper, and rub evenly over the steak. Leave to marinate for a good hour or two.

When you are ready to eat, set a griddle pan over a high heat (no oil) until it begins to smoke. (You may also use a barbecue, or failing both these things, pan-fry the steak in a hot frying pan over a high heat.) Rub the steak with a little olive oil, season with salt all over and place on the griddle. The sirloin should be medium rare to rare, so it is sufficient to sear the meat on both sides. If the griddle pan is very hot, the meat will need only about 45 seconds to a minute on each side. Season with a little more salt as the sirloin is turned. Remove from the heat and set aside to rest for a minute or so while you assemble the dish.

Spread the hummus on to a plate (it can be slightly warm if you prefer), then scatter the parsley leaves all over. With a sharp knife, cut the steak into thin slices about 5mm thick. Spread the steak evenly over the hummus and finish with a drizzle of olive oil and a sprinkling of black onion seeds. Serve immediately with pickled chillies on the side and some warm flatbread.

HUMMUS

Serves 4–8

       400g cooked, drained chickpeas (see page 59), plus their cooking
         liquor/water
       1 garlic clove, crushed to a paste with salt
       juice of 1 lemon
       3–4 tablespoons tahini
       3 tablespoons extra virgin olive oil
       sea salt and black pepper

Blend the chickpeas in a food processor, adding a few tablespoons of cooking liquor or water to help them on their way. When smooth, add the garlic, lemon juice, tahini, olive oil, salt and pepper, and more liquid if necessary. Taste for seasoning and eat as you wish.

MANTI

TURKISH RAVIOLI WITH SPICED LAMB AND YOGHURT

Manti is a ravioli of sorts from Turkey. Traditionally filled with lightly spiced lamb, manti are served with garlicky yoghurt and caramelised butter on top. Intrigued by the sound of those flavours, we asked our friend Engin to take us somewhere to try them. That evening we had a delicious dinner at her house, where we tasted, among other things, manti. They did not disappoint. If pasta came to Italy from China, then this dish might imply it first stopped in Turkey, where they made it their own.

Serves 6–8 as a mezze, 4 for a starter or light meal

MANTI PASTA DOUGH

200g strong white bread flour (Doves Farm or Shipton Mill), plus extra
   for dusting and rolling out
2 eggs, lightly beaten

LAMB MANTI STUFFING

240g finely minced lamb
1 rounded tablespoon finely grated onion
$^3/_4$ teaspoon ground allspice
$^1/_2$ teaspoon dried oregano
$^1/_2$ teaspoon dried mint
2 tablespoons finely chopped fresh flat-leaf parsley
2 tablespoons water
sea salt and black pepper

TO COOK AND SERVE

1.5 litres Chicken Stock (see page 313), or fresh frozen stock from the
   supermarket, spiced with $^1/_2$ teaspoon each of ground cinnamon and
   ground cumin
250g Greek yoghurt, thinned with 2 tablespoons milk, flavoured with
   1 garlic clove crushed with salt
1 quantity caramelised butter (see page 68)
2 tablespoons roughly chopped fresh flat-leaf parsley
1 teaspoon Turkish chilli flakes (kirmizi biber), or hot or sweet paprika

To make the manti dough, put the flour into a wide bowl to one side, and pour the eggs into the other side. With your fingertips, steadily work the flour into the egg. When the dough becomes too stiff to knead, add a splash of water to enable you to incorporate the remaining flour. If it is still too stiff, add another splash of water. When the dough has come together nicely, wash and dry your hands. Sprinkle flour on a work surface, your fingertips and the dough, and knead the pasta for 3 minutes. The dough's final texture should be firm, but have a pleasing softness and elasticity to it. Wrap with clingfilm and put it in the fridge for 20 minutes to relax. It will keep happily in the fridge for 24 hours.

For the stuffing, mix the lamb and all the other ingredients in a bowl. At this point, if you are feeling brave, taste a little of the lamb to see if it has sufficient salt. The mixture is now ready.

Cut the pasta dough in half. With your hands, shape one piece of pasta into a rectangle that is roughly 10cm long (cover the remainder with a cloth). Start to roll the shaped piece so you have a long strip of pasta that is now 10cm wide. If your strip gets unmanageably long, cut it in half and work on one half to get it as long and thin as possible. The finished pasta strips should be almost thin enough to see through. Put a small teaspoonful of lamb mixture at 10cm intervals along the whole length of the strip. With a sharp knife, cut between each dollop of lamb and the next to make rough squares. Lightly moisten the pasta around the meat of each square and then fold over each square to make a triangle. Push down the pasta around the meat so there are no air bubbles. When you have finished one batch, place on a floured board or plate (we use semolina flour). Roll out the other half of the dough and repeat the process. Manti will keep in this state, loosely covered with greaseproof paper, for up to 12 hours provided the board is well floured. It does not matter if they dry out a little.

When you are ready to cook the triangles, bring the spiced stock to a steady boil and add the manti. Cook for about 2–3 minutes, or a little longer if dry, then drain in a colander. Serve immediately with a little of the stock spooned over the top, followed by the garlic yoghurt, caramelised butter, parsley and chilli flakes or paprika.

KHLII WITH GREEN BEAN SALAD

Khlii is a spiced, dried meat delicacy from Morocco, which we like to serve with green beans. Dressings made with Dijon mustard are common in Morocco, probably because of the strong French influence from colonial times.

Serves 6–8 as a mezze, 4 for a starter or light meal

> 1 quantity Khlii (see page 275), cut into thinnish strips no
> wider than 1cm
>
> 4 tablespoons whole coriander leaves (optional)

GREEN BEAN SALAD

> 2 teaspoons Dijon mustard
>
> $1/2$ tablespoon sweet red wine vinegar, or red wine vinegar with
> a pinch of caster sugar (see page 287)
>
> 6 tablespoons extra virgin olive oil
>
> 300g fine green beans, topped
>
> sea salt and black pepper

Put the mustard, sweet vinegar and $1/2$ tablespoon water into a medium bowl and season with salt and pepper. Whisk in the olive oil a bit at a time so that it emulsifies with the mustard. Taste for seasoning.

Bring a large pot of well-salted water to the boil. Boil the beans until they are just tender, but not al dente. They should lose the raw vegetable taste and become slightly sweet. Drain and place in a bowl with half the coriander leaves. Pour over the vinaigrette, toss well and season with a little salt and pepper. Serve immediately with the shredded khlii on top and the remaining coriander leaves.

POTATO CAKES STUFFED WITH MINCED LAMB AND PINE NUTS

We think this street food comes from Iran, but these flavours could just as easily appear in the Lebanon or Syria. At the restaurant, we serve these potato cakes with a little yoghurt and salad. If you wish to, you can follow this recipe to make a type of shepherd's pie for two. Omit the flour with the potatoes and instead add 300ml warm milk, then just assemble and cook as you would a shepherd's pie.

Makes 4 cakes

POTATO DOUGH

700g potatoes (Desirée, Cyprus or King Edwards), skins on

sea salt

1 rounded tablespoon plain flour plus extra for dusting

LAMB FILLING

25g butter

2 tablespoons olive oil

$^1/_2$ large or 1 medium onion, finely chopped

1 teaspoon ground cinnamon

2 pinches freshly ground black pepper

2 pinches freshly grated nutmeg

3 cardamom pods, black seeds only, ground to a fine powder

3 cloves, ground with a pinch of salt to a fine powder

200g finely minced lamb shoulder

50g pine nuts, lightly toasted or fried in oil until just golden

1 tablespoon tomato purée

3 tablespoons chopped fresh flat-leaf parsley

sea salt and black pepper

TO COOK AND SERVE

olive oil

1 bunch or 150g wild rocket or other salad, dressed with 1 tablespoon lemon juice, 2 tablespoons extra virgin olive oil, salt and pepper

200g Greek yoghurt, thinned with 2 tablespoons milk and seasoned with 1 garlic clove crushed to a paste with salt

a few pickled chillies, or 1 lemon, cut into wedges

To make the dough, boil the potatoes whole in salted water until cooked but not mushy: if they start to break up, they will absorb more water, which may affect the way they handle and fry. Drain well in a colander for 10 minutes. Then, while they are still warm, peel and mash thoroughly. Stir in the flour and season with a little salt. The potato dough is now ready.

While the potatoes are boiling, make the filling. Melt the butter with the olive oil over a medium to high heat. When the butter begins to foam, add the onion and soften until it is sweet and slightly caramelised. Now add all the spices and cook for a minute. Add the lamb, stirring and breaking it up with a spoon as it begins to cook. Stop stirring for a minute or two, so the lamb has a chance to stick to the pan and colour. This will add depth of flavour to the dish. You should cook the lamb for about 5-8 minutes until nicely browned. Finally stir in the pine nuts, tomato purée, 2 table-spoons water and the parsley, and season with salt and pepper to taste. Set aside until cool enough to handle.

To prepare the potato cakes, first wash and dry your hands, then flour them. Divide the dough into four balls. Keeping the surface well dusted with flour, flatten one ball to a disc 1cm thick. Put 2 tablespoons of filling in the centre, and bring up the sides of the dough to enclose the meat. Place on a floured surface. Neaten the shape of the cake and patch up any cracks and gaps. The result should look like a round patty 10cm across and 3-4cm thick. Repeat this process with the other balls of dough. These potato cakes will keep in the fridge for one or two days as long as there's enough flour to prevent them from sticking (although the fresher they're eaten, the better).

Cover the bottom of a large frying pan generously with oil, about 3-4mm deep, and place over a medium to high heat until hot and nearly smoking. Gently and care-fully lift up the cakes with a fish spatula and lower into the oil one by one. Do not disturb until they are a dark golden colour and crispy, then turn carefully with the spatula to colour the other side. When they are done, take out and dab off any excess oil with kitchen paper. Keep warm in a low oven, or serve immediately with the rocket, yoghurt, and chillies or lemon.

HIGADO CON OLOROSO

CALF'S LIVER WITH OLOROSO SHERRY, PINE NUTS AND RAISINS

The combination of nutty oloroso sherry and offal is a classic, not only with liver, but also with kidneys and sweetbreads. We tend to use calf's liver in the restaurant, but lamb's liver or chicken livers are good alternatives. Make sure the lamb's liver is pink, though. If you decide to use chicken livers, place in a colander and run under a cold tap for 5–10 minutes until the water runs clear. Carefully separate the livers, discarding any sinewy bits, and try to keep them as whole as possible. Drain well and dry on kitchen paper.

Serves 6–8 as a tapa, 4 for a starter or light meal

- 2 thick slices calf's or lamb's liver, total weight 300g, or prepared chicken livers (see above)
- 6 tablespoons olive oil
- $1/2$ large mild onion, finely chopped
- 50g pine nuts, lightly toasted until golden
- 1 garlic clove, thinly sliced
- 50g raisins, soaked in warm water to swell, then drained
- 100ml medium dry oloroso sherry
- sea salt and black pepper

TO SERVE

- 1 bunch or 150g watercress, dressed with 2 tablespoons extra virgin olive oil, 1 tablespoon sherry vinegar, salt and pepper, or 250g spinach, braised with garlic

To prepare the liver, cut into strips about 4–5cm long and 1cm wide, or small pieces, removing any sinew as you go. Set aside.

Place a large frying pan over a medium heat and add 4 tablespoons of the olive oil. When it is hot, add the onion and a small pinch of salt and turn the heat to low. Fry for 5–10 minutes, stirring occasionally, until the onion has softened and is golden in colour and sweet in smell. Now stir in the pine nuts and garlic and fry for a further 2 minutes. Add the drained raisins, cook for 1 more minute, then remove from the heat. Scrape this onion mixture into a bowl, draining off any excess oil, and set aside.

When you are ready to cook the liver, return the same frying pan to a medium heat and add the remaining 2 tablespoons of olive oil. When the oil just begins to smoke, season the liver with salt and pepper and fry quickly on one side until sealed (about 1 minute). Turn over and season the other side. After another minute (when the second side is also sealed), return the onion mixture to the pan. Stir around with the liver, then carefully pour in the sherry. Beware, it may spit. Sizzle for a minute or so to burn off the alcohol, then check for seasoning. We serve this in the restaurant with dressed watercress or braised spinach, and bread to mop up the juices.

SWEETBREADS WITH ARTICHOKES, CARDAMOM AND PRESERVED LEMON

Serves 6–8 as a mezze, 4 for a starter or light meal

 400g lamb's or calf's sweetbreads

 6 small, 3 medium or 2 large globe artichokes

 $^1/_2$ lemon

 6 tablespoons olive oil

 2 large garlic cloves, thinly sliced

 150ml water

 10 green cardamom pods, black seeds only, finely ground

 2 tablespoons plain flour

 rind of $^1/_2$ large Preserved Lemon (see page 281), washed, pulp discarded
  and finely chopped (1 heaped tablespoon)

 1 tablespoon roughly chopped fresh flat-leaf parsley

 sea salt and black pepper

TO SERVE (optional)

 1 bunch or 100g rocket leaves, dressed with a squeeze of lemon, extra virgin
  olive oil, salt and pepper

To prepare the sweetbreads, rinse in a colander under cold water for a minute or so. Place in a saucepan, cover with water and bring to the boil. Simmer for 5–8 minutes until they feel just firm to the touch. Cool in their cooking liquid, then drain. Now pick off and discard the outer membrane and any sinewy bits. If using calf's sweetbreads, slice into 1.5cm medallions.

 Follow the instructions on page 126 to prepare the artichokes. Cut each prepared artichoke in half lengthways and then each half into small wedges no more than 1cm thick. Place in cold water with a squeeze of lemon juice to stop them discolouring. Heat half the oil in a frying pan over a medium to high heat, and, when it is hot, add the drained artichokes. Fry, stirring every minute for about 5 minutes, or until they begin to colour. Now add the garlic and a pinch of salt and continue to cook until the garlic begins to colour, stirring all the while. Pour in the water, cover with a piece of damp greaseproof paper and steam the artichokes for about 3 minutes or until they are tender and the water has almost evaporated. Season with salt and pepper, remove from the heat and set aside.

To finish the dish, place the remaining oil in a large frying pan over a high heat. Season the blanched sweetbreads with the ground cardamom, salt and pepper. Toss the sweetbreads in the flour, and, when the oil is hot, fry them on one side until golden. Turn over and add the chopped preserved lemon in between the sweetbreads. When the second side of the sweetbreads is golden, add the artichokes and any of their remaining cooking liquid along with a tiny squeeze of lemon and the chopped parsley. Cook for 30 seconds more, check the seasoning and serve the sweetbreads with the rocket salad if you wish.

VEGETABLES, CHEESE AND EGGS

Ajo caliente (Warm tomato, bread and garlic purée)

Ensaladilla rusa (Russian salad)

Morels with butter beans, tomatoes and sweet herbs

Espárragos con dos salsas (Asparagus with two sauces)

Alcachofas y guisantes con oloroso (Artichokes and peas with oloroso sherry)

Moroccan bread salad with grilled green peppers and tomatoes

Ensalada de setas (Mushroom salad with sherry vinegar and oregano)

Turkish poached sweet and sour leeks

Turkish chopped salad

Carrot purée with caraway and feta

Feta with anise bread, tomatoes and oregano

Courgette fritters with feta and dill

Chicory salad with Picos blue cheese, walnuts and Pedro Ximénez dressing

Revueltos (Scrambled eggs)

Moroccan eggs with tomatoes and cumin

AJO CALIENTE

WARM TOMATO, BREAD AND GARLIC PURÉE

This dish is similar to the Tuscan thick tomato and bread soup, pappa pomodoro, only it is not really a soup but more of a tapa. We had this in Sanlúcar de Barrameda around late spring. It is a seasonal dish made with the new season's tomatoes and served with fresh crunchy radishes.

Serves 6–8 as a tapa, 4 for a starter or light meal

      5 tablespoons olive oil

      3 garlic cloves, sliced

      1 kg vine-ripened tomatoes or any sweet-tasting tomato, peeled (see
         page 42), and cut into quarters or sixths, depending on size

      a pinch of caster sugar (optional)

      100g ciabatta bread, preferably a day old, crusts removed, torn into
         bite-sized pieces

      sea salt and black pepper

TO SERVE

      extra virgin olive oil

      1 large bunch fresh radishes, preferably with leaves on

In a large saucepan, heat the olive oil over a medium heat. When it is hot, add the garlic and sizzle in the oil until most of the garlic turns golden. Then add the tomatoes and a pinch of salt. Cook the tomatoes, stirring occasionally, until they have dissolved into a sauce. Taste for seasoning. You can add a pinch of caster sugar if the tomatoes are not sweet enough. Add the bread and stir around until the bread softens and absorbs the tomato liquid (if there is too little liquid to soften the bread, add water a splash at a time until you're happy the bread will mush). When it is a thick paste, check the seasoning once again, and serve immediately with a drizzle of extra virgin olive oil over the top and the radishes on the side.

ENSALADILLA RUSA
RUSSIAN SALAD

When new chefs start at the restaurant and are told we will make Russian salad, a look of bewilderment comes over their faces. Ensaladilla Rusa is one of Spain's most popular tapas, sometimes served with picos (Andalucían breadsticks). Accompanied by cold beer, it tastes delicious. At its most simple, it consists of good salad potatoes, mayonnaise made with vinegar, and some finely chopped onion. This is a more elaborate restaurant version. At Moro we often serve Russian salad with Spanish smoked anchovies, whole leaves of white chicory or treviso dressed with a little lemon and olive oil, and a large handful of picos or bread.

Serves 6–8 as a tapa, 4 for a starter or light meal

> 150g fresh or frozen petits pois
>
> 500g waxy salad potatoes (Ratte, Charlotte or Pink Fir), peeled
>
> $^1/_2$ medium red onion, finely chopped
>
> 1 tablespoon sweet red wine vinegar or normal red wine vinegar with a pinch of caster sugar (see page 287)
>
> 2 tablespoons roughly chopped fresh flat-leaf parsley
>
> 2 tablespoons roughly chopped fresh tarragon
>
> 150g mayonnaise (use recipe for Alioli on page 86, but omit the saffron and garlic, and add 1 tablespoon chilled water)
>
> 2 tablespoons small capers in salt or vinegar, prepared as on page 154
>
> extra virgin olive oil
>
> sea salt and black pepper

Bring a large saucepan of salted water to the boil and add the petits pois. Simmer for about a minute or until tender, then scoop them out with a fine-mesh sieve, drain and set aside. Now add the potatoes to the same boiling water and cook for about 15-25 minutes until tender. Drain in a colander. Allow to cool, then dice the potatoes about 1cm square. Transfer to a large mixing bowl and add the peas, red onion, vinegar and chopped herbs. Stir in the mayonnaise and capers until they are mixed evenly with the vegetables, add a good drizzle of extra virgin olive oil, and finally season with salt and pepper.

Variation

You could also serve Ensaladilla Rusa spooned inside whole cooked artichoke hearts (see page 157).

MORELS WITH BUTTER BEANS, TOMATOES AND SWEET HERBS

When it comes to seasons, morel mushrooms are an exception to the rule that most mushrooms arrive in the autumn with the first rains, for they appear in the spring. Last time we were in Marrakech in April, boxes of sandy morels from the foothills of the Atlas Mountains were available in the markets and were somewhat cheaper there than they are here. We brought back 2kg. This dish is actually Turkish in origin.

Serves 6–8 as a mezze, 4 for a starter or light meal

250g fresh morel mushrooms, or 60g dried, rehydrated by covering with
   boiling water

12–16 sweet cherry tomatoes, quartered

2 tablespoons roughly chopped fresh flat–leaf parsley

1 tablespoon roughly torn fresh basil

1 tablespoon each of roughly chopped fresh tarragon and dill

$1/2$ red onion, chopped

300g cooked butter beans, such as Spanish judión beans, or
   white beans (see page 17)

3–4 tablespoons olive oil

sea salt and black pepper

DRESSING

$1/2$ garlic clove, crushed

1 tablespoon lemon juice

4 tablespoons extra virgin olive oil

Trim the ends of the morels, then fill a sink with cold water, add the morels and toss for a minute to remove the grit. If they are still dirty, rinse one more time. Leave to drain thoroughly in a colander. If using dried morels, lift them out of the soaking liquid so as not to disturb any grit that might have settled at the bottom of the bowl. Put them into a small saucepan, then pour in the soaking liquid through a fine-mesh sieve to get rid of any grit. Heat the pan until you are left with roughly 1 tablespoon of liquid. Season with a little salt.

Meanwhile, make the dressing. Combine the garlic, vinegar and olive oil with some salt and pepper, and whisk together. Now mix the tomatoes, herbs and onion with the dressing and set aside to let the flavours mingle.

When you are ready to eat, warm up the beans in their cooking liquid and season with salt. Place a large frying pan over a medium to high heat and add the olive oil. When it is hot, add the morels and juice and fry for 2–3 minutes, stirring occasionally, until the mushrooms are soft and have a tiny bit of colour. Remove from the heat and taste. Now toss the warm drained beans, half the mushrooms and any juice with the dressed tomatoes. Taste for seasoning and serve immediately with the remaining mushrooms on top.

ESPÁRRAGOS CON DOS SALSAS
ASPARAGUS WITH TWO SAUCES

Spanish country lanes or roadsides are perfect places to forage for wild things in the spring, and we particularly love finding wild asparagus and artichokes. Wild asparagus stalks are thin and require cooking for a while to get rid of some of the bitterness. In Spain, the classic way of eating them is chopped into small pieces and stewed in olive oil with garlic and jamón, or in Revueltos (see page 141). The following dish calls for normal green asparagus, served with a twist on the traditional two sauces that often accompany it.

Serves 6–8 as a tapa, 4 for a starter or light meal
>   1kg firm green asparagus
>   1 tablespoon lemon juice
>   4 tablespoons extra virgin olive oil
>   sea salt and black pepper

TO SERVE
>   Jamón Serrano and Parsley Sauce (see opposite)
>   Almond and Sherry Vinegar Sauce (see opposite)

As the root end of large asparagus can be woody and stringy, gently flex until the stems snap off at their natural break, or peel the ends. Rinse, drain and bunch the stalks loosely with string.

Now prepare the two sauces (see opposite).

When you are ready to eat, bring a tall saucepan of salted water to the boil, add the asparagus (tips up) and put on the lid. Boil for 2–3 minutes or until tender, depending on the thickness. They should not be crunchy. Drain carefully. Dress immediately with the lemon juice, olive oil, salt and pepper, and serve with both the following sauces at the same time.

JAMÓN SERRANO AND PARSLEY SAUCE

Serves 4–8

    1–2 garlic cloves

    5 tablespoons roughly chopped fresh flat-leaf parsley

    4 tablespoons extra virgin olive oil

    80g jamón serrano, very finely chopped

    juice of $1/2$ lemon

    sea salt and black pepper

Crush the garlic with a good pinch of salt in a mortar until a smooth paste is formed. Now add the parsley to the mortar, a tablespoon at a time, and continue to pound until the parsley has become part of the paste. Add the olive oil and jamón, and stir well before adding the lemon juice. Always add the lemon juice after the oil, otherwise it will discolour the parsley. Season with salt and pepper.

ALMOND AND SHERRY VINEGAR SAUCE

Serves 4–8

    150g whole blanched almonds

    approx. 120ml water

    1 garlic clove, crushed to a paste with salt

    1 tablespoon extra virgin olive oil

    $1/2$–$3/4$ tablespoon sherry vinegar

    sea salt

In a food processor, grind the almonds until as fine as possible. Now add 3 tablespoons of the water and process until the almonds form a paste. Grind in the garlic, followed by the rest of the water and the olive oil, poured in very slowly, and continue until really smooth. The consistency should be thick and smooth but not too solid, similar to double cream, so it clings to the asparagus tips nicely. Transfer to a bowl and season with the sherry vinegar and salt to taste.

ALCACHOFAS Y GUISANTES CON OLOROSO

ARTICHOKES AND PEAS WITH OLOROSO SHERRY

The mother of our friend Lidia from Jerez cooked up this dish for us. We watched how she quartered peeled baby artichokes and stewed them slowly in olive oil with onions, peas and oloroso sherry. The result was sublime – so sweet and complex from the nutty oloroso. This is delicious on its own or with some sliced jamón or cecina (smoked cured beef from Castille) on the side.

Serves 6–8 as a tapa, 4 for a starter or light meal

6 small, 3 medium or 2 large globe artichokes

juice of $^1/_2$ lemon

4 tablespoons olive oil

1 medium onion, thinly sliced

2 large garlic cloves, thinly sliced

150ml medium dry oloroso sherry

200ml water

300g shelled peas, fresh or frozen

3 tablespoons roughly chopped fresh mint

sea salt and black pepper

To prepare the artichokes, cut off the stalks from the base. The general rule when preparing artichokes is that what is green is tough and what is yellow is tender. Now carefully snap or pull off enough layers of the tough, green outer leaves until you reach the ones that are mostly yellow and therefore tender. Cut the tips off these, then peel the tough green outside of the base (heart) of the artichoke, using a potato peeler or sharp knife, until you see yellow. Scrape out all the furry choke inside the artichoke with a teaspoon. Cut each prepared artichoke in half lengthways, and then each half into small wedges no more than 1.5cm across. Place in cold water with a squeeze of lemon juice to stop them discolouring.

Place a large, heavy saucepan over a medium heat and add the olive oil. When it is hot, stir in the onion and a pinch of salt and turn the heat to medium–low. Fry for 10–15 minutes, stirring occasionally, until the onion has softened, is golden in colour and sweet in smell. Now add the garlic and cook for 1 more minute, then add the drained artichokes and an extra pinch of salt and pepper. Fry for about 3 minutes, then pour in the sherry and reduce almost totally while stirring. Add the water, peas and half the mint and cover with a piece of damp greaseproof paper. Steam the artichokes for about 3 minutes or until they are tender. You should have a little bit of sauce with the artichokes, otherwise add an extra splash of water. Check the seasoning and sprinkle on the remaining mint. Serve either warm or at room temperature.

MOROCCAN BREAD SALAD WITH GRILLED GREEN PEPPERS AND TOMATOES

This is an adaptation of the classic Moroccan salad of grilled green peppers and tomatoes with the addition of bread and nutty argan oil. If you cannot source argan oil, use olive oil.

Serves 6–8 as a mezze, 4 for a starter or light meal

    4 green peppers, grilled and peeled (see page 78)
    225g ciabatta bread, half the crust removed
    600g cherry or any sweet tomatoes, peeled (see page 42), cut into
        quarters or eighths
    4 tablespoons fresh coriander leaves
    2 tablespoons roughly chopped fresh flat-leaf parsley
    120g oily black olives
    sea salt and black pepper

DRESSING

> 1 garlic clove, crushed to a paste with salt
>
> 1 rounded teaspoon lightly pan-roasted cumin seeds, roughly ground
>
> $1^1/_2$ tablespoons sweet red wine vinegar (see page 287)
>
> 100g tomatoes, sliced and puréed to juice in a food processor
>
> 4 tablespoons extra virgin olive oil
>
> 3 tablespoons argan oil (see page 315), plus 1 extra tablespoon mixed
>> with $^1/_2$ tablespoon extra virgin olive oil

Preheat the oven to 220°C/425°F/Gas 7.

While the peppers are charring, break up the bread into bite-sized pieces and place on a roasting tray. Put in the oven for 10 minutes until lightly toasted. While the bread is in the oven, peel and tear the peppers into strips and make the dressing. In a bowl, mix the garlic with the cumin, vinegar, tomato juice and some salt and black pepper. Now add the olive oil and the 3 tablespoons argan oil and whisk well. Taste for seasoning.

When the bread is ready, transfer to a large salad bowl and pour over half the dressing. Give it a good toss and allow to sit for a few seconds before adding the peppers, tomatoes, herbs and olives. Pour on the remaining dressing, give everything another good toss and check the seasoning. Serve with the remaining argan and olive oil drizzled on top.

ENSALADA DE SETAS
MUSHROOM SALAD WITH SHERRY VINEGAR AND OREGANO

Sherry vinegar may be an unusual choice for mushrooms, but it works and is really delicious.

Serves 6-8 as a tapa, 4 for a starter or light meal

> 500g wild mushrooms, mixed or one variety, such as ceps, morels,
>> chanterelles, pieds de mouton or oyster, or a mixture of wild and field
>> mushrooms
>
> 5 tablespoons olive oil
>
> 1 garlic clove, finely chopped
>
> 1 tablespoon roughly chopped fresh oregano
>
> 2 tablespoons roughly chopped fresh flat-leaf parsley
>
> 2-3 teaspoons sherry vinegar, to taste
>
> sea salt and black pepper

First pick over the mushrooms for any bits. If they are particularly dirty, wipe them with a damp cloth. (Do not wash them as it makes them go soggy when cooked.) Slice the mushrooms up roughly (chanterelles can be cooked whole, oyster mushrooms and morels should have the tough white stalk removed). Set a very large frying pan over a medium heat. (If you don't have a large enough pan to amply accommodate all the mushrooms, cook in two batches.) Add the olive oil and, when it is hot, add the garlic and fry for a minute until it begins to colour. Immediately add the mushrooms and half the oregano and stir well. Fry for 3–5 minutes until the mushrooms are soft (if using field mushrooms as well, they will need about 10–15 minutes, so add the wild mushrooms towards the end). Season with a little salt and pepper and transfer to a bowl. Now add the remaining oregano, the parsley and 2 teaspoons of the sherry vinegar and toss well. Taste for seasoning once more, and add more vinegar if you feel it needs more of a kick (you may need more salt to balance out the vinegar).

TURKISH POACHED SWEET AND SOUR LEEKS

Leeks, artichoke hearts, cauliflower, white cabbage and green beans are all wonderful cooked in this way, in a sweet and sour poaching liquor. At Moro we serve a combination of new season's leeks and artichoke hearts as a starter, but generally these vegetables are also suited to accompany fish or white meat. Think of the dish as vegetables poached in a light sweet and sour dressing. In the summer it is often eaten at room temperature. The liquor left over from the vegetables can be kept in the fridge and used as a dressing for pulses or salads.

Serves 6–8 as a mezze, 4 for a starter or light meal

> 8 tablespoons olive oil
> 3 garlic cloves, peeled and sliced
> 600g young leeks, washed and trimmed
> 3 rounded teaspoons caster sugar
> juice of 1 lemon
> 300ml water
> 2 level tablespoons roughly chopped fresh flat-leaf parsley
> 2 level tablespoons roughly chopped fresh dill
> sea salt and black pepper

Place the olive oil in a medium saucepan over a medium heat and cook the garlic until lightly coloured. Add the leeks, sugar, lemon juice, water and a good pinch of salt. Cover with a piece of greaseproof paper, then a lid and simmer (with the lid on but slightly ajar) for 15 minutes or until soft and tender. Gently stir in the parsley and dill and check the seasoning. Serve with some of the poaching liquor spooned over.

Variation

The above recipe can easily be adapted to a combination of vegetables. Choose three or four from the following: 150–200g young leeks as above, 1 large or 2 small artichokes, trimmed (see page 126), $1/2$ small cauliflower in florets, 150g green beans, topped, $1/3$ small white or Turkish cabbage in wedges. Cook one at a time in the same batch of cooking liquid until tender, so it picks up all the flavours. Warm together, add the herbs and serve with some of the liquor spooned over.

TURKISH CHOPPED SALAD

Unlike most restaurant kitchens, the one at Mangal (our favourite Turkish café in Arcola Road, Stoke Newington) has an oblong charcoal grill that the chef sits in front of. When we go, we often order chopped salad, a refreshing, finely chopped mixture of tomatoes, peppers, cucumber and coriander offset with creamy yoghurt and nutty caramelised butter. Wonderful on its own, it is even better with some grilled or roasted marinated lamb. Visiting Mangal before Moro opened made us determined to cook over real charcoal.

Serves 6–8 as a mezze, 4 for a starter or light meal

> 12 cherry tomatoes, halved
>
> $1/2$ cucumber, peeled
>
> $1/4$ small red onion, peeled
>
> $1/2$ red pepper, halved and seeded
>
> $1/2$ green pepper, halved and seeded
>
> 2 heaped tablespoons each of roughly chopped fresh coriander and parsley

DRESSING

> $1/2$ garlic clove, crushed to a paste with salt
>
> 1 tablespoon lemon juice
>
> 4 tablespoons extra virgin olive oil
>
> sea salt and black pepper

TO SERVE

> 200g Greek yoghurt thinned with 1 tablespoon milk
>
> 1 quantity caramelised butter (see page 68)
>
> 1 teaspoon Turkish chilli flakes (kirmizi biber)
>
> warm Flatbread (see page 36) or pitta bread

For the dressing, whisk all the ingredients together and taste for seasoning.

Chop the tomatoes, cucumber, onion and red and green peppers very finely and place in a bowl. Do not be tempted to use a food processor. Add the herbs and dressing. Toss well and check for seasoning. Spread the chopped salad out on a large plate. Spoon the yoghurt over the centre of the salad, then drizzle the warm caramelised butter all over. Sprinkle with the chilli flakes. Eat with bread or grilled meats.

CARROT PURÉE WITH CARAWAY AND FETA

For this dish the flavour of the carrots is very important, so for that reason we would recommend you buy English organic carrots. At Moro we serve them with triangles of crisp pitta bread.

Serves 6–8 as a mezze, 4 for a starter or light meal

> 750g organic carrots, scrubbed
>
> 4 tablespoons extra virgin olive oil, plus extra for drizzling
>
> sea salt and black pepper
>
> 1 level tablespoon caraway seeds, roughly ground in a mortar
>
> 2 tablespoons roughly chopped fresh mint
>
> 100g feta cheese

CRISPBREAD

> 25g butter
>
> 2 pitta breads

Preheat the oven to 180°C/350°F/Gas 4.

For the crispbread triangles, melt the butter over a low heat. As it is melting, warm the pitta in the oven for a couple of minutes, then carefully split the pitta in half lengthways and brush the butter on both sides. Now place on a board and slice each half in half again lengthways and then cut four or five triangles out of each one. Place the triangles on a cooling rack and transfer to the middle shelf of the oven. Bake for about 10–15 minutes or until golden brown.

Now turn up the heat to 200°C/400°F/Gas 6. Slice the carrots into rounds no more than 2cm thick. Toss with half the olive oil and some salt and pepper, and place in a roasting tin. Cover with foil and roast for about 45 minutes, or until completely tender. Remove and cool a little before putting through a mouli or mashing by hand or whizzing in a food processor. Transfer the puréed carrot to a bowl, stir in the caraway, half the mint and the remaining olive oil, and season with salt and pepper.

To serve, spread the purée on a plate, crumble the feta on top, drizzle with a little more olive oil, and finally sprinkle on the remaining mint. Serve with the crispbread triangles round the edge of the plate.

FETA SALAD WITH ANISE BREAD, TOMATOES AND OREGANO

This salad is a cross between the Tuscan bread salad panzanella, and Greek salad. When tomatoes are in season, it is definitely worth making and can be done a little in advance.

Serves 6–8 as a mezze, 4 for a starter or light meal

> 6 x 1.5cm thick slices Anise Bread (see page 34), broken into bite-sized pieces
>
> 400g sweet vine-ripened cherry tomatoes, cut into halves or quarters
>
> $^1/_2$ medium red onion, finely chopped
>
> 150g feta cheese
>
> 2 tablespoons fresh or dried oregano leaves
>
> 2 handfuls oily black olives

DRESSING

> 1 garlic clove, crushed to a paste with salt
>
> $1^1/_2$ tablespoons good-quality red wine vinegar (see page 287)
>
> 100g tomatoes, sliced and puréed to juice in a food processor
>
> 6 tablespoons extra virgin olive oil
>
> sea salt and black pepper

Preheat the oven to 150°C/300°F/Gas 2. Place the anise bread pieces on a baking sheet in the oven to dry out until almost hard but with a slight chewiness in the middle, about 20–30 minutes. Remove and cool.

For the dressing, whisk the garlic, vinegar, tomato juice and olive oil together, then season with salt and pepper.

Place the anise bread croûtons in a large bowl, pour on half the dressing, toss well and leave for 10 minutes. Now add the tomatoes and chopped onion, crumble on the feta, then add the oregano and olives. Add the rest of the dressing. Season with salt and pepper and toss.

Variation

Swedish Krisproll rusks can be used in place of the anise bread and do not need to go in the oven. Simply break them into bite-sized pieces, place in the serving bowl and mix with 2 teaspoons crushed anise or fennel seeds. Then combine with the rest of the ingredients as described above.

COURGETTE FRITTERS WITH FETA AND DILL

These fritters are a beautiful colour as they are cooked quite briefly. The flavour is fresh and light due to the herbs and lemony feta.

Serves 6–8 as a mezze, 4–6 for a starter or light meal (makes about 20 small fritters)

2 large courgettes (about 300–350g), ends removed

sea salt and black pepper

110g chickpea (gram) flour

$^1/_4$ teaspoon bicarbonate of soda

120ml soda water

6 level tablespoons roughly chopped fresh mint

6 level tablespoons roughly chopped fresh dill

5 spring onions, finely sliced

200g feta cheese, crumbled

10–12 tablespoons olive oil

TO SERVE

200g Greek yoghurt thinned with a little milk and seasoned with $^1/_2$ garlic clove crushed to a paste with sea salt

tomato salad dressed with extra virgin olive oil, a squeeze of lemon or 1 tablespoon red wine vinegar, a pinch of sugar, salt and pepper

Coarsely grate the courgettes. Place in a colander, salt lightly with $^3/_4$ teaspoon of sea salt and mix well. Leave to stand for 20 minutes. Meanwhile, make a batter by mixing the chickpea flour and bicarbonate of soda, then slowly whisking in the soda water with a balloon whisk. (This should make quite a thick batter.) Gently squeeze the courgettes in a clean, dry cloth to get rid of all the excess water, transfer to a bowl, pour on the batter and mix well. Add the mint, dill, spring onion and feta, mix well again, and check the seasoning (the mixture may need only a little black pepper).

In a large frying pan, heat 3–5 tablespoons of the oil over a medium to high heat until hot. Scoop up a tablespoon of the courgette mixture and gently lower into the oil. Fill your frying pan with a further 3–4 tablespoons of mixture, depending on the size of the pan, but make sure there is enough space in between so you can turn them easily. Press the mixture down with the back of the spoon to flatten slightly. Fry for 2 minutes or until golden brown on one side, then gently loosen the fritters from the bottom of the pan with a palette knife, turn over carefully and continue to fry for a further 2 minutes, adding more oil as necessary, as the fritters absorb some while cooking. Try not to disturb the fritters as they fry or they will break up. Remove, drain on kitchen paper and keep warm until all the mixture has been used (you will need to do this in two or three batches, adding more oil to the pan if necessary). We serve these fritters with seasoned yoghurt and a tomato salad.

CHICORY SALAD WITH PICOS BLUE CHEESE, WALNUTS AND PEDRO XIMÉNEZ DRESSING

This dressing is a perfect accompaniment to crisp, slightly bitter chicory and strong blue cheese, and is an easy starter to put together in minutes. If you cannot find a Spanish blue cheese, Roquefort or Gorgonzola are suitable substitutes.

Serves 6–8 as a tapa, 4 for a starter or light meal

3–4 heads white chicory

1 handful fresh flat–leaf parsley leaves

120g walnut quarters

150g Picos cheese

DRESSING

1 garlic clove

sea salt and black pepper

1 tablespoon sherry vinegar

1 tablespoon sweet–tasting Pedro Ximénez sherry or 2 tablespoons
sweet oloroso sherry

a squeeze of lemon (optional)

5 tablespoons extra virgin olive oil

For the dressing, crush the garlic with a good pinch of salt in a mortar until a smooth paste is formed. Then add the vinegar, sherry and lemon juice (if using), and whisk in the olive oil until emulsified. Season with salt and pepper. This can be made a few hours earlier, but not the day before because the garlic will taste a little stale. Make sure you give it a good whisk just before dressing.

To assemble the salad, cut each head of chicory across in roughly 3cm slices and place in a mixing bowl with the whole parsley leaves and walnut quarters. Toss with the dressing, put in a serving dish and crumble on the blue cheese. Season with a little salt and black pepper, toss once more and serve.

REVUELTOS

SCRAMBLED EGGS

In both Spain and Morocco, eggs have always been an important part of the people's diet – a miracle food often used as a substitute for meat and fish. Like any scrambled eggs, revueltos can vary from disgusting to heavenly, but the best simply seduce the classic Spanish flavours with which they are combined.

POINTERS FOR REVUELTOS

- Use quite a small proportion of egg compared to your other ingredients, a ratio of about 1:3.
- Have people ready to eat and the toast on the plates, as the eggs carry on cooking when ready, and don't improve for sitting around.
- When cooked, the egg should be quite soft and glistening.
- Most revueltos are overcooked in the time it takes to put them on the plate, so remove from the heat just before you think they are quite ready.
- The amount of olive oil may seem a lot, but it is necessary for the texture.

SCRAMBLED EGG WITH PRAWNS AND ASPARAGUS

Serves 4

> 600g frozen North Atlantic prawns, shells on, peeled (250g peeled weight)
> 200g thin asparagus stalks, any tough ends snapped off
> 6 tablespoons olive oil
> 1 garlic clove, sliced
> 4 medium organic or free-range eggs
> 2 tablespoons roughly chopped fresh flat-leaf parsley
> sea salt and black pepper

TO SERVE

> sourdough or ciabatta toast

Thoroughly defrost your prawns in a sieve. Peel them by first breaking off the head, then peeling off the middle part of the shell and finally pulling off the tail. Bring a saucepan of salted water to the boil. Slice the asparagus into 2cm pieces. Blanch the asparagus until it is just soft. (Undercooked, crunchy asparagus does not suit this dish.) Pour the olive oil into a saucepan and fry the garlic over a medium heat until golden. Add the drained asparagus and prawns to the garlic and cook for a minute or two, adding some salt and pepper. Break the eggs into a bowl and whisk. Stir the eggs and parsley into the asparagus and cook over a medium heat, stirring every 4 seconds. (This encourages some texture in the egg.) When your egg is still a little bit wet (80 per cent cooked), season with a little salt and pepper, then spoon it over your toast and eat straight away.

Variations

There are many revueltos in Spain; here are a few just in case you want to vary the ingredients. (The basic ingredients and method remain the same.)

• Prawns with peas or broad beans and a little mint
• Prawns with mushrooms
• Mushrooms with jamón serrano
• Artichoke hearts with jamón serrano
• Flaked cooked salt cod and potatoes
• Braised garlic shoots (ajetes) or wild garlic leaves with prawns or jamón serrano

MOROCCAN EGGS WITH TOMATOES AND CUMIN

In Marrakech we sought out a small kiosk restaurant we had read about, and through a miracle found it. The name of the place was Mustafa's, and Mustafa himself cooked this dish for us while we sat next to him perched on stools. He placed a battered frying pan on what seemed an ancient (but beautiful) calor gas burner. He then fried chopped onion and tomatoes together, delicately spicing them with cumin and paprika and some fresh coriander. When the mixture became soft, he cracked open an egg and folded it in. The dish was magical! When we returned from our trip we wanted to replicate it, so we described the dish to our Moroccan chef Mohammed. He nodded and said how these were the eggs that his mother cooked and that he ate every day when he was growing up.

Serves 6–8 as a mezze, 4 for a starter or light meal

600g ripe tomatoes

4 tablespoons olive oil

6 spring onions, trimmed and roughly sliced

4 garlic cloves, sliced

1 level teaspoon cumin seeds, roughly ground

a pinch of cayenne pepper or chilli flakes

$1/2$ teaspooon caster sugar (optional)

4 medium organic or free-range eggs

3 tablespoons roughly chopped fresh flat-leaf parsley (or coriander)

sea salt and black pepper

Peel the tomatoes (see page 42), then quarter and seed them. If they are large, cut each quarter in half again. Pour the olive oil into a medium frying pan over a medium heat and fry the spring onion, garlic and cumin until they just start to colour. Now add the tomatoes, cayenne or chilli, salt and pepper. You might find it necessary to add the sugar because the tomatoes may not be sweet enough. Simmer for 15 minutes or until the tomatoes are cooked but not totally broken up. Crack an egg in each quarter of the pan. Ruffle the whites with a fork so they are thinned over the surface of the tomato. Simmer until the eggs are as you like them (1–2 minutes). Serve with lots of parsley on top and some warm Moroccan bread (see page 33) or pitta bread.

SALADS AND COOKED MOROCCAN SALADS

As we walked into Restaurante El Dorado, a good fish restaurant near the port of Motril, the waiter gave us a quick glance up and down as if to single us out from the other customers who were eating there that evening. Unruffled, we sat at a table and asked for two tinto veranos (red wine with casera, a sort of Spanish cream soda), and the menu. After driving from Malaga in the quiet dark, the bright strip-lighting seemed all the more stark, and the thunderous cheers of men watching football in the tapas bar next door, all the louder. We ordered an ensalada mixta (mixed salad), the precursor to any Spanish meal. We dressed the mélange of gem lettuce, palm hearts, slices of sweet onion, green olives, sweetcorn, creamy local avocado and grated carrot with olive oil and vinegar scented with bay, and tucked in. It was delicious. We do enjoy these Spanish salads, but as they don't tend to vary that much, we crave a bit more choice. The salads in this section are all excellent on their own or in a group (particularly the Moroccan salads), or, where appropriate, served with meat or fish.

ENSALADA DE COGOLLOS AL AJILLO
GEM LETTUCE WITH CRISPY GARLIC

We ate this salad in a buzzing tapas bar that we stumbled across in Córdoba. There was nothing complex about the fan-shaped gem lettuce and roast red peppers that had been lovingly arranged on the plate, but what made it special were little nuggets of garlic fried until light brown and crisp and spooned over the top at the last minute.

Serves 4

> 4 gem lettuces
>
> 4 piquillo peppers, torn into 12 strips, or 3 roasted red bell peppers (see page 78), peeled, seeded and torn into 12 strips
>
> $1^1/_2$ tablespoons good-quality red wine vinegar (see page 287)
>
> 3 tablespoons extra virgin olive oil
>
> 4 garlic cloves, roughly chopped
>
> sea salt and black pepper

Remove any damaged outer leaves from the lettuces and discard. Cut each lettuce in half lengthways and then each half into three or four. Try to make sure that each slice has part of the stalk of the lettuce attached so it keeps together. Fan the slices out on a plate until most of the plate is covered. Now lay the peppers on top, season with salt and pepper and sprinkle on the vinegar. In a frying pan, warm the olive oil over a medium heat and when fairly hot add the garlic. Fry gently, stirring occasionally, until the garlic becomes an even golden brown in colour. Spoon the warm oil and garlic over the salad and serve immediately.

WINTER TABBOULEH

This is a winter version of the famous Lebanese bulgur salad, replacing the tomato with chicory, fennel, walnuts and pomegranate seeds. The dressing is made with pomegranate molasses – the treacly sweet-sour syrup from the reduced juice of fresh pomegranates. Winter tabbouleh is delicious as a salad or as an accompaniment for fish or chicken.

Serves 4

> 140g medium-coarse bulgur (cracked wheat)
>
> 1 head white chicory, finely chopped
>
> $1/2$ fennel bulb, trimmed and finely chopped
>
> 75g cauliflower, separated into tiny florets no more than 1cm in diameter
>
> 4 tablespoons roughly chopped fresh flat-leaf parsley
>
> 2 tablespoons roughly chopped fresh mint
>
> 2 tablespoons roughly chopped walnuts
>
> seeds of 1 pomegranate, preferably the deep-red Iranian or Turkish variety,
>   all bitter yellow membrane removed

POMEGRANATE MOLASSES DRESSING

> 1 garlic clove, crushed
>
> $1/4$ teaspoon ground cinnamon
>
> 2 tablespoons Pomegranate Molasses (see page 284)
>
> 1 tablespoon water
>
> 4 tablespoons extra virgin olive oil
>
> $1/2$ teaspoon caster sugar (optional)
>
> sea salt and black pepper

Sit the bulgur in warm water for 10–15 minutes to swell before putting it into a sieve to drain. For the dressing, mix the garlic with the cinnamon and pomegranate molasses, then add the water and whisk in the olive oil. It should emulsify. Check for seasoning. If the dressing is very tart (pomegranate molasses does vary in sourness), add a little sugar if you like.

Mix the bulgur, chicory, fennel, cauliflower, herbs, walnuts and pomegranate seeds together. Toss the salad with the dressing just before you are ready to eat, and check the seasoning once again.

ENSALADA DE HINOJO
FENNEL, POTATO AND ORANGE SALAD

At Moro we often serve roast pork (see pages 202-4) with the following salad, as it is clean, fresh-tasting and cuts through the richness of the pork.

Serves 4

750g firm, waxy small salad potatoes (Charlotte, Ratte, Anya, Pink Fir or
  Cyprus), peeled, unless very small

3-4 eating oranges

2 fennel bulbs

$^1/_2$ red onion, finely chopped

a handful of fresh flat-leaf parsley leaves

sea salt and black pepper

DRESSING

3 tablespoons olive oil

1 tablespoon red wine vinegar

$^1/_2$ teaspoon caster sugar

1 garlic clove, crushed with salt

To make the dressing, whisk the olive oil, vinegar, sugar and garlic together, and season with salt and pepper.

Place the potatoes in cold salted water and bring to the boil. Simmer for 10-20 minutes, depending on size, until tender. While the potatoes are cooking, prepare the rest of the salad. With a small, sharp knife, preferably serrated, cut the rind and pith off the oranges, keeping the fruit whole. Now slice into rounds and place in a large mixing bowl. Remove any damaged outer leaves from the fennel, then cut in half lengthways and cut each half into thin slices no more than 5mm thick. Place in the mixing bowl along with the onion and parsley leaves. When the drained potatoes are cool enough to handle, slice into rounds no more than 1cm thick. Place on top of the other ingredients in the bowl. Pour over the dressing, season with salt and pepper, mix well and taste.

TOMATO, WALNUT AND POMEGRANATE MOLASSES SALAD

Of all the Mediterranean countries, it is Turkey that cultivates and appreciates walnuts more than any other. They are used in every aspect of Turkish cuisine. This salad has the added exoticism of pomegranate molasses.

Serves 4

> 600g small sweet cherry tomatoes, cut in half horizontally
>
> 100g walnut halves
>
> 4 tablespoons roughly chopped fresh flat-leaf parsley
>
> 1 quantity Pomegranate Molasses (see page 148)
>
> sea salt and black pepper

Place the tomatoes, walnuts and parsley in a bowl. Pour over the dressing and toss well. Check for seasoning. Leave for half an hour in the fridge or serve immediately.

PARSNIP, YOGHURT AND DATE SALAD

This Lebanese salad can be thought of as half salad, half relish. It is concentrated, rich and sweet. We like to eat it as part of a mezze plate or with lamb.

Serves 4

> 600g parsnips
>
> 10 dates, stoned and roughly chopped
>
> 2 tablespoons roughly chopped fresh mint
>
> 150g Greek yoghurt with a squeeze of lemon, or Home-made Yoghurt (see page 279), or any slightly sour yoghurt
>
> 1 tablespoon lemon juice
>
> 2 teaspoons runny honey
>
> 2 tablespoons extra virgin olive oil
>
> sea salt and black pepper

Peel the parsnips, cut in quarters lengthways, and get rid of any woody centre (only if the parsnips are large). Grate coarsely and place in a bowl. Add the chopped dates and mint, followed by all the remaining ingredients. Season with salt and pepper, toss well and taste. Serve immediately.

CHICKPEA, CAULIFLOWER AND PRESERVED LEMON SALAD

This is a classy salad that demonstrates the potential of the humble cauliflower. Zaatar (used in the dressing) is a blend of summer savory, sumac (see page 45) and sesame seeds – a flavouring common throughout the Middle East, especially in Lebanon. It is sprinkled on flatbreads, salads and kebabs, or mixed to a paste with olive oil.

Serves 4

    1 small cauliflower (about 500g), stalk and leaves discarded, broken into small florets

    240g home-cooked chickpeas (see page 59) or 1 x 400g can, drained

    $^1/_2$ Preserved Lemon (see page 281), rinsed, inner pulp removed, finely chopped (about 1 heaped tablespoon)

    3 tablespoons fresh coriander leaves

    sea salt and black pepper

DRESSING

    1 tablespoon lemon juice

    3 tablespoons extra virgin olive oil

    1 tablespoon zaatar (optional)

    $1^1/_2$ teaspoons cumin seeds, roughly ground

Whisk all the dressing ingredients together in a bowl and check for seasoning.

Blanch the cauliflower in boiling salted water for a couple of minutes or until tender. Drain well. Put the drained chickpeas, cauliflower, preserved lemon and coriander in a large bowl. Pour on the dressing, season with a little salt and pepper, and mix well.

ROAST RED PEPPER, PRESERVED LEMON AND CAPER SALAD

Claudia Roden told us about this Moroccan salad. It is delicious with fish or as a starter or part of a light lunch.

Serves 4

> 4 large red peppers (grilled or roasted, see page 78)
>
> 50g capers in salt or vinegar
>
> $^1/_2$ Preserved Lemon (see page 281), rinsed, inner pulp removed, finely
>> chopped (1 heaped tablespoon)
>
> 3 tablespoons fresh flat-leaf parsley, roughly chopped
>
> 1 garlic clove, crushed with salt
>
> 3 tablespoons extra virgin olive oil
>
> a squeeze of lemon
>
> freshly ground black pepper

To roast, peel and seed the peppers, see page 78. Tear the peppers into large strips and set aside. Place the capers in a sieve and rinse well under cold water for 1 minute. Transfer to a bowl filled with fresh cold water and leave on the side for 1 hour, changing the water a couple of times.

Place the peppers in a bowl with the lemon, parsley, garlic and drained capers, drizzle on the olive oil, and add lemon juice and black pepper. Toss well and taste for seasoning. This salad should be salty enough from the preserved lemon.

WHITE CABBAGE, MINT AND CARAWAY SALAD

The following salad is Lebanese, and an original way of using white cabbage. It is like a healthier, more interesting version of coleslaw.

Serves 4

 1 garlic clove

 2 tablespoons lemon juice

 4 tablespoons extra virgin olive oil

 300g white cabbage, cut in half, cored and finely shredded

 2 tablespoons roughly chopped fresh mint

 2 tablespoons roughly chopped fresh flat-leaf parsley

 1 tablespoon caraway seeds, half of them lightly crushed in a mortar

 sea salt and black pepper

Crush the garlic in a mortar with $1/2$ teaspoon sea salt until you have a smooth paste. Add the lemon juice followed by the olive oil. Place the cabbage, mint, parsley and caraway in a large mixing bowl. Pour over the dressing and toss well. Taste for seasoning. Serve immediately.

ARTICHOKE AND POTATO SALAD WITH HARISSA

This salad is delicious on its own or with a few salted anchovy fillets on top, or you can leave out the artichokes and serve it as a simple potato salad with the cooked Moroccan salads that follow.

Serves 4

 4 large or 8 small globe artichokes

 600g waxy small potatoes (Anya, Cyprus, Pink Fir, Ratte, Charlotte, Linzer
 or Jersey Royals), peeled unless very small

 2 tablespoons fresh coriander leaves

 1 tablespoon finely shredded fresh mint

 Harissa (optional, see page 282)

 sea salt and black pepper

HARISSA DRESSING

    1 garlic clove, crushed with salt

    1 tablespoon lemon juice

    1–2 tablespoons Harissa, depending on how hot it is

    1 tablespoon roughly chopped fresh coriander

    5 tablespoons extra virgin olive oil

For the dressing, mix all the ingredients together thoroughly. Season with a little salt and pepper.

To cook the artichokes, break or cut off the stalks at the base, put in a large saucepan and cover generously with cold water and a pinch of salt. Put a lid from a smaller saucepan on top of the artichokes to weigh them down, and place over a medium heat. Simmer for 15–25 minutes, depending on size or until you are able to pull out one of the leaves near the base of the artichoke (be careful, it will be hot). When a leaf comes away easily it means it is tender. You can also test to see if it is cooked by sliding a small knife into the heart: if it goes in easily, it is cooked. Drain in a colander and cool with cold water. Now gently pull off all the leaves (the ends of the large ones are rather delicious dipped in a mustard dressing), until you are left with the furry choke. Scrape away this thistly choke with a teaspoon. Cut the heart into slices about 5–7mm thick and place in a bowl.

While the artichokes are simmering away, put the potatoes in a separate saucepan and cover with salted cold water. Bring to a gentle simmer and cook until tender, roughly 15–20 minutes, depending on size. When the potatoes are tender, drain, and when cool enough to handle, but still warm, cut into rounds about the same thickness as the artichoke hearts and place on top of the artichokes. Pour the harissa dressing over the potatoes, preferably whilst they are still warm, as they absorb the flavour better, add the coriander and mint and toss well. Check the seasoning. We prefer to serve this salad whilst still slightly warm, but it is equally good at room temperature. Sprinkle with harissa if you like.

COOKED MOROCCAN SALADS

In Morocco, mezze as such do not exist. However, one of the delights of a Moroccan table are the cooked salads. This colourful array of textures and tastes is often shared to start a meal. These are very simple recipes, but we find the result startlingly exotic and satisfying. Serve at room temperature with a Moroccan bread or a type of flatbread, or use to accompany simply cooked meat or fish. Cooked salads can be made in advance.

GRILLED AUBERGINE SALAD

This cooked aubergine salad is wonderfully intense, not only because of the spice, but also because of the aubergines, which are grilled beforehand for a smoky taste and then slow-cooked to concentrate the flavours.

Serves 4

> 1 kg (or approx. 4 large) aubergines
>
> 5–6 tablespoons olive oil
>
> 3 garlic cloves, cut into thin slivers
>
> 1 teaspoon coriander seeds, roughly ground
>
> 2 teaspoons cumin seeds, freshly ground
>
> 1 large tomato, skinned (see page 42) and chopped, or 1 teaspoon
> tomato purée
>
> $1^1/_2$ teaspoons sweet paprika
>
> 5 tablespoons roughly chopped fresh flat-leaf parsley
>
> 6 tablespoons roughly chopped fresh coriander
>
> $1^1/_2$ tablespoons lemon juice
>
> sea salt and black pepper

Grill the aubergines whole over a hot barbecue, a diffuser over gas, directly on the naked flame of a gas hob, or under the grill, turning until the skin of the aubergines is charred and crispy all over and the flesh is soft. If none of these options is available, place dry in a very hot oven at 220°C/425°F/Gas 7 for about 45–60 minutes until soft inside, though they will not char much. Remove from the heat. When cool enough to handle, cut off the tops and peel off the skin, scraping the flesh off the back of the skin if necessary. Roughly chop the aubergine and set aside on the chopping board.

Now place a large frying pan or saucepan over a medium to high heat, add the oil and, when it is hot but not smoking, add the garlic. Fry for a few seconds until it begins to colour, then add the coriander and cumin seeds. Stir a little and cook for a further 10–20 seconds to bring out the flavour of the spices, then add the chopped aubergine, tomato (or tomato purée), paprika, parsley, 3 tablespoons of the fresh coriander, and finally the lemon juice. Give everything a thorough stir so that all the ingredients are evenly mixed, and season with a little salt and pepper. Turn the heat to low and continue to cook for 20–30 minutes, stirring every 5 minutes to scrape off any caramelised bits that have stuck to the bottom of the pan. The aubergine is ready when it is no longer watery. To finish, stir in the remaining coriander and taste for seasoning once more.

COURGETTE AND AUBERGINE SALAD WITH CHARMOULA

Blanching aubergines and courgettes together is unusual, but when dressed with charmoula it all makes sense.

Serves 4

    600g small to medium courgettes, washed and trimmed both ends

    1 large or 2 small aubergines

    sea salt and black pepper

CHARMOULA MARINADE

    2 teaspoons cumin seeds

    2 garlic cloves

    1 level teaspoon salt

    juice of $1/2$–1 lemon

    $1/2$ tablespoon good-quality red wine vinegar (see page 287)

    1 teaspoon sweet paprika

    3 tablespoons roughly chopped fresh coriander

    3 tablespoons extra virgin olive oil

We make the charmoula in a mortar. First, roughly pound the cumin and set aside. Now add the garlic to the mortar and crush with the salt until a smooth paste is formed. Return the cumin to the mortar, followed by the lemon juice, vinegar, paprika, coriander and olive oil. Set aside.

    Slice the courgettes in half lengthways and then each half across widthwise into slices about 1–1.5cm thick. Now slice the aubergines into sixths lengthways and then again into small wedges about 1–1.5cm thick, roughly the same as the courgettes.

Bring a large saucepan of salted water to the boil and add the courgettes and aubergines. Put on the lid immediately and boil for 2 minutes or until both vegetables are tender (they should cook in roughly the same time). Drain well in a colander and leave to stand for 5 minutes in the sink. To remove any excess water, gently press the courgettes and aubergines with the back of a large spoon. While still warm (it is always best to marinate these vegetables when still warm), transfer the courgettes and aubergines to a large bowl, pour over the charmoula marinade and toss well. Taste for seasoning and either eat immediately or serve at room temperature. Also good with fish or chicken.

CAULIFLOWER SALAD WITH TOMATO AND CUMIN

Cauliflower is a wonderful vehicle for spiced tomato. Its delicate flavour combines beautifully with more assertive ingredients.

Serves 4

> 6 tablespoons olive oil
> 1 medium onion, finely chopped
> 2 garlic cloves, finely chopped
> 4 tomatoes, peeled (see page 42) and roughly chopped
> 2 teaspoons cumin seeds
> 30 threads saffron, infused in 2 tablespoons boiling water
> 500g cauliflower, leaves and stalk discarded, broken into small florets
> 1 tablespoon roughly chopped fresh flat-leaf parsley
> sea salt and black pepper

Heat the olive oil over a medium heat and, when hot, add the onion and a pinch of salt. Fry for 10 minutes, stirring occasionally, until the onion begins to caramelise, then add the garlic and cook for another 2 minutes. Now stir in the tomato and cumin seeds and simmer for 5 minutes. Add the saffron infusion and the cauliflower, season with salt and pepper, stir well and put on the lid. Simmer for 10–20 minutes, stirring occasionally, until the cauliflower has softened. Add the chopped parsley and serve at room temperature.

CARROT SALAD WITH
ORANGE-BLOSSOM WATER

Try to use organic or home-grown carrots whenever possible as their flavour tends to be much superior, especially the home-grown variety.

Serves 4

600g organic carrots, peeled and left whole

1 tablespoon orange-blossom water

2 tablespoons finely chopped fresh mint

$^{1}/_{2}$ garlic clove, crushed with salt

$^{1}/_{2}$ teaspoon caster sugar

$^{1}/_{2}$ tablespoon lemon juice

3 tablespoons extra virgin olive oil

sea salt and black pepper

Bring a large saucepan of lightly salted water to the boil and add the carrots. Simmer until tender, turning down the heat if necessary, then drain in a colander and leave to cool. When cool enough to handle, slice each carrot across about 5mm thick and place in a mixing bowl along with the orange-blossom water, mint, garlic, sugar, lemon juice and olive oil. Season with salt and pepper, mix well and taste.

Variation

This salad is also delicious made with coarsely grated raw carrots.

BROAD BEAN SALAD

This salad is a delicious way of using up large broad beans that can be tough. You can buy frozen broad beans if fresh are not available.

Serves 4

> 4 tablespoons olive oil
>
> 2 garlic cloves, thinly sliced
>
> 2 teaspoons cumin seeds, roughly ground
>
> 3 tablespoons roughly chopped fresh coriander
>
> 1kg fresh broad beans, podded, or 500g frozen
>
> a squeeze of lemon
>
> sea salt and black pepper

Heat the olive oil in a frying pan or large saucepan over a medium heat. When hot, add the garlic and fry for roughly $1/2$ minute or until it begins to turn golden. Add the cumin, half the coriander and, shortly after, the broad beans. Stir well. Cover with cold water and simmer gently until tender. This can take from 5 minutes for small, young broad beans to 15 minutes for larger, tougher ones. The important thing is that whatever the size, they are ready when soft. Remove from the heat, season with salt and pepper and stir in the remaining coriander and a squeeze of lemon. Taste for seasoning once more and serve immediately or at room temperature.

CHARD SALAD WITH PRESERVED LEMON AND OLIVES

Spinach can be used instead of chard, and it does not need blanching

Serves 4-6

> 600g chard, leaves and young stalks only, washed
>
> 4 tablespoons olive oil
>
> 3 garlic cloves, thinly sliced
>
> $1/2$ medium Preserved Lemon (see page 281), washed well, inner pulp removed and discarded, finely chopped (1 heaped tablespoon)
>
> 150g purple olives, stoned and halved
>
> sea salt and black pepper

Bring a large saucepan of lightly salted water to a proper boil. (The salt fixes the green in the chard, as well as bringing out the flavour.) Add the chard and put on the lid to ensure the water will come back to the boil as quickly as possible. When the stalks are tender, about 1–2 minutes, immediately scoop out and place in a colander and cool briefly under running water. Drain and chop into roughly 2–3cm pieces. Place a large saucepan over a medium heat, add the olive oil and, when hot, the garlic. Fry gently until the garlic begins to turn golden, then add the chopped preserved lemon and the olives. Cook for a further 30 seconds, then add the chard. Stir around well and taste for seasoning (it might not need any extra salt because of the preserved lemon and olives).

PUMPKIN SALAD

At the restaurant we mix varieties of pumpkin or squash as some are a bit watery and some a little too starchy. Butternut is good mixed with Kabocha, and Iron Bark is good mixed with red onion squash. We use squash or pumpkin from early autumn to late winter because long after they are picked the flavour keeps on developing and becomes sweeter. Good with lamb or among a selection of cooked salads.

Serves 4

> **1kg pumpkin or squash, preferably a variety with dense flesh (butternut, Kabocha, Crown Prince)**
> **1 teaspoon ground cinnamon**
> **$^1/_2$ garlic clove, crushed to a paste with a pinch of salt**
> **2 tablespoons olive oil**
> **$^1/_2$ teaspoon caster sugar (optional)**
> **sea salt and black pepper**

Preheat the oven to 220°C/425°F/Gas 7.

Cut the pumpkin or squash in half lengthways and scoop out the seeds. Remove the skin with a sharp knife (or a potato peeler if the skin is tender enough), and divide up into large chunks. Put in a large mixing bowl and add the ground cinnamon, crushed garlic and olive oil and toss the pumpkin pieces so they are lightly coated. Season with salt and pepper. Place on a roasting tray in the hot oven for a good 20–30 minutes, or until the flesh is soft. Remove and cool a little before mashing well or putting through a mouli. Check the seasoning, including the cinnamon. If the pumpkins are not particularly sweet, add a little caster sugar, and if the mixture is very thick, thin it down with a little hot water.

SWEET TOMATO JAM

In Morocco this spiced tomato jam is often served as an accompaniment to salads. However, we like to eat it with bread or grilled sardines, or any roast or grilled fish. Because of its high sugar content, it will keep in the fridge forat least two weeks.

Serves 4-6

> 1.5kg ripe, good-quality tomatoes in season, peeled (see page 42)
> 50g butter
> 2 tablespoons olive oil
> 2 garlic cloves, thinly sliced
> 1 teaspoon ground cinnamon
> 2-3 tablespoons caster sugar
> sea salt and black pepper

Prepare the tomatoes as described on page 42. If they are big, remove the seeds. Chop the tomatoes roughly and place in a bowl.

Put a large frying pan or saucepan over a medium heat and add the butter and olive oil. When the butter begins to foam, add the garlic and cinnamon. Cook for a minute or two until the garlic is golden, then add the tomatoes and sugar and stir well. Still over a medium heat, bring the tomatoes up to a gentle simmer and cook for approximately 30-40 minutes, stirring occasionally, until most of the liquid has evaporated and the tomatoes are the consistency of strawberry jam. Let the tomatoes caramelise slightly on the bottom of the pan before stirring, but do not let them burn. Taste for seasoning.

CELERY AND PRESERVED LEMON SALAD

Serves 4

       4 tablespoons olive oil

       1 garlic clove, thinly sliced

       rind of $^1/_2$ Preserved Lemon (see page 281), rinsed well, inner pulp
          removed and discarded, finely chopped (about 1 tablespoon)

       1 head celery, trimmed and sliced into roughly 1cm pieces

       100ml water

       1 tablespoon roughly chopped fresh flat-leaf parsley

       sea salt and black pepper

In a large frying pan heat the oil over a medium heat and, when hot, add the garlic and preserved lemon. Fry for 30 seconds before adding the celery. Fry for a further 5–10 minutes, stirring occasionally. When the celery begins to soften, add the water and cook for a further 5 minutes or until all the liquid has almost evaporated. Add the parsley and season with a little pepper and salt.

RADISH SALAD WITH ORANGE-BLOSSOM WATER

This salad is the exception to the others as it is not cooked. It can be made with cucumber, radish or turnip, or a mixture of all three. Refreshing and exotic.

Serves 4

       750g radishes (or cucumber or turnip)

       finely grated zest of 1 orange

       1 tablespoon orange-blossom water

       1 tablespoon roughly chopped fresh flat-leaf parsley

       $^1/_2$ tablespoon roughly chopped fresh mint

       3 tablespoons extra virgin olive oil

       sea salt and black pepper

If using radishes, just wash and slice into thin rounds, no thicker than 5mm. (For cucumber, wash, peel the skin off in strips, then slice the flesh into thin rounds. For turnips, peel, cut into quarters, then slice each quarter into thin strips.)

       Place in a bowl and add the remaining ingredients. Serve immediately.

FISH MAIN COURSES

Although we sometimes suggest a particular fish in the following recipes, you can easily use substitutes, depending on what is available and freshest on the day.

RAYA CON SALSA DE JEREZ
ROAST SKATE WITH SHERRY SAUCE AND CRISPY CAPERS

The butter sauce is made with fino and sherry vinegar for a more robust flavour.

Serves 4

> 4 portion-sized skate wings, about 250g each, or 4 cod/monkfish
>   steaks/fillets, about 200g each
> 3 tablespoons olive oil
> sea salt and black pepper

SHERRY SAUCE

> 200ml fino sherry
> 1 banana shallot, or 2 normal shallots, very finely chopped
> a sprig of fresh thyme
> 2 bay leaves (preferably fresh)
> 5 tablespoons sherry vinegar plus 1 extra teaspoon
> 10 black peppercorns
> 200g good-quality unsalted butter, cold, cubed

TO SERVE

> 1 quantity Crispy Capers (see opposite)
> 4 level tablespoons finely chopped fresh flat-leaf parsley
> 1 lemon, quartered

First, prepare the Crispy Capers as described opposite. This can be done well in advance.

To make the sauce, place the fino, shallot, thyme, bay leaves, 5 tablespoons vinegar and the peppercorns in a small saucepan and simmer over a low to medium heat until you are left with roughly 5 tablespoons of liquid. Strain out the thyme, bay leaves and peppercorns. Over a very low heat, stirring constantly, add the cubes of butter, a couple at a time. Add more when the butter has melted into the sauce and continue to do so until all the butter has been used and a light emulsion has formed. Add the remaining teaspoon of vinegar and a little salt, and taste. Keep warm over the stove or in a bain-marie while you cook the fish, but do not allow to bubble.

Preheat the oven to 220°C/425°F/Gas 7. When you are ready to cook the skate, heat a large metal roasting tin on the hob until very hot. Season the skate with salt and pepper on both sides, drizzle the olive oil into the pan to cover the bottom, and gently ease each wing into it, shaking the pan as you do so to prevent the skate from sticking. Place in the oven for about 10 minutes, depending on the thickness of the wing, or until cooked through. Remove and serve immediately with the warm sauce spooned over the fish, the capers and chopped parsley sprinkled all over, and lemon wedges on the side. Delicious with braised spinach or chard and new season's boiled potatoes.

CRISPY CAPERS

80g capers in salt or vinegar
4 tablespoons olive oil

Prepare the capers as described on page 154. Heat the olive oil over a medium heat in a small saucepan and, when it is hot, add the drained capers. Fry, stirring occasionally, until they are slightly browned and crisp. Remove from the heat and drain on kitchen paper. Set aside.

POTAJE DE PESCADO CON ANÍS

FISH STEW WITH ANÍS, FENNEL, SAFFRON AND ALMONDS

Serves 6

8 tablespoons olive oil

1 onion, roughly chopped

3 fennel bulbs, trimmed and finely diced (keep any feathery tops aside)

2 garlic cloves, thinly sliced

2 bay leaves (preferably fresh)

$1/2$ teaspoon fennel seeds

150ml Spanish dry anís or Pernod or ouzo

750ml Fish Stock (see page 313)

80 strands saffron, infused in 3 tablespoons boiling water

150g whole blanched almonds, lightly toasted and roughly ground

650g monkfish fillets, cut in chunks about 5cm square

500g clams, venus or palourdes, washed (discard any that are broken or
   open)

juice of about $1/2$ lemon to taste

the roughly chopped fennel tops, or 2 tablespoons roughly chopped fresh
   flat-leaf parsley

sea salt and black pepper

In a large saucepan, heat the oil over a medium heat. When the oil is hot (just beginning to smoke), add the onion and a pinch of salt. Lower the heat and cook the onion, stirring occasionally, until golden and sweet (about 15 minutes). Now add the fennel and cook for 10 minutes, stirring occasionally. Then add the garlic, bay and fennel seeds and cook for 10 minutes more until it has reduced by one-third and is golden. Pour in the anís and let the alcohol bubble away for a couple of minutes before adding the fish stock and the saffron-infused water. Finally, add the almonds and taste for seasoning. This base can be prepared earlier and set aside until you are ready to eat.

Warm the base through over a medium heat until it is just beginning to bubble, add the monkfish and cover with a lid. Simmer for 5 minutes, then add the clams and continue to cook until the fish is cooked through and the clams have steamed open (this should take another 3-5 minutes). Add the lemon to taste. Sprinkle on the chopped fennel leaves or the parsley. Serve with some new potatoes and/or a raw fennel salad and lots of bread to mop up the sauce.

BESUGO AL HORNO

BAKED BREAM WITH POTATOES AND TOMATOES

Bream cooked in the oven this way is traditional in Spain for Christmas. It is easy to make and a treat to eat. This dish is also good made with cod or hake steaks or filleted sea bass (as these fish will take about 15 minutes less to cook, you will have to roast the other ingredients for 15–20 minutes before you place the fish on top).

Serves 4

> 2 bream (red, golden or black), each big enough for 2 (around 500g each), scaled and gutted
>
> 4 large firm Cyprus potatoes (about 1kg), sliced into rounds 3mm thick
>
> 2 medium red onions, thinly sliced
>
> 6 medium sweet tomatoes, sliced in rounds about 5mm thick, or 12–18 small cherry tomatoes, cut in half
>
> 2 garlic cloves, crushed to a paste with salt
>
> 2 bay leaves (preferably fresh), halved
>
> 6 tablespoons olive oil
>
> a few parsley stalks
>
> 4 slices lemon
>
> $^1/_2$ fennel bulb, finely chopped, or $^1/_2$ tablespoon fennel seeds
>
> sea salt and black pepper

TO SERVE

> 1 lemon, quartered
>
> 2 tablespoons roughly chopped fresh flat-leaf parsley

Preheat the oven to 220°C/425°F/Gas 7.

Season the fish well with salt and pepper inside and out, and lightly salt the potatoes. Place the onions, potatoes, tomatoes, garlic and bay leaves in a large mixing bowl. Pour on half the olive oil, season well with salt and pepper and carefully toss together. Stuff the parsley stalks, lemon and fennel inside the cavity of each fish. Cover the bottom of a very large and roomy roasting tray with half the onions, potatoes and tomatoes, and spread out in a single layer. Now place the bream on top, cover with the rest of the vegetables and drizzle on the remaining olive oil. Place in the middle of the hot oven and roast for 35 minutes or until the fish is cooked. Serve with lemon and chopped parsley on top, with a salad.

VIEIRAS CON MIGAS
SCALLOPS WITH BREADCRUMBS

It makes complete sense to cook scallops in their shells as they are the perfect individual baking dishes. The scallop shell is the symbol of Galicia, which is quite apt as this dish is a variation of a Galician recipe. The jamón included below is by no means essential, but is there for those who like it.

Serves 4

> 80g white breadcrumbs
>
> 4 tablespoons olive oil
>
> 4 garlic cloves, finely chopped
>
> 6 tablespoons roughly chopped fresh flat-leaf parsley
>
> 75g jamón serrano, finely chopped (optional) or 2 tablespoons fresh oregano
>
> 12 scallops with their orangey-pink corals, cleaned and halved
>
> 8 scallop shells, if possible
>
> 8 tablespoons fino sherry or white wine
>
> 50g butter, cut into 8 pieces
>
> sea salt and black pepper

Preheat the oven to 180°C/350°F/Gas 4.

Spread the breadcrumbs out on a baking tray, drizzle roughly with 2 tablespoons of olive oil and lightly toss. Place in the middle of the oven for 15–20 minutes or until the crumbs have more or less dried out and are slightly golden. Transfer to a mixing bowl and allow to cool. Now add the chopped garlic, parsley and jamón or oregano, and season with salt and pepper.

Turn the oven up to 230°C/450°F/Gas 8.

To cook the scallops, season with a little salt and place three halves in each shell or all in an ovenproof dish. Sprinkle the fino sherry over the scallops, then place a knob of butter on each one. Scatter the breadcrumb mixture on top until most of the scallops are covered. Drizzle on the remaining oil and place in the oven for 10–15 minutes until the scallops are just cooked. Serve with braised or blanched spinach dressed with lemon and oil, or some green beans, and a glass of chilled fino.

MERLUZA CON LIMÓN

HAKE WITH LEMON AND BAY

We had this dish at a famous restaurant near Cádiz called El Faro. Try to use fresh bay leaves as they are wonderfully aromatic and key to this recipe.

Serves 4

4 thick hake or cod steaks, about 225–250g each

25g butter

3 tablespoons olive oil

$^1/_2$ tablespoon plain flour

3 bay leaves (preferably fresh), halved

75ml white wine

125ml Fish Stock (see page 313)

2 tablespoons finely chopped fresh flat-leaf parsley

a squeeze of lemon

sea salt and black pepper

MARINADE

2 garlic cloves

2 bay leaves (preferably fresh), finely chopped

a good pinch of sea salt

juice of 1 lemon

1 tablespoon olive oil

First marinate the fish. Crush the garlic and bay to a paste with the salt and mix in the lemon juice. Rub all over the fish, followed by the olive oil, and place in a bowl. Leave to stand in the fridge for approximately 1–3 hours.

When you are ready to cook, place a large frying pan over a medium to high heat, and add the butter and olive oil. Season the fish with salt and pepper, and when the butter begins to foam, carefully slide the fish into the frying pan. Fry on one side for about 2–4 minutes until sealed and golden brown in places; gently turn over with a spatula, and fry for another 2–4 minutes, again until sealed. Turn the heat to low and add the flour and bay leaves in between the pieces of fish, cook for 30 seconds, then slowly stir in the wine, any remaining marinade and the fish stock, shaking the pan quite vigorously to prevent lumps forming. Cook for another 5 minutes, or until the fish is cooked through. When cooked, the flesh of the fish should flake easily and be white all the way through. (If it is still slightly translucent, it might need a little more time.) Sprinkle on the parsley and add the lemon juice to taste. (Just a little squeeze should be enough, otherwise the sauce may taste too acidic.) Season with salt and pepper.

This is delicious served with some mashed potato and watercress salad or Slow-cooked Fennel, without the dill (see page 240), or spinach.

MERLUZA A LA GALLEGA
HAKE WITH HOT PAPRIKA DRESSING

The hake is simply poached, then brought alive with a hot dressing of smoky paprika, olive oil, caramelised garlic and vinegar. Wonderful!

Serves 4

4 large firm potatoes (Cyprus or Wilja), peeled and cut in wedges

4 thick hake or cod steaks, about 225–250g each

3 tablespoons roughly chopped fresh flat-leaf parsley

sea salt and black pepper

POACHING STOCK

1.5 litres Fish Stock (see page 313) or water

1 onion, quartered

approx. 20 parsley stalks

2 bay leaves (preferably fresh)

$^1/_2$ head garlic

100ml white wine

5 black peppercorns

HOT PAPRIKA AND OIL DRESSING

125ml extra virgin olive oil

4 garlic cloves, thinly sliced

3 tablespoons sweet red wine vinegar (see page 287)

3 teaspoons sweet paprika (preferably smoked)

2 teaspoons hot paprika (preferably smoked)

Place all the ingredients for the poaching stock in a saucepan, bring to a simmer and cook gently for 20 minutes. Strain and season with salt, add the potatoes and simmer for a further 15–20 minutes, until the potatoes are cooked. Meanwhile, make the hot paprika dressing.

Place a small saucepan over a medium heat and add the olive oil. When it is

quite hot, but not at all smoking, add the garlic and fry until the slices are golden all over. Take care not to burn the garlic as it will taste bitter. If you think the garlic is frying too fast, turn down the heat. When the garlic is golden, remove the saucepan from the heat and add the red wine vinegar all at once to stop the garlic from cooking any longer. Take care as the oil may spit. Wait a couple of seconds and add the paprikas. They should dissolve into the oil, turning it a distinctive orangey-red colour. Season with a little salt and pepper.

When the potatoes are cooked, remove from the stock with a slotted spoon and keep aside. When you are ready to cook the hake, bring the stock to a gentle simmer, and lower in the fish. Cook gently (it's fine if the water isn't bubbling at all) for 10–15 minutes, depending on the thickness of the fish, or until the flesh just comes away from the bone. A couple of minutes before you think the fish is ready, return the potatoes to the pot to warm through. Remove the fish and potatoes carefully with the slotted spoon and place on a plate, spooning 3 tablespoons of the stock on top of each portion of fish followed by the paprika oil and caramelised garlic. Sprinkle over the roughly chopped parsley and serve with braised spinach or sprouting broccoli, a bit of salad or just on its own.

GINGER AND CARDAMOM FISH

We like to eat this with Beetroot and Potato Salad (see page 246) and a wedge of lime.

Serves 4

> 4 thick hake, sea bass or cod steaks, about 225–250g each
> 4 tablespoons plain flour
> 6 tablespoons olive oil
> sea salt and black pepper

MARINADE

> 2 garlic cloves
> 5cm chunky piece fresh root ginger, peeled and finely chopped
> juice of 2 limes and finely grated zest of 1
> 1 teaspoon crushed cardamom seeds, green husks removed
> 2 tablespoons extra virgin olive oil

For the marinade, crush the garlic with a pinch of salt in a mortar until a paste has formed. Then add the ginger and lime zest and crush again, followed by the lime juice and crushed cardamom seeds. Stir well. Place the fish in a bowl, rub the marinade (except the oil) all over the fish, then drizzle on the olive oil and mix in. Leave the fish to marinate for 4–8 hours.

When you are ready to cook the fish, lift out each piece and dry on kitchen paper. Spread the flour out on a plate, season it well and coat each piece of fish. Shake off any excess, and set the fish aside on a clean, dry plate. Put a large frying pan over a medium to high heat and add the olive oil. When the oil is hot, carefully place the fish in the pan and fry for 4–5 minutes on each side or until cooked through, depending on the thickness of the steaks. When cooked, the flesh should flake easily and be white all the way through. If it is slightly translucent it might need a little more time. Place on kitchen paper to absorb any excess oil. Serve immediately.

LUBINA CON ANCHOAS

SEA BASS WITH ANCHOVIES AND TOMATO AND PEPPER SAUCE

A simple dish, but the combination of anchovies with tomatoes and peppers is superb.

Serves 4

> 4 sea bass or cod fillets, 150–180g each, or 1 whole fish, enough for 4
>
> 6 salted anchovy fillets, each cut into 3 or 4 pieces
>
> 3 tablespoons olive oil
>
> sea salt and black pepper

TOMATO AND RED PEPPER SAUCE

> 1 kg ripe fresh tomatoes, peeled (see page 42)
>
> 5 tablespoons olive oil
>
> 2 garlic cloves, thinly sliced
>
> 2 large red bell peppers, roasted, peeled and seeded (see page 78),
>
>   or 8 piquillo peppers, roughly chopped
>
> a pinch of caster sugar (optional)

With a small knife, make little incisions in the fleshy side of the sea bass (if using fillets, don't go through the skin), and stuff a piece of anchovy inside each cut.

For the sauce, cut the tomatoes in half horizontally and seed them. Strain away any juice from the tomatoes and discard. Place the tomatoes in a bowl and mash up with your hands, throwing away any remaining bits of skin or core. In a medium saucepan, heat the olive oil over a medium to high heat. When the oil is hot, but not smoking, add the sliced garlic and fry until it begins to colour. Add the mashed tomatoes, chopped peppers and a pinch of salt to balance the acidity of the tomatoes. Simmer over a medium heat until most of the liquid that the tomatoes give out has evaporated. Taste for seasoning. If the tomatoes are not particularly sweet, add a pinch of sugar.

To cook the fish, season with salt and pepper, then heat the oil in a frying pan over a high heat. When it is hot and beginning to smoke, add the fish skin-side down (carefully as the oil may spit), and fry over a medium heat for 3–4 minutes until the skin is crispy and golden in places, then turn over gently and finish cooking through for another 5 minutes. When cooked, the flesh of the fish should flake easily and be white all the way through. If it is slightly translucent, it might need a little more time.

Serve with the warm sauce on the side. This dish is delicious with a salad of olives or braised spinach, sprouting broccoli and a few potatoes dressed with lemon and olive oil.

SWORDFISH WITH POMEGRANATE MOLASSES

The sweet and sour nature of the pomegranate molasses works well with the dense meaty quality of swordfish or tuna.

Serves 4

> 4 swordfish steaks, 2–3cm thick (about 200–225g each)
>
> sea salt and black pepper

MARINADE

> 1 garlic clove
>
> 4 tablespoons Pomegranate Molasses (see page 284)
>
> 1 level teaspoon ground cinnamon
>
> 2 tablespoons chopped fresh coriander
>
> a good pinch of ground black pepper
>
> 1 tablespoon extra virgin olive oil

TO SERVE

> 4 teaspoons Pomegranate Molasses
>
> 2 tablespoons extra virgin olive oil
>
> 4 tablespoons fresh coriander leaves
>
> seeds of 1 pomegranate (about 4 tablespoons)

To make the marinade, crush the garlic in a mortar with a pinch of salt until smooth. Stir in the pomegranate molasses. Transfer to a large bowl and add the cinnamon, coriander and pepper. Rub all over the fish. Drizzle on the olive oil. Leave to marinate in the fridge for at least an hour or two.

If you are grilling the fish over charcoal, light the barbecue 45 minutes before you wish to cook, or use a very hot griddle pan or frying pan. Grill (or fry) the fish for about 2–3 minutes either side, basting with any excess marinade, until the outside is slightly charred but the inside is still pink and juicy. (If we use tuna instead of swordfish, we like to serve it medium rare to rare.) Drizzle the extra pomegranate molasses and olive oil over the fish, and scatter the coriander leaves and pomegranate seeds on top. This is delicious with a simple pilav (see page 259) and salad.

DEEP-FRIED SARDINE BALLS

We ate this dish in the middle of the main market in Essouira on the west coast of Morocco. Essouira is famous for its small, sweet, juicy sardines. As we walked through the market, we noticed a man dropping small patties into a large copper cauldron of boiling oil. We asked for some and they turned out to be these richly spiced sardine balls. They were served broken open in a pitta bread with chopped salad, pickled chillies and extra cumin and salt sprinkled on top.

Serves 4

> 12 sardines, scaled and filleted
>
> 5 tablespoons roughly chopped fresh coriander
>
> 1 tablespoon cumin seeds
>
> 2 garlic cloves, crushed to a paste with salt
>
> juice of 1 lemon
>
> sea salt and black pepper

TOMATO SAUCE

> 1 kg ripe fresh tomatoes, peeled (see page 42),or
>
>   2 x 400g cans whole plum tomatoes
>
> 4 tablespoons olive oil
>
> 2 garlic cloves, thinly sliced
>
> 1 tablespoon cumin seeds, roughly ground
>
> a pinch of caster sugar (optional)

TO FINISH AND SERVE

> fine semolina flour or instant polenta
>
> sunflower oil, for deep-frying
>
> 3 tablespoons fresh coriander leaves

Finely chop the sardine fillets with the coriander and cumin seeds until the skin is hardly visible. (Hand-chopping gives a better texture than a food processor.) Add the garlic, lemon juice and seasoning and mix well. Transfer to a bowl.

Generously sprinkle some fine semolina flour on to a plate. Add a couple of pinches of salt and mix well with your fingers. Wash your hands. Now take little bits of the sardine mixture and roughly shape to a size just smaller than a golf ball. Coat well with the semolina and leave uncovered in the refrigerator for at least 2 hours to firm up for deep-frying. If you prefer to shallow-fry the fish, flatten the balls in the palm of your hand to make patties 1cm thick.

To make the tomato sauce, follow the instructions on page 182, using the cumin instead of the peppers.

To cook, heat enough sunflower oil in a saucepan to just cover the balls. (For safety reasons, never fill your saucepan more than half-full.) Test the temperature of the oil by adding a small bit of the mixture. If it colours very quickly, turn down the heat; if it seems to do nothing, turn up the heat a little. Fry the balls in batches – for 3–4 minutes – until the outside has started to turn golden but the inside is still moist. Sprinkle with the coriander and serve with the tomato sauce and some bread.

FIVE SAUCES FOR FISH

Choose between the following five sauces to give your fish the accent you wish.

PAPRIKA AND ANCHOVY BUTTER

This is a simple and versatile accompaniment to white fish, trout or tuna, and we also like it with veal chops or sirloin steak.

Serves 8

>125g unsalted butter, not too hard
>
>12 salted anchovy fillets (about 30g)
>
>1 small garlic clove, very finely chopped
>
>zest and juice of $^1/_2$ lemon
>
>2 tablespoons finely chopped fresh flat–leaf parsley
>
>2 teaspoons paprika
>
>a pinch of freshly ground black pepper

Put all the ingredients in a food processor and blend well. Transfer to a bowl and place in the fridge to harden slightly. When still pliable, shape into a block or roll, wrap in clingfilm and chill again. When the fish is cooked, simply slice the butter and place on each piece of fish. Serve immediately.

MUHUMMRA

This pepper, walnut and pomegranate sauce is Turkish in origin. Acili biber, a paste made from a slightly hot variety of red pepper, is available from Turkish food shops and is like the pepper equivalent of tomato purée.

Serves 6

>150g walnut halves
>
>2 tablespoons Turkish pepper paste (acili biber), or 8 piquillo peppers,
>   very finely chopped
>
>2 garlic cloves, crushed to a paste with salt
>
>1 tablespoon red wine vinegar
>
>1 tablespoon Pomegranate Molasses (see page 284)
>
>1 teaspoon Turkish chilli flakes (kirmizi biber), or 1 teaspoon hot paprika

$^1/_2$ teaspoon ground allspice

3–4 tablespoons water

$1^1/_2$ tablespoons extra virgin olive oil

sea salt and black pepper

Put the walnuts and pepper paste or peppers in a food processor and blend until more or less smooth. Transfer to a bowl and stir in the remaining ingredients. Check for seasoning. The consistency should be thick but not solid. Add extra water if necessary.

PINE NUT TARATOR

Tarator is a garlicky nut sauce from Turkey. It can be made with walnuts, almonds or, as in this version, pine nuts. We prefer to use the longer, thinner pine nuts from the Mediterranean pine tree instead of the fatter, shorter Chinese pine nuts. The texture and flavour tend to be better and more interesting, but don't go to huge lengths trying to find them. At Moro, we like to serve this with roast skate or monkfish, but really any white fish will do.

Serves 4–6

150g pine nuts

1 garlic clove, crushed to a paste with salt

$1^1/_2$ tablespoons good-quality red wine vinegar (see page 287)

$^1/_4$ teaspoon ground allspice (optional)

juice of $^1/_2$ lemon

8 tablespoons water

$1^1/_2$ tablespoons extra virgin olive oil

sea salt and black pepper

Put the pine nuts in a food processor and blend well. This is slightly a matter of taste. The finer the nuts are chopped, the more mayonnaise-like the end result is. Combine the other ingredients and stir. The consistency should be a little thicker than double cream. Season with salt and pepper.

PRESERVED LEMON AND OLIVE SAUCE

The preserved lemon is just as distinctive in flavour as the olives.

Serves 4–6

> 1 medium Preserved Lemon (see page 281)
> 200g olives (purple kalamata, violets, or hard green olives, Lucques), stoned
> 1 garlic clove, crushed to a paste with salt
> 3 tablespoons roughly chopped fresh coriander or flat-leaf parsley
> 4 tablespoons olive oil
> a small squeeze of lemon
> freshly ground black pepper

Under cold water, rinse the preserved lemon well. Remove the soft pulpy flesh inside and discard. Chop the rind finely and transfer to a small bowl. Now chop the olives finely and add to the lemon along with the garlic and chopped coriander or parsley. Pour on the olive oil and the lemon juice and stir well. Season with a little pepper (the sauce should be salty enough).

GARUM

We have had this olive sauce in Spain, although it is a legacy not of the Moors but of the Romans.

Serves 4–6

> 200g olives, a mixture of firm green and black/purple, stoned
> 1 garlic clove, crushed to a paste with salt
> 2 teaspoons finely chopped fresh rosemary
> 2 teaspoons finely chopped fresh oregano
> 4 salted anchovy fillets, finely chopped
> 1 tablespoon sweet red wine vinegar (see page 287)
> 4 tablespoons olive oil
> sea salt and black pepper

Finely chop the olives, then transfer to a bowl and add the crushed garlic, rosemary, oregano, anchovies and red wine vinegar. Mix well, then stir in the olive oil. Taste for seasoning.

MEAT MAIN COURSES

دجاج المزرعة
أثمان مناسبة :
الحي :
15,00
المطبوخ :
21,00

Here are eighteen dishes for different meats. They range from simple to marginally complicated. We hope you find something right for you in this chapter.. grilled marinated meats, and the choices are endless.

LAMB

For each recipe, we suggest which cut works best. As there is more than one recipe for lamb, here is a guide to cooking your meat once you have chosen what cut to use.

- **To slow-roast a 2.5kg shoulder of lamb, trimmed and bone in, that will serve about 6-8** (1.6-1.8kg would serve 4-6)

Rub the meat with marinade. Season with 2 teaspoons sea salt per kilo and roast at 160°C/325°F/Gas 3 for a minimum of 3 hours, adding a small glass of water (125ml) to the pan after the first half-hour and each subsequent hour, and basting every 45 minutes. Test the lamb's doneness by inserting a skewer into the centre: if the meat is soft and has a lot of give, it is done. Leave to rest for 15 minutes, as it's too hot to eat when it comes out of the oven.

- **To fast-roast a 2.5kg leg or shoulder of lamb, boned, that will serve about 6-8** (1.6-1.8kg would serve 4-6)

Ask the butcher to remove the thigh bone and trim the skin off the meat. Rub with marinade, and season with 2 teaspoons sea salt per kilo. Roast at 230°C/450°F/Gas 8 for 30 minutes per kilo for medium-well done; 25 minutes per kilo for medium; 20 minutes per kilo for rare. To determine if the lamb is cooked, gently push a metal skewer into the centre of the meat: if it is hot and the juices run slightly pink, it is cooked. A meat probe (basically a thermometer) will give you a more accurate reading and is particularly useful for those who are not very confident cooks. Take the meat out of the oven and slide the probe into the middle: as long as it registers 60-65°C, the meat is cooked through. The temperature may continue to rise while it is resting. Rest for 15-20 minutes before serving.

- **To grill chops or fillet**

Season the meat well and place under a hot grill or on a smoking griddle pan, or on a barbecue that is not too hot, for about 5-8 minutes either side for pink, turning once or twice. Remove and rest before serving. For butterflied (flattened) leg of lamb, grill slowly on a barbecue until sealed on all sides (or seal in a roasting tin on the hob), and finish it off in a hot oven 220°C/425°F/Gas 7 for approximately 15-20 minutes or until pink. Rest the meat, covered, for 10 minutes before slicing.

CORDERO AL ROMERO Y MIEL

ROAST LAMB WITH HONEY AND ROSEMARY

Really this is just good old-fashioned roast lamb, but the honey makes it taste very eastern. The sweet gravy works in the same way that redcurrant jelly works with lamb. This dish was originally made with wild rosemary gathered from the scrubby hillsides, and mountain honey to satisfy the sweet tooth of the Moors.

Serves 6–8

    1 shoulder or leg of lamb, about 2.5kg, trimmed for roasting (see page 194)

    3 garlic cloves, sliced into thin slivers, 10–12 in total

    10–12 tiny sprigs fresh rosemary (3–4 leaves to each sprig)

    1 garlic clove, crushed to a paste with salt

    3 tablespoons scented runny honey, such as Greek flower honey

    3 tablespoons olive oil

    2 tablespoons finely chopped fresh rosemary

    150ml white wine

    sea salt and black pepper

Preheat the oven to 230°C/450°F/Gas 8.

Make 10–12 small incisions in the lamb (depending on the size of the meat) all over with a narrow sharp knife, and gently push a sliver of garlic and a sprig of rosemary into each hole. In a small bowl, mix the crushed garlic, honey and 2 tablespoons of the olive oil together. Place the lamb in an oiled roasting tray, and spread the sticky mixture all over the lamb, followed by the chopped rosemary. Season well with salt and pepper. Place in the oven and roast for half an hour, then add half the white wine to the tin to stop the honey from burning, and roast until it is pink or medium, depending on how you like your lamb cooked. (See page 194 for guidance on cooking times.) Add a little extra water if the wine evaporates. Remove, transfer the lamb to a board and let it rest for 15–20 minutes, loosely covered with foil.

Meanwhile, make the gravy. Pour off any fat, return the roasting tray to the hob and heat over a medium heat. Add the remaining white wine and bring to a gentle simmer, scraping any caramelised juices off the bottom of the pan. Taste for seasoning, transfer to a small saucepan or bowl and keep hot.

When you are ready to eat, slice the lamb and serve with the gravy over the top, some whole parsley leaves and roast vegetables.

CORDERO CON GARBANZOS Y SALSA DE HIERBABUENA

LAMB WITH CHICKPEA PURÉE AND HOT MINT SAUCE

Most of us are fond of mint sauce with lamb, so this dish feels familiar yet with an exotic slant. The cut of lamb used is up to you: roast whole shoulder or leg (bone in), or boned, butterflied and grilled or roasted, or just simple lamb chops all work well.

Serves 4–6

    1 shoulder or leg of lamb, about 1.6–1.8kg, ready for roasting (see page 194),
      or 12–16 lamb chops, depending on size
    sea salt and black pepper

MARINADE

    4 garlic cloves, crushed to a paste with a pinch of salt
    juice of $1/2$ lemon
    2 tablespoons red wine vinegar
    4 tablespoons fresh thyme leaves
    $1/2$ medium red onion, finely grated
    2 teaspoons sweet paprika
    1 tablespoon olive oil

TO SERVE

    1 quantity Chickpea Purée (see overleaf)
    1 quantity Hot Mint Sauce (see overleaf)

Mix all the marinade ingredients together, except the olive oil, season with salt and pepper, and rub all over the meat. Now add the olive oil (it can prevent the acidity of the lemon and vinegar from penetrating the meat), and leave to marinate for a minimum of 2 hours, turning occasionally, or in the fridge overnight so that the flavours really get into the meat. If using a shoulder, you can score the surface very lightly 1–2mm deep in a 1cm criss-cross pattern to help the marinade penetrate.

Depending on what cut of meat you use, prepare the chickpea purée and mint sauce in time for when the meat is ready. To cook the meat, see page 194.

When the meat has rested, carve and serve with the warm chickpea purée and hot mint sauce.

CHICKPEA PURÉE

The rich complexity of these chickpeas is obtained by frying the cumin, garlic and onions together until they are all brown.

Serves 4–6

> 2 x 400g cans cooked chickpeas, drained and rinsed, or about
>   400g drained weight home–cooked chickpeas (see page 59)
> 4 tablespoons olive oil
> $1/2$ large onion, finely chopped
> 3 garlic cloves, finely chopped
> $1^1/2$ rounded teaspoons cumin seeds, roughly ground
> 30 threads saffron, infused in 2 tablespoons boiling water
> 2 tablespoons roughly chopped fresh flat–leaf parsley
> sea salt and black pepper

Using either an electric hand–held blender or a processor, purée the chickpeas until quite smooth. Add enough cooking liquor or water so they are similar to wet mashed potato. Put aside.

In a medium saucepan, heat up the olive oil over a medium to high heat and add the onion, garlic and cumin. Fry, stirring quite regularly, until evenly golden brown. When ready, mix the chickpea purée into the saucepan along with the saffron infusion. Simmer for 5 minutes (take care as it can spit). Check the salt and add some pepper. Serve warm, sprinkled with parsley at the last minute.

HOT MINT SAUCE

Do not be alarmed if the mint becomes discoloured; it is just the action of the vinegar.

Serves 4–6

> 4 tablespoons extra virgin olive oil
> 2 garlic cloves, finely chopped
> 8 tablespoons finely chopped fresh mint
> 1 teaspoon cumin seeds
> 2 tablespoons good-quality sweet red wine vinegar (see page 287)
> $1/2$ teaspoon caster sugar (optional)
> sea salt and black pepper

Place a small saucepan over a medium heat and add the olive oil. When the oil is hot but not smoking, add the garlic and fry for a couple of minutes until golden brown. Stir once or twice to make sure the garlic is colouring evenly. Now add half the chopped fresh mint and all the cumin, fry for a further minute, then add the red wine vinegar (it may spit). Simmer for 30 seconds more, then remove from the heat. Stir in the remaining mint, season with salt and pepper and taste. If the vinegar is rather acidic, add the sugar to help balance the flavours. Set the sauce aside until you need it, but remember it should be served hot.

LAMB MECHOUI WITH CUMIN AND PAPRIKA SALT

The last time we were in Marrakech, we went to a bustling outdoor market about 15 kilometres outside the city. Against the backdrop of the snow-covered Atlas Mountains, we wandered around with our guide, Khalid, for what seemed like hours. When we stopped for lunch, we were given a bowl of steaming chickpeas with calf's feet by a friend of his who ran the oldest 'restaurant' in the market. Whilst we were scooping up mouthfuls of this gelatinous stew with bread, we noticed one man ask the owner to grill him some chops he had just bought from a butcher on the other side of the market. Simply sprinkled with a mixture of cumin, salt and paprika, the chops were grilled either side over charcoal and served with a small pile of extra cumin salt on the side, and bread. 'This is real mechoui,' Khalid said. He was referring to the famous mechoui of whole lambs spit-roasted over the embers of an open fire, basted with a mixture of butter, saffron, cumin, salt and paprika. Still feeling a little hungry ourselves, we too went off to buy some chops for him to grill for us.

Serves 4

> 2 tablespoons whole cumin seeds, freshly ground
>
> 1 teaspoon sweet paprika
>
> $1/2$ teaspoon hot paprika
>
> 1 tablespoon sea salt, roughly crumbled
>
> 12–16 lamb chops, depending on size
>
> 40g butter, melted

Mix the spices and salt together in a bowl. Just before you are ready to grill the chops, brush them with the melted butter, sprinkle liberally with half the cumin mixture and follow the cooking instructions on page 194. Serve immediately with some of the remaining cumin salt on the side. This is delicious on its own with bread and/or with a Moroccan salad (see pages 159–66).

Variation

Instead of chops, you could cover a whole shoulder of lamb with the mix and roast it in the oven at 160°C/325°F/Gas 3 for 4–5 hours until the meat is falling off the bone. Keep basting the meat with the buttery, spicy juices that collect in the roasting tin. Serve with extra cumin salt on the side.

PORK

LOMO CON VINAGRE DE JEREZ
PORK LOIN POT-ROASTED WITH SHERRY AND SHERRY VINEGAR

The complex flavours of sherry and sherry vinegar make a wonderful sweet–sour sauce to complement this pot-roasted pork. If you prefer simple roast pork with crackling, follow the instructions opposite, and make the sauce by adding the sherry and sherry vinegar instead of white wine, and omit the onions, raisins and extra thyme.

Serves 4-6

> 1–1.5kg boned organic or free-range pork loin, trimmed of most of its fat, or lean belly, skin off
> 2 tablespoons olive oil
> 75g butter
> 2 medium red onions, halved and thinly sliced
> 4 sprigs fresh thyme, or a pinch of dried thyme
> 2 bay leaves (preferably fresh)
> 300ml Pedro Ximénez or sweet oloroso sherry
> 100ml sherry vinegar
> 100g raisins
> sea salt and black pepper

Season the pork well with salt and pepper. Place a large saucepan over a medium heat and add the olive oil. When hot, lower the pork into the pan and seal until just golden brown on all sides and both ends. Remove the pork and set aside briefly. Still over a medium heat, add the butter and, when it foams, the onion with a pinch of salt, and fry for 10 minutes until sweet, stirring occasionally. Pour off any excess oil, then add the thyme, bay leaves, sherry, sherry vinegar and raisins and turn the heat to low. Return the pork to the pan, cover with greaseproof paper or tin foil and put the lid on. Cook slowly for 1–1$^1/_4$ hours or until the meat is just cooked through but still juicy, turning occasionally, so it cooks evenly. To determine whether the pork is cooked, gently push a sharp knife or metal skewer into the centre of the meat. Count to ten and pull out. Touch the area above your top lip gently with the end of the skewer. If it is hot, the meat is cooked. A meat probe (see page 194) will give you a more accurate reading and is particularly useful for those who are not very confident cooks. Simply slide the probe into the middle of the joint: as long as it registers 60–65°C degrees, the meat is cooked through but still juicy.

If using belly pork, double the cooking time, or cook until it is tender. Make sure the juices do not simmer dry. Just add a little water from time to time.

Let the pork rest for 10 minutes, covered loosely with foil, before slicing. Turn the heat under the sauce to high and reduce it for 5 minutes, until it is still runny but delicious. Taste the sauce and adjust the seasoning if necessary. We serve this with mashed potato and braised spinach.

CERDO CON MEMBRILLO
ROAST PORK WITH QUINCE PURÉE

Apple sauce is a traditional accompaniment to roast pork. A purée made out of fresh quince is a delicious alternative and definitely worth trying. For this recipe, use either pork loin or pork belly.

Serves 4-6

    1.5kg organic or free-range pork loin (bone in), or 2kg pork belly, skin on

    2 garlic cloves, crushed to a paste with salt

    1 heaped teaspoon fennel seeds, roughly ground

    1 tablespoon fresh thyme leaves

    1 tablespoon olive oil

    150ml white wine or fino sherry

    sea salt and black pepper

QUINCE PURÉE

    500g quinces

    4 tablespoons water

    20g butter

    2 pinches ground cinnamon

    2-4 teaspoons caster sugar (to taste)

    a squeeze of lemon (to taste)

Preheat the oven to 230°C/450°F/Gas 8.

Score through the skin and fat, but not the muscle, with a very sharp knife, making lines no more than 1cm apart and about 5mm deep (or ask your butcher to do it). Mix the garlic and fennel seeds together and rub over the flesh (not the skin), then rub in the thyme. Season well with salt and pepper. Place on a board skin-side up and dry the skin thoroughly. Sprinkle the top liberally with fine sea salt and leave for half an hour, then dust off excess salt. Make sure the skin is dry again.

Transfer the pork to a shallow roasting tin lightly oiled with the olive oil and place in the hot oven for 30–45 minutes, or until the skin has blistered and crisped all over to form crackling. Lower the heat to 180°C/350°F/Gas 4 and roast for a further 20–25 minutes for each 500g of weight. For loin, the total cooking time should be about 1 hour or a little more, until the meat is just the other side of pink but still juicy. (To test whether the meat is cooked, see page 202.) For belly, roast for a further hour for each 500g of weight, making the total roasting time about 3–3$^1/_2$ hours, until the meat is soft and tender. If the pork is a tight fit in the pan, it is less likely to burn on the bottom. If it is burning, pour in 50ml of the wine or sherry. When the pork is ready, remove from the oven, transfer to a board and let it rest in a warm place for at least 15–20 minutes, loosely covered with foil.

To make the gravy, pour off the excess oil, place the roasting tray over a medium heat on the hob and add the white wine or sherry. Bring to a gentle simmer and scrape any caramelised juices off the bottom of the pan. Season with a little salt and pepper, and taste. Set aside.

While the pork is cooking, make the quince purée. Peel, core and slice the quinces as thinly as possible and transfer them straight into a small saucepan with the water. Place over a medium heat, put on the lid and steam for 20–30 minutes, stirring occasionally to prevent sticking. When the quince becomes tender, remove from the heat and mash by hand until smooth or use an electric hand-held blender. Add the butter and cinnamon and keep stirring until the butter has melted, then taste. Depending on the natural sweetness of the quince, add some sugar to taste and finally a squeeze of lemon.

Serve the quince purée warm or at room temperature with the pork and some roast potatoes cooked with thyme or chopped rosemary.

Variation
Pears with clove instead of cinnamon also make a delicious sauce if you cannot get fresh quince; otherwise use puréed cooking apples and melt in 100g finely chopped membrillo, the Spanish quince cheese.

BEEF

BUEY CON RÁBANO PICANTE
BEEF WITH HORSERADISH AND SHERRY VINEGAR SAUCE

What cut of beef you use is determined partly by the occasion – whether it is individual sirloin steaks for a quick meal, or roast rib of beef for a grander event.

Serves 4-6

> 4-6 sirloin steaks (or fillet or rib eye), approx. 2.5cm thick for grilling or frying, or a double rib joint, approx. 1.6–1.7kg in weight
>
> 2 tablespoons olive oil, plus 2 extra tablespoons for oiling the roasting tin (for the rib joint only)
>
> 1 tablespoon fresh thyme leaves
>
> 150ml good red wine (for the rib joint only)
>
> sea salt and black pepper

TO SERVE

> 1 quantity Horseradish and Sherry Vinegar Sauce (see overleaf)

Rub the olive oil over the meat, followed by the thyme leaves and freshly ground black pepper.

GRILLED (OR FRIED) SIRLOIN STEAKS

Place a hot griddle over a high heat, and when it is very hot and begins to smoke, season the steaks well with salt on both sides and place immediately in the pan. For a better flavour, use a hot barbecue, or, failing both of these, a hot frying pan over a high heat. For rare, sear the meat on both sides for 60 seconds; for pink 2 minutes each side; for medium to medium-well done, 3-4 minutes each side.

Remove from the heat and let the meat rest for a few minutes before eating with the horseradish sauce.

ROAST RIB OF BEEF ON THE BONE

Remove from the refrigerator at least 2 hours before roasting to bring the joint up to room temperature. Preheat the oven to 230°C/450°F/Gas 8. Weigh the joint and calculate the cooking time as outlined overleaf:

- Rare: 12 minutes per 500g
- Medium-rare: 15-18 minutes per 500g
- Medium: 20 minutes per 500g
- Medium-well done: 23 minutes per 500g
- Well done: 25+ minutes per 500g

Season the meat with a $^1/_4$ teaspoon freshly ground black pepper and 1 teaspoon fine sea salt per 500g meat. If the total roasting time for your joint is less than an hour, sear well on all sides over a medium-high heat before putting it in the oven. Put it fat-side up in a roasting tray just large enough for the joint. If the tray is too big, scatter in a few roughly chopped vegetables (carrots, celery, onions, etc.) to keep the juices from burning and spoiling your gravy.

Once in the oven, if the total roasting time is longer than $1^1/_2$ hours, turn the oven down to 180°C/350°F/Gas 4 after the first hour has elapsed.

After the joint is cooked, remove it from the oven and transfer it to a carving board to rest, loosely covered with foil, for 20-30 minutes.

Meanwhile, make your gravy in the roasting tray. Pour off any excess oil and place the tin over a medium heat on the hob. Pour in the red wine, let it simmer for a few minutes and scrape off any caramelised juices from the bottom. Season with salt and pepper. To serve the beef, either remove the bone and then slice, or carve right off the bone. Serve with hot gravy on top, the horseradish sauce on the side, and some roast vegetables and watercress salad dressed with oil and a squeeze of lemon.

HORSERADISH AND SHERRY VINEGAR SAUCE

To do this sauce justice, you really need fresh horseradish. You could ask your green-grocer to pick up some in the market. It lasts for ages in the fridge if wrapped in clingfilm. Be careful when you grate fresh horseradish, as it is particularly pungent and can make you weep if inhaled too deeply. If you have to use bottled horseradish, use the grated variety rather than the creamed sauce.

Serves 4-6

> 3 tablespoons fresh horseradish, finely grated (or 5-6 tablespoons
>   bottled grated horseradish, as a last resort)
> 1 tablespoon sherry vinegar
> 70ml double cream
> sea salt and black pepper

Place the grated horseradish in a small bowl, stir in the vinegar and season with salt and pepper. Now add the cream, and stir until evenly mixed. Do not overmix as the sauce will become solid.

CHICKEN AND OTHER BIRDS

POLLO AL AJILLO CON PIÑONES Y PASAS
CHICKEN BRAISED WITH PINE NUTS, RAISINS AND SAFFRON

There are many variations on the al ajillo theme, whether one uses chicken, rabbit, guinea fowl, quail, goat, lamb, or even fish, shellfish or vegetables, but the main ingredients – namely, olive oil, garlic and wine – remain the same, as does the method. Once you have cooked this dish a couple of times, you should feel confident enough to experiment with the ingredients, just remembering that brown meat needs longer to become tender and juicy than white meat, and that lamb and kid are better stewed (in more liquid) until tender.

Serves 4

> 6 tablespoons olive oil
>
> 12 garlic cloves, peeled
>
> 1 medium organic or free-range chicken, jointed into 8 pieces
>
> 150ml light white wine or fino sherry
>
> 50 threads saffron, infused in 7 tablespoons boiling water
>
> 100g raisins, soaked in warm water
>
> 75g pine nuts, very lightly toasted or fried until light golden
>
> sea salt and black pepper

Over a medium heat, heat the olive oil in a large saucepan until hot. Add the garlic, fry until golden, then remove and set aside. Now season the jointed chicken pieces and add the breasts to the pan. Brown nicely on both sides until the skin is crisp and deep golden. Remove from the pan and set aside. Still over a medium heat, add the jointed legs and seal until they are also golden and crisp. Now add the wine and saffron-infused water, shaking the pan vigorously to help the wine emulsify with the oil. Bring to a gentle simmer, reduce the heat and cook for 15–20 minutes until the legs are beginning to become soft and tender. Return the breasts to the pan along with the garlic, drained raisins and pine nuts and season with salt and pepper. Cover and simmer for a further 5–10 minutes or until the breasts are cooked through but still juicy. The sauce should be the consistency of single cream. Add a little water if too thick, or reduce if too thin. Remove the meat temporarily as you do not want to over-cook it. Taste for seasoning.

In Spain we have often eaten pollo al ajillo with fried potatoes and a salad. We also like boiled new season's potatoes.

ROAST CHICKEN WITH PRESERVED LEMON

Preserved lemons have such a distinctive flavour that they provide an easy way to give a unique twist to a simple roast chicken.

Serves 4

> 1 medium organic or free-range chicken, about 1.5kg
> freshly ground black pepper
> 1 tablespoon olive oil, for the roasting tin
> 100ml water

MARINADE

> 2 medium or 3 small Preserved Lemons (see page 281)
> juice of $^1/_2$ lemon (keep the squeezed lemon half to put inside the chicken)
> 2 garlic cloves, crushed to a paste with salt
> 3 tablespoons roughly chopped fresh coriander
> 1 teaspoon cumin seeds, roughly ground
> 1 teaspoon sweet paprika
> 2 tablespoons olive oil

Wash the preserved lemons well under cold water. Remove the inside pulp and discard. Put all the marinade ingredients into a food processor or large mortar and work until smooth. Smear the mixture all over the chicken and season lightly with pepper, stuffing the squeezed lemon half into the body cavity. (You will not need salt as the preserved lemons are already very salty.) Transfer the chicken to a dish and leave to marinate in the fridge for approximately 6 hours, or overnight if you prefer.

When you are ready to roast the chicken, preheat the oven to 180°C/350°F/Gas 4. Put the chicken in an oiled roasting tray and roast for about $1^1/_4$ hours, basting every now and then. If the marinade begins to burn a little on the top of the chicken, cover loosely with foil. After about 1 hour, test whether the chicken is cooked by piercing the leg with a skewer or sharp knife. If the juices run clear, the chicken is ready; if they are still pink, it will require a little more time. Transfer the chicken to a board and leave to relax in a warm place for 10 minutes, loosely covered in foil.

Meanwhile, make some gravy. Pour off most of the oil from the pan, place the tin over a medium heat on the hob, add the water and bring to a gentle simmer. Empty the inner juices from the resting chicken into the gravy. Scrape up any caramelised bits and check the seasoning. If the gravy is strong, add a little more water.

Serve the chicken with steamed couscous or fried potatoes or a simple pilav (see page 259) or bulgur wheat and some salad.

CHICKEN FATTEE WITH RICE, CRISPBREAD AND YOGHURT

This is a glorious layered dish from the Lebanon, ideally suited to sharing at home with family and friends. As there are so many simple components in this dish, one chicken goes a long way. In the Lebanon, the bird is poached rather than roasted.

Serves 8

ROAST CHICKEN

1 medium organic or free-range chicken, about 1.5kg

3 tablespoons olive oil

$^1/_4$ teaspoon ground cloves

sea salt and black pepper

TOMATO SAUCE

5 tablespoons olive oil

5 garlic cloves, sliced

4cm cinnamon stick

2 x 400g cans plum tomatoes, drained and the tomatoes squashed well

RICE

300g basmati rice, unwashed

sea salt

75g butter

4cm cinnamon stick

$^1/_2$ large onion, halved and thinly sliced

1 x 400g can cooked chickpeas, drained and rinsed

485ml water or Chicken Stock (see page 313)

FRIED AUBERGINE

2 medium aubergines, cut into 3cm cubes and tossed with 1 teaspoon salt

8 tablespoons olive oil

TO LAYER UP THE FATTEE

1 quantity Crispbread (see page 135)

500g Greek yoghurt, mixed with 1 garlic clove crushed with salt

8 tablespoons roughly chopped fresh flat-leaf parsley

75g pine nuts, very lightly toasted or fried in olive oil until golden

Preheat the oven to 220°C/425°F/Gas 7. Rub 2 tablespoons of the olive oil all over the chicken, season well with salt and pepper and sprinkle the ground cloves over the top. Oil a baking tray with the remaining tablespoon of oil, then insert the chicken and roast according to the instructions on page 208. When cooked, transfer the chicken to a board to rest. Deglaze the roasting tray with 150ml water. Again, see the instructions on page 208. When cool enough to handle, take the meat off the bone and slice into manageable pieces. Keep warm until you are ready to serve.

Meanwhile, make the tomato sauce. Heat up the olive oil in a frying pan over a medium heat and fry the garlic until light brown. Add the cinnamon and prepared tomatoes, simmer for half an hour, then season well with salt and a little pepper. Keep the sauce warm.

Rub the rice in three changes of cold water to wash off the starch. Cover with warm water, stir in the salt and let it soak for 30–60 minutes. Melt the butter over a medium heat and add the cinnamon and onion. Fry for 10–15 minutes until golden brown, stirring every now and then. Remove from the heat and set aside.

About 15 minutes before you are ready to eat, replace the saucepan with the golden onions over a high heat. Drain the rice well and stir into your onions. Fry the rice while stirring for 1 minute. Add the measured water or chicken stock and the chickpeas to the saucepan. Add salt (about $^1/_2$ teaspoon) and cover the top of the water with either baking parchment or foil followed by a lid. Boil fast for 5 minutes, then turn the heat to a low to medium temperature for a further 5 minutes. At this point the rice should be cooked, but it will sit happily for 15 minutes.

Rinse the salt off the aubergines, then dry with kitchen paper. Heat up the olive oil in a large frying pan or wok over a medium to high heat and fry the aubergine until soft and brown. Cover and keep warm.

At this stage, you just have to layer things up on one or more big platters or serving dishes. Everything needs to be hot apart from the crispbread and yoghurt.

The order to layer your plate is first the crispbread, then the rice, then the chicken and juices from the roasting pan (about 4–5 tablespoons), then the aubergine, then a scattering of tomato sauce, then a scattering of yoghurt and finally lots of chopped parsley and the pine nuts. Eat right away.

ROAST CHICKEN STUFFED WITH SAGE AND LABNEH

Labneh, a thick strained yoghurt cheese mixed with sage, makes a delicious stuffing for chicken. This recipe was inspired by a Turkish combination of ingredients: yoghurt, sage and paprika.

Serves 4

> 1 medium organic or free-range chicken, about 1.5kg
>
> 1 garlic clove, crushed to a paste with salt
>
> 250g Labneh (see page 280), or half cream cheese, half Greek yoghurt
>
> 3 tablespoons finely chopped fresh sage leaves
>
> 1 level teaspoon sweet paprika
>
> 3 tablespoons olive oil
>
> 100ml water
>
> a squeeze of lemon
>
> sea salt and black pepper

Preheat the oven to 220°C/425°F/Gas 7.

For the stuffing, mix together the garlic, labneh or cream cheese mixture, two-thirds of the sage and all the paprika, and season with salt and pepper. With your hands, working from the tail end of the bird, gently ease the skin of the chicken away from the breast and thigh to form a pocket on either side. Place the stuffing under the skin a teaspoon at a time until as much of the area is filled as possible. Try to get some stuffing in and around the thigh and drumstick – you can massage it around once it is under the skin. Use four or five toothpicks to stop the stuffing running out.

To cook the chicken, rub the outside of the chicken with 2 tablespoons of the olive oil and the last tablespoon of chopped sage, and season with salt and pepper. Transfer to a lightly oiled roasting tin and put in the hot oven to roast for $1-1^1/_2$ hours, basting every now and then. After about an hour, test the leg with a skewer. If the juices run clear the chicken is cooked, if they are still pink it will require a little more time. Transfer the chicken to a board, loosely cover with foil and leave for 10 minutes.

To make a simple gravy, skim off most of the fat from the roasting tray, then add the water, a small squeeze of lemon and some salt and pepper. Put the roasting tray on a medium heat and when it begins to simmer, scrape off any caramelised juices from the bottom. Tilt the open end of the resting chicken downwards over the roasting tin so any juices that have collected inside the bird also become part of the gravy. Taste for seasoning and pour into a warm jug. Good with braised spinach and bulgur wheat or wild rice.

QUAIL STUFFED WITH COUSCOUS, RAISINS AND ALMONDS

One mouthful of this dish and you know it could come only from Morocco. It tastes heavenly!

Serves 4-6

8 free-range or organic quails, rinsed under cold water and drained

3 tablespoons olive oil

1 cinnamon stick

a small pinch of saffron (about 30 threads)

1 small red onion, roughly chopped

a handful of golden sultanas

$1^{1}/_{2}$ teaspoons ground cinnamon

1 dessertspoon runny honey

$^{1}/_{2}$ teaspoon caster sugar

sea salt and black pepper

COUSCOUS STUFFING

375g fine couscous

3 tablespoons sunflower oil

300g golden raisins, soaked for 10 minutes in hot water

150g almonds, soaked for 10 minutes in hot water and roughly chopped

60g butter

$2^{1}/_{4}$ teaspoons ground cinnamon

1 quantity Crushed Sweet Almonds (see page 216)

$1^{1}/_{2}$ tablespoons runny honey

$^{1}/_{2}$ tablespoon icing sugar

$1^{1}/_{2}$ teaspoons orange-blossom water

For the stuffing, place the couscous in a bowl and pour over the sunflower oil. Mix well, then cover with cold water. When the water has been absorbed (5-10 minutes), delicately work with the palms of your hands to make the couscous light and fluffy, breaking up any lumps as you go. Fill the bottom half of a couscoussier or steamer a third full with water and put on a high heat to boil. Turn down the heat to a steady simmer, and put on the top half of the pan. Gently scatter a layer of couscous 5mm thick on the bottom, wait for 1 minute, then add a second layer. Wait for 5-10 minutes until the steam begins to rise above the two layers of couscous, then put on the rest. Steam for 10 minutes.

Put the hot couscous in a bowl and season with salt. Add the raisins, almonds and butter. Cover the butter with some of the hot couscous so that it melts, then add the ground cinnamon, 200g of the crushed sweet almonds, the honey, icing sugar and orange-blossom water. Mix well, add a little salt and pepper and taste to check the seasoning. Put some of this stuffing inside the cavity of each quail and a little under the skins. Secure the open cavity of the tail with foil or a couple of wooden toothpicks and brush off any excess stuffing. You will be left with sufficient stuffing to serve on the side.

To cook the quails, choose a saucepan that will fit the eight birds snugly, and put over a medium heat. Add the olive oil and, when hot but not smoking, add the cinnamon stick, saffron and chopped onion. Season with salt and pepper, then add the quails breast-side down and enough water almost, but not quite, to cover them. Bring to a steady simmer and cook for about 30 minutes, turning once halfway through the cooking time. At this stage preheat the oven to 230°C/450°F/Gas 8. When the birds are cooked, transfer them to a baking dish (keep the cooking liquor aside) and place in the hot oven until golden, a few minutes. Meanwhile, add the sultanas and ground cinnamon to the cooking liquor and reduce for 10–15 minutes. Then add the honey and sugar. Check for seasoning. You should taste a balance between the savouriness of the stewed quail, the sweetness of the honey and the spice.

When the quails are golden, warm up the couscous left over from the stuffing and serve on the side with the hot sauce (spoon a little of the sauce over the quail just before serving). Sprinkle the remaining whole lightly roasted almonds on the couscous for an attractive finish.

CRUSHED SWEET ALMONDS

10 tablespoons olive oil
250g whole blanched almonds
5 tablespoons granulated sugar

Place a frying pan over a medium heat and add the oil. When hot but not smoking, add the almonds and stir around until lightly toasted (light brown, approximately 2–3 minutes). Take care not to make them too dark as they will be bitter and unusable (the almonds will carry on cooking a bit out of the oil). Remove the pan from the heat and spoon the almonds on to a piece of kitchen paper to absorb any excess oil. Transfer about 200g of the almonds to a mortar along with the sugar, and crush until the nuts are almost fine. Alternatively, do this in a food processor, but make sure the almonds are not too smooth. Reserve the extra 50g almonds whole for decorating the dish.

QUAIL WITH GRAPES AND GINGER

This is a recipe adapted from Claudia Roden's wonderful 'A New Book of Middle Eastern Food' (Penguin). Jointed guinea fowl or chicken can be used instead of quail.

Serves 4

  6–8 quails

  4 tablespoons olive oil

  25g butter

  1 garlic clove, crushed to a paste with a pinch of salt

  2 tablespoons fresh root ginger juice (finely grate and squeeze the root)

  250g white grapes without pips, such as Muscat or seedless

  juice of 2 oranges

  2 tablespoons finely chopped fresh flat-leaf parsley

  sea salt and black pepper

Season the birds with salt and pepper. Place a large saucepan with a heavy bottom over a high heat and add the olive oil. When the oil is hot, add the quails, and fry for about 5 minutes, turning occasionally until sealed and golden brown on most sides. Pour off any excess oil from the birds and add the butter. When it has melted, add the garlic, ginger juice, grapes and orange juice. Cover and simmer for 10–15 minutes or until the quails are cooked. Check for seasoning, then add the parsley. We serve this with couscous or rice and rocket salad.

  If using guinea fowl or chicken, remember that dark meat always takes longer to become tender than white meat, so once sealed, cook the dark meat until tender, then return the breast to the pan to finish off the cooking (see page 207).

PERDIZ CON OLOROSO

PARTRIDGE WITH OLOROSO SHERRY

We ate this delicious dish in late September in Ronda near the beginning of the shooting season. The small birds were simply braised with garlic, sweet onion and oloroso sherry.

Serves 4

    4 partridges, plucked and cleaned

    4 sprigs fresh thyme

    6 tablespoons olive oil

    1 head garlic, broken into cloves, skin on

    2 medium onions, thinly sliced

    250ml oloroso sherry, sweet or dry, depending on your taste

    sea salt and black pepper

Put a sprig of thyme in the body cavity of each bird, and season all over the outside with salt and pepper. Place a large saucepan over a high heat, add the olive oil and when it is hot, add the partridges. Brown well on all sides, then remove the birds, lower the heat to medium and add the garlic cloves. Fry gently until golden, remove with a slotted spoon and keep aside, then add the onion with a pinch of salt. Cook for 15 minutes, stirring occasionally, until golden and sweet. Return the garlic to the pan, followed by the partridges and oloroso. Turn the heat to low and simmer gently with the lid ajar for 30–45 minutes, turning the birds every 5 minutes, or until tender and barely pink. Add a splash of water if the sauce is too strong, and taste for seasoning.

SLOW-COOKED DISHES

In Morocco, as you lift the lid of a tagine, there is often a mound of green beans or cardoons, and, hidden underneath, a couple of pieces of lamb. As you eat the tagine, you realise that this small amount of meat is all you need, for the vegetables and spice have enough richness to make a satisfying meal. The bean stews (potajes or pucheros) of Spain are similar. One chorizo, a piece of fat (manteca) and salted belly, for example, are sufficient (along with a few vegetables) to make the beans gutsy and flavoursome. On the next few pages are some recipes we cook in the restaurant. The great thing about these is that you are actively encouraged to cook them in advance. For most of the lamb dishes here we recommend using lamb shank and the neck for undisputed succulence and flavour.

RABO DE TORO CON RIOJA

OXTAIL WITH RIOJA AND CHORIZO

Oxtail stew was always a favourite at home when I (Samantha) was young. Like many children, I shunned the idea of eating the tail of an animal, and Saturday lunchtime was always a misery because it was usually oxtail (or tongue). Then one day, perhaps a sign of growing up, I tried some and realised what I had been missing all these years. Rabo de toro is something one sees quite a lot in Spain, especially in bars close to the bullrings. Like many stews, it should be cooked the day before, if possible, as the flavours definitely improve with age.

Serves 4–6

THE DAY BEFORE

> 3 tablespoons olive oil
>
> 1.5kg oxtail, sliced into 5cm chunks
>
> 1 carrot, cut into chunks
>
> 1 onion, quartered
>
> 1 celery stick, cut into chunks
>
> 5 black peppercorns
>
> 2 bay leaves
>
> 4 sprigs fresh thyme
>
> 4 cloves
>
> 2 garlic cloves
>
> 1 bottle red Rioja
>
> 10 parsley stalks
>
> sea salt and black pepper

ON THE DAY OF EATING

> 2 tablespoons olive oil
>
> 1 medium onion, finely diced
>
> 1 medium carrot, finely diced
>
> 120g chorizo, preferably cooking chorizo, cut into 1cm rounds
>
> 2 tablespoons plain flour
>
> 1 teaspoon sweet paprika
>
> $1/_4$ teaspoon hot paprika or dried red chilli flakes (kirmizi biber)
>
> $1/_4$ teaspoon fennel seeds, ground
>
> 1–2 tablespoons tomato purée

The day before serving, heat the oil in a large saucepan over a medium to high heat. Season the oxtail pieces with salt and pepper and brown well on all sides – you will probably need to do this in two batches. Remove the oxtail from the pan and pour off the excess fat before adding the carrot, onion and celery. Fry for 5 minutes until starting to colour, then add the aromatics (peppercorns, bay, thyme, cloves and garlic) and fry for 2 minutes more. Return the oxtail to the pan, add the Rioja and parsley stalks, and cover with water. Bring to a gentle simmer, reduce the heat to low and cook until tender – about 2 hours, or longer if necessary, adding water if the liquids boil down below the top of the meat. Season. The meat is ready when it can be easily pulled from the bone, but not so soft as to fall off of its own accord. Transfer the oxtail to a bowl or suitable container and strain the juices through a sieve over the meat. Cool and put in the fridge overnight.

On the day of eating, remove as much fat as possible from the chilled oxtail. Heat the olive oil in a large saucepan over a medium to high heat. When hot, add the onion and carrot, and cook for about 10 minutes until they begin to caramelise, stirring occasionally. Add the chorizo and fry for 5 more minutes. Now stir in the flour, fry for a couple more minutes and add the paprikas, fennel seeds and tomato purée. Add the oxtail with its stock to the pan and season with salt. Bring to a simmer and cook for 15 minutes. Serve with mashed potato or, as is usual in Spain, with fried potatoes.

MUTUMMA

LAMB STEW WITH WHITE BEANS AND CORIANDER

We used to cook this stew early on in Moro. One of our chefs, Raviv Hadad, whose father is Algerian, taught us how to make mutumma. It has a wonderful, earthy flavour thanks to the coriander and white beans. We use shank so as not to waste what remains from the legs of lamb we grill. If you cannot get lamb shank, then try diced shoulder or neck (bone in).

Serves 4

   1 kg lamb shank (boneless), trimmed of any excess fat, cut into 2cm cubes
   2 large bunches fresh coriander, leaves and stalks chopped, but kept separate
   $^1/_2$ medium onion, grated
   3 garlic cloves, thinly sliced
   3 tablespoons olive oil
   2 teaspoons sweet paprika
   1 teaspoon hot paprika
   750g chard, stalks cut into 2cm pieces, washed
   500g cooked white beans (see page 17), such as cannellini or butter beans
   sea salt and black pepper

Place all the ingredients except half the chard, the beans and the leafy parts of the coriander in a large pot, cover with a tight-fitting lid and simmer over a low heat for 2–2$^1/_2$ hours until the meat is tender. There is no need to add water, as plenty will come from the chard and coriander stalks. However, if it does become dry, add a little. Add half the coriander leaves, the remaining chard and the beans and cook for 20 minutes more. Taste for seasoning at the end. We serve this with a mixed herb salad and bread.

TANGIA

LAMB STEAMED WITH PRESERVED LEMON AND CUMIN

We had originally read about tangia in Paula Wolfert's book 'Moroccan Cuisine' (Grub Street), and were immediately captivated by the exotic idea of a stew being slow-cooked in the ashes of a hammam (steam bath). A few years later in Marrakech, we were led to the depths of a great furnace, to the side of which, neatly sitting in piles of hot grey ash, were two or three tangia pots. Tangia is a speciality of Marrakech and a favourite dish during Ramadan, when there can be more than a hundred of these pots steaming away silently in the dusty heat of the furnace.

Serves 6

> 6 whole lamb shanks, or 1 shoulder of lamb on the bone, about 1.8kg, trimmed and sawn into 6 pieces
>
> 1 large or 2 small Preserved Lemons (see page 281), washed, flesh discarded, rind roughly chopped (about 2 tablespoons)
>
> 1^1/$_2$ large onions, sliced
>
> 1 tablespoon cumin seeds, roughly ground
>
> 2 small heads garlic, cloves halved
>
> 3 tablespoons roughly chopped fresh coriander
>
> 75g butter
>
> 150ml water
>
> sea salt and black pepper

Preheat the oven to 230°C/450°F/Gas 8.

Blitz the preserved lemon, onion, cumin, garlic and coriander in a food processor. Place all the ingredients in a heavy-bottomed medium-sized saucepan (or earthenware pot) and mix together thoroughly. Season. Cover the top of the meat with baking parchment, then cover the top of the saucepan or pot with foil and then put on a tight-fitting lid. Place in the hot oven and immediately turn the heat down to 140°C/275°F/Gas 1. Cook for 5-6 hours. Remove and check for seasoning. The meat should be falling off the bone. We like to serve this with a mixed herb salad and some flatbread, but couscous, although not traditional, would also be suitable.

BEEF TAGINE WITH PRUNES

Of all the many Moroccan tagines, this one is a classic, and with good reason. Last time we ate it in Morocco, it was served with warm rice vermicelli instead of bread.

Serves 4

>   40g unsalted butter
>
>   2 tablespoons olive oil
>
>   1 teaspoon ground ginger
>
>   2 teaspoons ground cinnamon
>
>   3 tablespoons finely grated onion
>
>   4 tablespoons roughly chopped fresh coriander
>
>   1.2kg stewing beef, cut into 3cm cubes, trimmed of excess fat
>
>   40 threads saffron, infused in 2 tablespoons boiling water
>
>   400g stoned prunes, soaked in cold water
>
>   2 tablespoons runny honey
>
>   sea salt and black pepper

TO SERVE

>   1 tablespoon sesame seeds, lightly roasted
>
>   180g whole blanched almonds, fried in olive oil until just golden
>
>   4 tablespoons fresh coriander leaves (optional)

Put the butter and olive oil in a large saucepan over a medium to high heat, and when the butter starts to foam, add the ginger, $^1/_2$ teaspoon black pepper, the cinnamon, onion and coriander. Fry for 30 seconds, then add the beef and stir well for a minute or two so it is coated in the spice mixture. Cover the meat with water and the saffron infusion, bring to the boil, then lower the heat to a gentle simmer. Add half the prunes (drained), and cook for $1^1/_2$ hours, until the meat just begins to become tender and juicy. Add the remaining prunes along with the honey and some salt and pepper. Simmer for a further 30 minutes, or until the meat is tender and the liquid has thickened and reduced. Serve with sesame seeds, almonds and coriander leaves sprinkled over the top.

LAMB TAGINE WITH PEAS AND TOMATOES

We had this dish for lunch one day in an outside market. When we arrived at the market we ordered our tagine, then went off for a couple of hours to look around. We returned to a steaming dish of delicately spiced lamb and the peas that were in season at the time.

Serves 4

       4 tablespoons olive oil

       2 teaspoons cumin seeds, freshly ground

       1 cinnamon stick

       1 teaspoon sweet paprika

       $1/4$ teaspoon hot paprika

       2 medium red onions, roughly chopped

       2 tomatoes, peeled (see page 42) and roughly chopped

       3 lamb shanks (on the bone), or 1 large neck of lamb (on the bone,
         cut into 4 equal chunks, about 750g)

       1 litre cold water

       40 threads saffron, infused in 2 tablespoons boiling water

       600g fresh peas, podded

       sea salt and black pepper

In a large saucepan, put the olive oil, cumin, cinnamon stick, paprikas, chopped onion, tomatoes and some salt and pepper. Cook for 10 minutes, stirring occasionally, then add the meat. Stir well over a medium heat, then pour on the cold water and add the saffron infusion. Cover and cook for $1^1/2$–2 hours, or until the meat is almost tender. Now add the peas and simmer, uncovered, for a further 20–30 minutes until the lamb is soft and the peas sweet. Check the seasoning and serve with bread or couscous.

VEGETABLES

Each one of the dishes in this section has enough personality to 'hold' a plate. This means that if you are eating simply cooked meat or fish, you need nothing but one of these vegetable dishes to accompany it. Such simple recipes demand great ingredients, so we recommend that you choose the best of seasonal vegetables before you decide what to cook (see page 313).

We are very proud of this chapter because all the dishes have individuality and a strong regional identity. They also include some of our favourite foods.

PATATAS CON AZAFRAN
SAFFRON POTATOES

These potatoes are delicious with grilled or baked fish and a lemony home-made alioli (see page 86) or mayonnaise on the side .

Serves 4

> 200ml olive oil
>
> 2 large mild Spanish onions, thinly sliced
>
> sea salt and black pepper
>
> 5 garlic cloves, peeled and sliced
>
> 2 dried ñoras peppers, stalks and seeds removed, broken into small
>
>   pieces, or $^1/_2$ teaspoon sweet paprika
>
> 4 bay leaves (preferably fresh)
>
> $^1/_2$ tablespoon finely chopped fresh rosemary
>
> 1 kg firm Cyprus potatoes, peeled
>
> 50 threads saffron, infused in 4 tablespoons boiling water

Set a large saucepan over a medium heat and add half the olive oil. When the oil is hot, add the onion and a pinch of salt. Cook the onion for 5 minutes, then turn down the heat to low and cook for a further 5-10 minutes, stirring occasionally, until golden and sweet in smell and taste. Now add the garlic, dried peppers (or paprika), bay and rosemary and cook for 5 more minutes to release their flavours. Meanwhile, cut the potatoes in half lengthways and each half into two or three long wedges, depending on the size of the potato. Salt them lightly and pour on the saffron infusion. Toss well and leave for about 5 minutes before adding to the pan. Let everything simmer gently, covered, stirring occasionally and scraping the bottom of the pan until the potatoes are tender, around 30 minutes. If there is any excess oil in the pan, drain through a colander or sieve and reserve for further use (in tortillas or caramelised onions, for example).

Variation

As in the Alpujarras, instead of using saffron, sprinkle fresh (wild) oregano on top just before serving.

PATATAS ALIÑADAS

WARM POTATO SALAD WITH RED ONION AND SWEET VINEGAR

The Spanish variety of green 'goat's horn' pepper is perfect for salads such as this classic tapa, which is often served with fish roes. In London, because of the large Turkish community, it is easy to get similar varieties, such as kizarmis biber or carliston biber. At Moro we serve patatas aliñadas with roast pork or grilled marinated lamb.

Serves 4

> 1kg firm, waxy small salad potatoes (Cyprus, Ratte, Anya or Pink Fir)
> 1 small red onion, finely chopped
> 2 small green peppers, stalks and seeds discarded, roughly chopped
> 2 tablespoons roughly chopped fresh flat-leaf parsley
> sea salt and black pepper

DRESSING

> 1 small garlic clove, crushed to a paste with salt
> 6–7 tablespoons extra virgin olive oil
> 1–2 tablespoons good-quality sweet red wine vinegar (see page 287)

Wash or scrub the potatoes, don't peel them, and make sure they are more or less the same size (cut any large ones in half) so that they all cook in the same time. Bring a large saucepan of salted water to the boil over a medium to high heat, add the potatoes and put on the lid. Simmer for approximately 15–20 minutes or until tender, turning down the heat if necessary. Drain in a colander.

Meanwhile, place the onion and green pepper in a large mixing or salad bowl. When the potatoes are still warm, cut into 1cm rounds and put in the bowl. Whisk all the dressing ingredients together and pour over the potatoes. Season with salt and black pepper and add the chopped parsley. Toss well, check for seasoning once more, then serve immediately or at room temperature.

COL CON CASTAÑAS
BRAISED CABBAGE, PANCETA AND CHESTNUTS

When chestnuts are gathered in the woods of one of our neighbouring villages, there is a fiesta to celebrate the harvest. We fry the panceta (the Spanish equivalent of Italian pancetta or French lardons/cured bacon) with garlic and cabbage, and stir in cooked chopped chestnuts. This is delicious with roast partridge or Partridge with Oloroso (see page 218), pheasant, guinea fowl or even pork.

Serves 4

> 800g cabbage (Savoy or cavolo nero), or spring greens, quartered, heart removed, roughly shredded
>
> 4 tablespoons olive oil
>
> 150g panceta, smoked or unsmoked, cut into 10mm x 5mm pieces
>
> 2 garlic cloves, thinly sliced
>
> 200g cooked chestnuts (vacuum-packed or fresh roasted or boiled), peeled and chopped
>
> 1 teaspoon chopped fresh thyme leaves
>
> 50ml medium oloroso sherry (optional) or water
>
> sea salt and black pepper

Set a large covered pan of salted water over a high heat and bring to the boil. Add the cabbage to the saucepan, replace the lid and when the water comes to the boil again, boil for 1 minute. Drain the cabbage and spread out on a kitchen towel to dry. When you are ready to fry the cabbage, set the same large saucepan or a frying pan over a medium to high heat and add the olive oil. When hot, add the panceta and fry for a few minutes, like bacon, until the fat renders and it begins to go crisp. Now add the garlic, turn down the heat and fry for a minute or so until golden. Add the chestnuts and thyme, stir well and fry for 2 minutes more. Pour in the oloroso or water and simmer for a minute, then stir in the cabbage and toss well until it is warmed through. Taste for seasoning and serve.

COLES CON ALCAPARRAS
SPRING CABBAGE WITH CAPERS, BUTTER AND PAPRIKA

Perfect for when spring greens or cabbage have just come into season and the tops are young, sweet and tender. This dish can also be made with sprouting broccoli, and is delicious on its own or with some white fish or chicken.

Serves 4

> 700g spring greens or spring cabbage, cut into small wedges or chunks
> 75g butter
> 70g capers in salt or vinegar, prepared as on page 154
> 2 garlic cloves, thinly sliced
> juice of $^1/_2$ lemon
> $^3/_4$ teaspoon sweet smoked paprika
> sea salt and black pepper

Place a large saucepan of salted water over a high heat and bring to the boil. Put your greens into the pan, submerge under the water and simmer until cooked. To test, the stalks should not be too hard, yet the leaves not too soft. Fill a large bowl with cold water and lift the greens from the pan into the water to refresh. Let them sit for a minute, then transfer them to a colander to drain.

Set a frying pan over a medium heat, add the butter, and when it begins to foam, the capers and garlic. Fry for a minute until they go slightly crisp. Now add the greens and fry for a minute or two, turning once or twice, until they are hot. Season with salt and pepper and stir in the lemon juice. Sprinkle the paprika on top just before serving.

BERENJENAS FRITAS

FRIED AUBERGINES WITH HONEY

Having read about this dish for years, we finally tried it at the El Rey de Copas restaurant in Ribera Alta, Jaén. The 'honey' was actually miel de caña, a light molasses made from sugar cane that is grown around Almuñecar. On our return to Moro, we immediately made our version, which we serve with grilled or roast lamb.

Serves 6

  3 large aubergines

  sea salt

  sunflower oil, for deep-frying

  4 tablespoons runny honey, preferably scented with rosemary, chestnut or
    thyme

BATTER

  150g chickpea (gram) flour

  $^1/_2$ teaspoon bicarbonate of soda

  200ml soda/fizzy water

  1 tablespoon finely chopped fresh rosemary (an option if serving with lamb)

Slice the aubergines into rounds no more than 1–1.5cm thick. Salt lightly and leave in a colander for 20 minutes to drain. Meanwhile, make the batter. Place the chickpea flour, bicarbonate of soda and a pinch of salt in a bowl. Make a well in the middle with your hand and then, with a balloon whisk, slowly whisk in the water, stirring constantly until it has all been amalgamated into the flour. Keep whisking for another minute to make sure the batter is completely smooth, then stir in the rosemary. Cover and put in the fridge for 20 minutes. Now dry the aubergines well on kitchen paper and set aside on a plate.

When you are ready to fry the aubergines, heat a 3cm depth of oil in a large saucepan (making sure the oil comes no more than halfway up the pan). While it is heating, blot the aubergines dry on kitchen paper once more. When a very light haze begins to appear above the oil (180–190°C/350–375°F), dip the aubergine in the batter, making sure each slice is lightly covered, and gently ease into the hot oil. Add only as many slices as needed to make a single layer. Fry until light brown on one side, then turn and fry the other. Remove with a slotted spoon, drain off any excess oil on kitchen paper, then salt and transfer to a warm oven while you fry the rest of the aubergines. As soon as the last ones are ready, drizzle over the honey and eat immediately.

VERDURAS DE MURCIA

AUBERGINES WITH OREGANO AND PINE NUTS

When peering over a bar in Murcia at different tapas that smelt fantastic, we enquired about a murky-coloured dish with pine nuts on top. Verduras de Murcia they called it, which, as Murcia is indeed famous for its vegetables, did not give much insight into what this dish actually was! It turned out to be this wonderful tapas of braised aubergine with pine nuts and oregano. If you replaced the oregano with a little paprika and cumin, it would be indistinguishable from a cooked Moroccan salad. This dish is also a treat with grilled or roasted lamb or chicken, or, indeed, as a tapa for 6–8.

Serves 4

> 3 large aubergines
> $1^1/_2$ teaspoons fine sea salt
> 8 tablespoons olive oil
> 1 medium to large onion, finely chopped
> 3 tablespoons pine nuts
> 2 garlic cloves, thinly sliced
> $^1/_2$ teaspoon dried oregano
> $1^1/_2$ tablespoons sweet vinegar (see page 287)
> 2 tablespoons chopped fresh oregano
> sea salt and black pepper

Preheat the oven to 230°C/450°F/Gas 8.

Cut the stalks off the aubergines and peel off the skin with a potato peeler. Slice the flesh into cubes the size of large sugar lumps (2cm square), then sprinkle with the fine salt. Leave to sit in a colander for at least 20 minutes, then blot dry with kitchen paper. Toss with half the olive oil, spread out on a large baking tray and roast for around 25–30 minutes until they start to brown and are completely tender. Put the remaining oil in a frying pan over a medium to low heat. Add the onion, pine nuts and a pinch of salt to the pan and soften for 10 minutes, stirring every now and then. Add the garlic and dried oregano and cook until the garlic, onions and pine nuts have taken on an amber colour – be careful not to burn anything. Add the cooked aubergine to the pan, increase the heat slightly and stir briskly for a minute or two. Stir in the vinegar and most of the fresh oregano and cook for 2 minutes more, until some of the pungency of the vinegar has gone. Taste for seasoning, and serve with the remaining fresh oregano scattered on top.

LEEKS WITH YOGHURT

There are a few recipes in which we use dried mint because it has a particular flavour that somehow feels more authentic for certain dishes. Turkish or Lebanese dried mint is particularly good.

Serves 4

> 50g butter
>
> 3 tablespoons olive oil
>
> 4–6 medium leeks (total weight 800g), trimmed, halved lengthways, washed, drained and thinly sliced
>
> 1 teaspoon Turkish chilli flakes (kirmizi biber) or hot paprika
>
> 1 rounded teaspoon dried mint
>
> 1 egg yolk
>
> $^1/_2$ tablespoon cornflour
>
> 350g Greek yoghurt
>
> sea salt and black pepper

Place a large saucepan over a medium heat and add the butter and olive oil. When the butter begins to foam, stir in the leeks and add a pinch of salt. After 10 minutes add the chilli flakes or paprika and dried mint, and continue to cook the leeks for another 20–30 minutes, stirring occasionally, until they are sweet. Set aside.

In a large bowl, whisk the egg yolk with the cornflour until a smooth paste is formed (this will stabilise the yoghurt when it is heated). Now stir in the yoghurt and pour the mix on to the leeks. Return the saucepan to the hob and warm gently over a low to medium heat, stirring every now and then. Remove just before it bubbles and check for seasoning. Add a little water if too thick.

SLOW-COOKED FENNEL WITH DILL

Serves 4

>   5 tablespoons olive oil
>   4 firm, medium fennel bulbs, trimmed, cut into sixths, keeping green
>   leaves aside
>   2 garlic cloves, thinly sliced
>   3 tablespoons roughly chopped fresh dill, plus 1 extra tablespoon if no
>   fennel leaves
>   4 tablespoons water
>   a squeeze of lemon
>   sea salt and black pepper

Heat the oil in a very large saucepan over a high heat. When the oil is hot but not smoking, add the fennel and a pinch of salt and cook for 5 minutes to colour, then turn down the heat and continue for another 15 minutes, turning occasionally until the fennel is nicely golden and caramelised all over. Now add the garlic and dill, and cook for another 5 minutes. Add the water and continue for a further 10 minutes, stirring occasionally, until most of the water has evaporated and the fennel is soft and tender. Just before serving add a squeeze of lemon, check for salt and add a few grinds of black pepper. Serve immediately with the chopped fennel leaves (or dill) on top.

Variation

For a Spanish version of this Middle Eastern recipe, substitute dried ñoras peppers for the dill. Simply break open 2 ñoras peppers, discarding the stalk and seeds, and break into small pieces into a bowl. Pour over boiling water and leave to infuse for 5 minutes until soft. When you come to add the garlic, drain and chop the soaked peppers and add to the pan. If you cannot get hold of ñoras peppers, use 4 finely chopped piquillo peppers or 1 roasted red bell pepper (see page 78), peeled, seeded and chopped, or 1 teaspoon sweet paprika.

WARM PUMPKIN AND CHICKPEA SALAD WITH TAHINI

This warm salad has lots of textures and tastes bouncing off each other. Tahini is an oily paste made from pounded sesame seeds. It has a rich, nutty flavour and is used throughout the Middle East.

Serves 4

1kg pumpkin or squash (800g prepared weight), peeled, seeded and cut into 3cm cubes

1 garlic clove, crushed

$^1/_2$ teaspoon ground allspice

2 tablespoons olive oil

250g home-cooked chickpeas (see page 59), or 1 x 400g can cooked chickpeas, drained

$^1/_2$ small red onion, finely chopped

4 tablespoons roughly chopped fresh coriander

sea salt and black pepper

TAHINI SAUCE

1 garlic clove, crushed to a paste with salt

$3^1/_2$ tablespoons lemon juice

3 tablespoons tahini paste

2 tablespoons water, to taste

2 tablespoons extra virgin olive oil

Preheat the oven to 220°C/425°F/Gas 7.

Toss the pumpkin with the garlic, allspice, olive oil and some salt and pepper. Place on a tray in the oven for about 15–25 minutes or until soft. Remove and cool.

While the pumpkin is cooking, make the tahini sauce. Mix the crushed garlic with the lemon juice and add the tahini. Now thin with the water and olive oil and check for seasoning. You should taste a balance between the nutty tahini and lemon.

To assemble the salad, place the pumpkin, chickpeas, red onion and coriander in a mixing bowl. Pour on the tahini sauce and remaining oil and toss carefully. Season with salt and pepper.

ESPINACAS CON NUECES

SPINACH WITH WALNUTS

Spinach was one of the many key ingredients that the Moors brought to Spain. In this recipe the spinach is combined with other hallmark Moorish ingredients: fried bread, garlic, saffron and walnuts.

Serves 4

> 8 tablespoons olive oil
>
> 750g spinach, washed and drained well
>
> 75g white bread, crusts removed, cut into 1cm cubes
>
> 3 garlic cloves, thinly sliced
>
> 100g shelled walnuts, roughly chopped
>
> 1 teaspoon cumin seeds
>
> 2 tablespoons roughly chopped fresh oregano
>
> 1 tablespoon red wine vinegar
>
> $^1/_2$ teaspoon sweet Spanish paprika
>
> 40 threads saffron, infused in 4 tablespoons boiling water
>
> sea salt and black pepper

Place a large saucepan over a high heat and add 3 tablespoons of the olive oil. When the oil is hot, add the spinach with a pinch of salt and stir well. Remove when the leaves are just tender, drain in a colander and, when cool, chop roughly. Set aside.

Heat the remaining olive oil in a frying pan over a medium heat. Fry the bread for about 3–5 minutes until golden brown all over, then add the garlic, two-thirds of the walnuts and all of the cumin and oregano, and cook for 1–2 more minutes until the garlic is nutty brown. Transfer to a mortar or food processor along with the vinegar, paprika and saffron infusion and mash roughly. Return the chopped spinach to the pan over a medium heat, then add the mashed bread and season with salt and pepper. If the consistency is too thick, add some more water. Serve with the remaining chopped walnuts on top.

WARM BEETROOT IN YOGHURT

As the beetroot bleeds into the yoghurt in this recipe, a wonderful bright purple colour emerges; it looks unnatural, but the flavour definitely is not.

Serves 4

      600g fresh raw beetroot

      a squeeze of lemon

      2 tablespoons extra virgin olive oil

      2 tablespoons roughly chopped fresh flat-leaf parsley

      1 tablespoon chopped fresh mint

      1 egg

      1 tablespoon cornflour

      500g Greek yoghurt

      sea salt and black pepper

Wash the beetroot carefully. Place in a saucepan of cold salted water and bring to the boil. The time it takes for the beetroot to cook will depend on the size, but allow from 30 minutes to $1^1/_2$ hours. They will be ready when you can slip a sharp knife easily into the centre, rather like testing to see if a potato is cooked. Drain, place under a running cold tap and rub away the skin with your fingers. Cut the beetroot into 2cm rounds, then dress with the lemon juice, olive oil, half the parsley, the mint, and some salt and pepper.

In a large bowl, whisk the egg with the cornflour until a smooth paste is formed, then add the yoghurt (this will stabilise the yoghurt when it is heated). Place the yoghurt in a saucepan and put over a medium heat to warm through, stirring occasionally. Do not boil, but remove from the heat just before it bubbles. Add the beetroot and stir over the heat again until warm. Check the seasoning, and serve sprinkled with the remaining parsley.

BEETROOT AND POTATO SALAD WITH MINT AND SPRING ONION

Serves 4

    400g fresh raw beetroot

    300g firm potatoes, peeled

    1 tablespoon roughly chopped fresh flat-leaf parsley

    2 tablespoons finely chopped fresh mint

    5 spring onions, finely sliced

    1 tablespoon sweet wine vinegar (see page 287)

    a squeeze of lemon

    4 tablespoons extra virgin olive oil

    sea salt and black pepper

Prepare and cook the beetroot as described in the previous recipe. While they are simmering, boil the potatoes in salted water, and when both vegetables are ready, cut into 2cm wedges and place in a large bowl. Add the parsley, mint and spring onions and dress with the vinegar, lemon juice, olive oil and some salt and pepper. Give everything a good toss while still warm. Taste and leave for a little while for the flavours to infuse and the potatoes to absorb some of the beetroot colour. Toss once more just before serving.

GRAINS AND PULSES

GRAINS

The versatility of rice is undisputed, and is demonstrated here in a selection of Spanish and eastern dishes that are quite different from each other. Spanish arroces are pungent and sweet from the pepper base and stock, while pilavs are more varied in texture, lighter and subtly perfumed with spice.

PAELLA WITH CHICKEN AND PRAWNS

If you are cooking paella for two people, a large frying pan will do well. If, however, you fancy cooking paella for four, six or even eight people, it is necessary to buy the right-sized pan. We like the black enamel paella pans with white spots. If you want to cook a paella outside, the traditional way, see the notes on page 14.

Serves 6 as a starter, 4 as a main course

300g North Atlantic prawns, preferably in their shells

1 litre Light Chicken Stock (see page 313)

a small pinch of saffron (about 20 threads)

6 tablespoons olive oil

350g boned and skinned chicken, cut into 2cm cubes

$1^1/_2$ large Spanish onions, finely chopped

1 green pepper, halved, seeded and finely chopped

4 garlic cloves, finely chopped

150g runner beans or green beans, cut into 3cm pieces

2 dried ñoras peppers, seeds and stalks removed, broken into small pieces
   and covered with boiling water, or 1 teaspoon sweet paprika

250g calasparra (paella) rice

75ml white wine

sea salt and black pepper

TO SERVE

2 tablespoons roughly chopped fresh flat-leaf parsley

1 lemon, cut into wedges

Peel the prawns as described on page 141 and put in the fridge. Transfer the shells to a large saucepan over a high heat and add the chicken stock. Bring to a gentle simmer and cook for 15 minutes for the seafood flavour to infuse the stock. Remove from the heat, strain the stock and add the saffron. Set aside.

Heat 2 tablespoons of the olive oil in a 30–40cm paella pan or frying pan over a medium to high heat. When the oil is hot and just beginning to smoke add the pieces of chicken and stir-fry for about 2 minutes until sealed on all sides but fractionally undercooked in the centre. With a slotted spoon remove the chicken and put to one side. Add the remaining olive oil to the pan and, when it is hot, the onion and pepper. Cook for 5 minutes, then lower the heat to medium and cook for another 10–15 minutes, stirring every so often. Now add the chopped garlic, beans and ñoras peppers, and cook for a further 5 minutes or until the garlic and the onions have some colour and are sweet. Add the rice to the pan and stir for 1 minute to coat with the vegetables and oil. (Up to this point everything can be cooked in advance. The next stage should be started about 20 minutes before you wish to eat.)

When you are ready to cook the rice, bring the stock to the boil. Remove and keep aside. Place the paella pan over a medium to high heat and add the wine, followed by the hot stock, and season perfectly with salt and pepper. Do not stir the rice after this as it affects the channels of stock, which allow the rice to cook evenly. Simmer for 10 minutes or until there is just a little liquid above the rice. Spread the pieces of chicken evenly over the rice and push each piece under the stock. Gently shake the pan to prevent sticking and turn the heat down to low. Cook for 5 more minutes or until there is just a little liquid left at the bottom of the rice. Sprinkle the prawns on top, turn off the heat and cover the pan tightly with foil. Let the rice sit for 3–5 minutes before serving with the chopped parsley over the top and the lemon on the side. We would eat this with a cold glass of fino or manzanilla sherry.

VEGETABLE PAELLA WITH ARTICHOKES AND PIQUILLO PEPPERS

We certainly can't pretend this is authentic, but the challenge was to produce the classic rice dish without any fish or meat and yet retain its integrity. The artichokes give complexity of texture and taste, while the peppers give colour and sweetness.

Serves 6 as a starter, 4 as a main course

> 6 tablespoons olive oil
>
> 1 large Spanish onion, finely chopped
>
> 1 green pepper, seeded and finely chopped
>
> 2 dried ñoras peppers, seeds and stalks removed, broken into small pieces and covered with boiling water, or 1 teaspoon sweet paprika
>
> 3 large globe artichokes
>
> 6 garlic cloves, finely chopped
>
> 1 level teaspoon finely chopped fresh rosemary
>
> 1 litre Vegetable Stock (see page 313)
>
> a pinch of saffron (about 40 threads)
>
> 1 teaspoon finely chopped dried porcini mushrooms (which give richness to the stock, optional)
>
> 1 dessertspoon tomato purée
>
> 250g calasparra (paella) rice
>
> 1 teaspoon sweet paprika
>
> 5 piquillo peppers (85g) sliced into strips, or 3 red peppers, grilled, skinned and seeded (see page 78)
>
> sea salt and black pepper

TO SERVE

> 2 tablespoons roughly chopped fresh flat-leaf parsley
>
> 1 lemon, cut into wedges

Heat the olive oil in a 35–40cm paella pan or frying pan and start to soften the onion, green pepper and ñoras peppers in the olive oil over a medium to high heat. Cook for 20–30 minutes, stirring occasionally.

Meanwhile, prepare the artichokes (see page 126). Cut each artichoke in half and each half into six wedges. Add these, along with the garlic and rosemary, to the softening onion and peppers, fry for a couple of minutes, then cover with foil or a lid and cook for a further 8–10 minutes over a medium heat, stirring every now and then.

Bring the vegetable stock to the boil and add the saffron, mushrooms and tomato purée to infuse.

It is time to start cooking the paella, which takes about 20 minutes plus 10 minutes 'resting' covered with foil. Over a medium heat add the rice and paprika to the vegetables in the pan. Stir the rice thoroughly for 2 minutes before adding the stock mixture. Bring to the boil and at this point take the time to season the liquor adequately. When the rice appears above the stock, don't be tempted to stir it: just turn down the heat to low to prevent it sticking to the bottom of the pan. Continue cooking for another 5–10 minutes until 80 per cent of the stock has been absorbed into the rice. Remove from the heat. Scatter the strips of pepper evenly over the top of the paella and cover the pan tightly with foil before letting it rest for 10 minutes.

Take off the foil, sprinkle with the parsley and serve with the wedges of lemon and perhaps a green salad made with a sherry vinegar dressing.

ARROZ A LA MARINERA
WET FISH RICE

This is more of a ricey stew, which cooks happily in a large pot. If you don't possess a paella pan, then this may be the rice for you.

Serves 6 as a starter, 4 as a main course

    300g North Atlantic prawns, preferably in their shells

    1 litre Fish Stock (see page 313)

    a small pinch of saffron (20 threads)

    6 tablespoons olive oil

    $1^1/_2$ large Spanish onions, finely chopped

    1 green pepper, seeded and finely chopped

    2 dried ñoras peppers, seeds and stalks removed, broken into small pieces
       and covered with boiling water, or 1 teaspoon sweet paprika

    5 garlic cloves, finely chopped

    $^1/_2$ teaspoon fennel seeds

    250g calasparra (paella) rice

    75ml white wine

    300g monkfish fillets, trimmed and cut into 2cm pieces

    2 medium squid, the size of your hand (prepared exactly as on page 84)

    sea salt and black pepper

TO SERVE

    2 tablespoons roughly chopped fresh flat-leaf parsley

    1 lemon, cut into wedges

Peel the prawns as described on page 141 and put in the fridge. Transfer the shells to a large saucepan over a high heat and add the fish stock. Bring to a gentle simmer and cook for 15 minutes for the seafood flavour to infuse the stock. Remove from the heat, strain the stock and add the saffron. Set aside.

Heat the olive oil in a large saucepan over a medium to high heat. When the pan is hot, add the onion and both the green and ñoras peppers, and cook for 5 minutes. Lower the heat to medium and cook for another 10–15 minutes, stirring every so often. Now stir in the chopped garlic and fennel seeds and cook for a further 5 minutes or until the garlic and the onions have some colour and are sweet. Add the rice to the pan and stir for 1 minute to coat with the vegetables and oil. (Up to this point everything can be cooked in advance. The next stage should be started about 20 minutes before you wish to eat.)

When you are ready to cook the rice, bring the stock to the boil. Remove and keep aside. Place the paella pan over medium to high and add the wine, followed by the hot stock, and season with a little salt and pepper. Simmer for 15 minutes, stirring every now and then to prevent sticking, then add the pieces of monkfish and squid and turn the heat down to medium to low. Cook for 2 more minutes, then add the prawns, turn off the heat and cover with a lid. Let the rice sit for 3–5 minutes, then check the seasoning. (The rice should be tender and surrounded by a soupy sauce.) Serve with chopped parsley sprinkled over the top and wedges of lemon.

FIDUEA

If you like the flavours of Spanish rice dishes but want a change, try making fiduea. The Spanish pasta known as 'fideos' comes in varying degrees of thickness, but is like short, thin spaghetti. (You can use spaghettini if you can't find fideos.) A good stock is vital because the pasta absorbs it as it cooks. The first time we made this dish, traditionally served with alioli, we were bowled over by how delicious it was.

Serves 6 as a starter, 4 as a main course

- 300g North Atlantic prawns, preferably in their shells
- 1 litre Fish Stock (see page 313)
- a small pinch of saffron (20 threads)
- 6 tablespoons olive oil
- 300g monkfish fillets, trimmed and cut into 2–3cm pieces
- 1 large Spanish onion, finely chopped
- 1 green pepper, seeded and finely chopped
- 5 garlic cloves, finely chopped
- $^1/_2$ teaspoon fennel seeds
- 1 x 400g can plum tomatoes, drained and chopped
- 2 dried ñoras peppers, seeds and stalks removed, broken into small pieces and covered with boiling water, or 1 teaspoon sweet paprika
- 250g fideos (grade 2 thickness) or spaghettini, snapped into 3–4cm lengths
- 250g clams, such as palourdes (optional), washed well and any broken or open clams discarded
- sea salt and black pepper

TO SERVE

2 tablespoons roughly chopped fresh flat-leaf parsley

1 quantity Alioli (see page 86, replacing the saffron infusion with
   1 tablespoon water)

1 lemon, cut into wedges

Peel the prawns as described on page 141 and put in the fridge. Transfer the shells to a large saucepan over a high heat and add the fish stock. Bring to a gentle simmer and cook for 15 minutes for the seafood flavour to infuse the stock. Remove from the heat, strain the stock and add the saffron. Set aside.

Heat 2 tablespoons of the olive oil in a 30–40cm paella pan or frying pan over a medium to high heat. When the oil is hot and just beginning to smoke add the pieces of monkfish and stir-fry for about 2 minutes until sealed on all sides but fractionally undercooked in the centre. Transfer the monkfish and any juices to a bowl and put to one side. Wipe the pan clean with kitchen paper and put back on the heat. Add the remaining olive oil and, when it is hot, the onion, green pepper and ñoras peppers, and cook for 5 minutes, then lower the heat to medium and cook for another 10–15 minutes, stirring every so often. Now add the chopped garlic and fennel seeds and cook for 1 minute. Add the tomatoes and cook for a further 5 minutes. Now add the fideos to the pan and stir for 1 minute to coat with the oily base. (Up to this point everything can be cooked in advance. The next stage should be started about 20 minutes before you wish to eat.)

When you are ready to cook the fideos, heat up your stock. Put the paella or frying pan over a medium to high heat, add the hot stock and season perfectly with salt and pepper. Simmer for 10 minutes, stirring occasionally, depending on the thickness of the fideos, or until al dente. Add the pieces of monkfish and clams, pushing them down into the pasta, and turn the heat to low. Cook for 5 more minutes, then add the prawns, turn off the heat and cover the pan tightly with foil. Let the fiduea sit for 2–3 minutes, check the seasoning and sprinkle the parsley over the top. Serve with alioli and wedges of lemon. Some people like to finish off fiduea in a hot oven or under a grill to get the pasta crispy and coloured on top.

PINE NUT, RAISIN AND DILL PILAV

In Turkey, this combination is used as a stuffing for mackerel and mussels. We like to serve it with fish (mackerel is delicious), some braised courgettes with mint and a simple yoghurt sauce.

Serves 4

> 200g white basmati rice
> 75g butter
> $1/3$ teaspoon ground allspice
> 3 tablespoons finely chopped fresh dill
> 6 spring onions, trimmed, peeled and chopped, green tops and all
> 50g currants, soaked in hot water
> 50g pine nuts
> sea salt and black pepper

Put the rice in a bowl and cover with cold water. Rub the rice with your fingertips until the water becomes cloudy with the starch. Strain off the cloudy water and repeat the process three times (or until the water runs clear). Finally, pour off the water, replace with warm water and stir in a teaspoon of salt. Leave to soak for 20 minutes to 1 hour. The salt stops the rice from breaking up, and the soaking reduces the cooking time by half. You can make pilav without soaking the rice, but a little more water and time is needed when it comes to cooking the rice.

Over a medium heat, melt the butter in a saucepan and when it begins to foam, fry the allspice and 2 tablespoons of the dill for 1 minute. Stir in the spring onions and cook for 5 minutes until soft, then add the drained rice, currants and pine nuts. Stir to coat with the butter and spices. Cover the rice with 5mm water and season with salt and pepper. Lay some damp greaseproof paper on the water and bring to the boil over a medium to high heat. When it comes to the boil, put a lid on the pan and cook quite fast for 5 minutes. Now turn down the heat to medium to low for another 5 minutes before it is ready to serve. Sprinkle the rest of the dill on top.

LENTILS AND RICE

The first time we had this classic Lebanese and Syrian dish, it was cooked by Joseph and Helene, two wonderful Lebanese cooks, who served it alongside lamb kibbeh and yoghurt sauce. Lentils and rice are a fantastic combination and very satisfying to eat. We often serve this dish with grilled lamb marinated in garlic, allspice and cinnamon, and offer yoghurt, chopped cucumber or tomatoes and crisp, caramelised onions on the side.

Serves 4

175g small brown lentils

75g butter

1 teaspoon ground cinnamon

1 teaspoon ground allspice

175g white basmati rice (prepared as in the preceding recipe)

sea salt and black pepper

TO SERVE

1 quantity Caramelised Crispy Onions (see opposite)

Put the lentils in a saucepan and cover generously with water. Bring to the boil, reduce the heat to a gentle simmer and cook for about 10 minutes or until the lentils are still a bit hard. Drain immediately. While they are cooking, make the caramelised onions as described opposite.

To finish the dish, melt the butter in a saucepan and add the spices plus 1 teaspoon freshly ground black pepper. Now stir in a third of the crispy onions, the drained lentils and drained rice. Gently toss them all together. Pour enough water into the saucepan to cover the lentils and rice by $^1/_2$ cm and season with salt to taste. Cover the top of the water with some damp baking parchment or foil so it touches the surface. Put a lid on the pan and bring to the boil over a high heat. After 5 minutes, turn down the heat to low and cook for a further 5 minutes. All the water should now have been absorbed. Serve with lots of crispy onions on top.

Variation

Chickpeas and rice are also a great combination. Follow the recipe above, simply substituting chickpeas for lentils, but make sure the chickpeas are properly cooked before you add the rice as they hold their structure better than lentils.

CARAMELISED CRISPY ONIONS

It is important that the onions are sliced quite thinly and evenly. We recommend using a mandolin or a food processor with a thin slicing attachment.

> 300ml sunflower oil
> 2 large onions, halved and sliced into rounds as thin and
>   even as possible

Heat the oil in a large saucepan or frying pan. (Unless you have a very large pan, it will be necessary to fry the onion in batches.) When the oil is hot, add enough sliced onion to make one layer, and cook over a medium heat, stirring occasionally. Towards the last stages of cooking, a lot of stirring will be required to help the onion cook evenly. When golden to mahogany in colour, remove the onion with a slotted spoon, draining as much of the oil as possible back into the pan. Spread out either on a rack or on kitchen paper. Repeat with the remaining onions. Strain the oil and keep it for another recipe, bearing in mind it will taste of onions.

TOMATO BULGUR

Pilavs made with bulgur instead of rice are quite common, especially in Turkey. The following recipe is wonderful with grilled lamb or chicken. It is very simple to make.

Serves 4

> 75g butter, plus 20g to finish
>
> 2 tablespoons olive oil
>
> 1 teaspoon ground allspice
>
> 1 teaspoon ground cinnamon
>
> 300g medium or coarse bulgur, washed 3 times in several changes of water
>
> 1 quantity Tomato Sauce, minus the peppers (see page 182)
>
> 300ml cold water
>
> sea salt and black pepper

Over a medium heat, melt the 75g butter with the olive oil in a saucepan. When the butter begins to foam, fry the allspice, cinnamon and 1 teaspoon freshly ground black pepper for 1 minute to release their flavours. Add the drained bulgur and the tomato sauce to the pan and stir. Cover the bulgur mixture with the water and season with salt and pepper. Lay some damp greaseproof paper on the water and bring to the boil over a medium to high heat. When it comes to the boil, put a lid on the pan and cook quite fast for 5 minutes. Now turn down the heat to medium to low for another 5 minutes. Add the remaining 20g butter and stir until melted. Let the pilav sit for 5 minutes before serving.

WALNUT AND RED PEPPER BULGUR

This dish resembles a punchy tabbouleh, flavoured with pepper and walnuts.

Serves 4

> 90g medium–coarse bulgur, washed and soaked in warm water for
>> 10–15 minutes
>
> 4 spring onions, trimmed, peeled and chopped
>
> 2 garlic cloves, crushed to a paste with salt
>
> 2 tablespoons Turkish pepper paste (acili biber, see page 189),.or 2 grilled
>> and peeled red peppers (see page 78), finely chopped
>
> $1/2$ teaspoon hot paprika
>
> 1 tablespoon tomato purée

2 tablespoons olive oil

50g shelled walnuts, finely chopped

2 tablespoons roughly chopped fresh flat-leaf parsley

2 tablespoons roughly chopped fresh mint

1 tablespoon roughly chopped fresh dill (optional)

sea salt and black pepper

TO SERVE

2 baby gem lettuces, washed and dried well

Drain the bulgur, squeeze dry and place in a large mixing bowl. Add the remaining ingredients, mix well and season. Place in the middle of a serving dish surrounded by individual leaves of the gem lettuce to scoop up the bulgur.

BARLEY BREAD

As we were leaving Tangiers on our camper-van trip, we bought a couple of breads on the street to eat for breakfast. One was flaky and oily, flavoured with onion and a little tomato; the other was a dense bread made of cracked barley. This bread felt primitive and ancient – more like polenta than bread. We like it lightly grilled and eaten with butter and other accompaniments (see below).

Serves 4

> 140g pearl barley
>
> 1.6 litres water
>
> 1 teaspoon fine sea salt
>
> olive oil, for grilling or frying

Combine the barley, water and salt in a medium to large saucepan and bring to a good simmer. Stir from time to time with a spoon to stop it sticking on the bottom, and cook for about 1 hour until the total volume has reduced by half. Take care at the end of cooking, as the mixture may bubble like hot lava and could burn you. Use an electric hand-held blender or food processor to roughly purée half the barley, then cook for 2 more minutes. Remove from the heat and spread out on to an oiled plate or baking dish so that the mixture is about 2–3cm thick. Leave until completely cold, then cut into wedges. Drizzle both sides with a little olive oil and grill on a hot griddle or barbecue until crisp and slightly charred on both sides. If frying, place a frying pan over a high heat and add olive oil to a depth of 1–2mm. Cook crust-side down for 3–5 minutes until browned and crisp, then turn to cook the other side for just a minute or two to warm through.

Serve with Fresh Cheese (see pages 278–9), or spiced Labneh (see page 280), cooked Moroccan salads (see pages 159–66), or yoghurt seasoned with garlic and ground cumin. Alongside this, offer cucumber, carrot and radish crudités, mixed olives and generous sprigs of fresh herbs (mint, flat-leaf parsley and tarragon).

Note

The brightly coloured enamel teapots that feature in many of the photographs come from Morocco. We collect them and use them for pouring olive oil.

PULSES

SYRIAN LENTIL PURÉE

We call this dish 'Syrian', but really the recipe is pretty common throughout the Middle East. It is delicious as part of a mezze spread, or with meat or fish, yoghurt and greens. If eaten hot, it is almost like a dahl of the Mediterranean.

Serves 4

> 6 tablespoons olive oil
> 4 garlic cloves, finely chopped
> 2 rounded teaspoons cumin seeds, roughly ground
> 250g small brown or Puy lentils
> 1.75 litres water
> 1 quantity Caramelised Crispy Onions (optional, see page 261)
> 125g fresh coriander, chopped and stalks set aside
> a squeeze of lemon
> sea salt and black pepper

In a large saucepan, heat 4 tablespoons of the oil over a medium heat. When it is hot but not smoking, add the garlic and cumin and fry for a minute until golden. Stir in the coriander stalks, followed by the lentils, water and half the caramelised onions. Bring to the boil, then reduce the heat to a gentle simmer and cook for 40–60 minutes or until the lentils are soft and start to mush, becoming sauce-like. Remove from the heat and stir in the coriander leaves, the remaining olive oil and a small squeeze of lemon. Season with salt and pepper, and taste. Serve warm or at room temperature with the remaining caramelised onions on top.

LENTEJAS

LENTILS WITH CHORIZO

Lentejas are an institution in Spain, the same way fish and chips are in Britain. We would happily eat a bowl of lentejas every day if we had to. It is a hearty mixture flavoured with chorizo and other Spanish ingredients, such as dried peppers, garlic and tocino. Tocino is hard pig fat, used to give flavour to a lot of Spanish soups and stews. If you cannot get hold of it, use slices of jamón instead.

Serves 4

> 4 tablespoons olive oil, plus extra for drizzling
>
> 2 sweet chorizo, each 10cm long, cut into rounds
>
> 1 medium onion, roughly chopped
>
> 2 medium carrots, diced
>
> 100g tocino, cut into small pieces 1cm x 2cm
>
> 2 garlic cloves, thinly sliced
>
> 2 bay leaves (preferably fresh)
>
> 2 dried ñoras peppers, seeds and stalks removed, broken into small pieces, and covered with boiling water
>
> 250g small dried lentils, brown or green
>
> 2 morcilla (Spanish black sausage), each 10cm long
>
> 2 tablespoons roughly chopped fresh flat-leaf parsley
>
> sea salt and black pepper

Heat the olive oil in a large saucepan over a high heat. As it begins to smoke, add the chorizo and fry until brown. Remove and reserve the chorizo, reduce the heat to medium and add the onion, carrot, tocino and a pinch of salt. Fry for about 10 minutes until the vegetables are sweet and beginning to colour. Add the garlic, bay leaves and drained ñoras peppers and cook for 2 minutes more. Return the chorizo to the pan, adding the lentils and whole morcillas at the same time. Cover with 1 litre water and simmer gently for 20–30 minutes until the lentils are tender, adding a little extra water if the liquid falls below the surface of the lentils. Season with salt and pepper, and serve with the parsley on top, an extra drizzle of olive oil and lots of bread. This recipe can be easily adapted to other pulses, such as white beans or chickpeas.

CHICKPEAS WITH POMEGRANATE MOLASSES

Serves 4

> 450g home-cooked chickpeas (200g dry weight, see page 59),
> or 2 x 400g cans cooked chickpeas, drained and rinsed
>
> 4 tablespoons olive oil
>
> 3 garlic cloves, thinly sliced
>
> 3 tablespoons Pomegranate Molasses (see page 284)
>
> 200ml cold water, or a mixture of chickpea liquor and water
>
> about 60 threads saffron, infused in 4 tablespoons boiling water
>
> 3 tablespoons roughly chopped fresh coriander
>
> seeds of 1 pomegranate
>
> sea salt and black pepper

Place a large saucepan over a medium heat and add the olive oil. When hot but not smoking, add the garlic and fry until nutty brown. Now add the drained chickpeas, pomegranate molasses, water and saffron infusion and simmer for 10 minutes. Stir in the coriander and season with salt and pepper. Finally, sprinkle in the pomegranate seeds. Taste and serve with fish or on its own as part of a selection of mezze.

HOME-MADE AND
HOME-CURED

It is not that we want to become completely self-sufficient, but we genuinely enjoy making our own things, whether it is bread or yoghurt, or our new discoveries, cheese and pomegranate molasses. When you buy pomegranate molasses, it is delicious but brown in colour, whereas a fresh, home-made molasses is electric purple. None of the recipes below are difficult, just fun.

HOME-SALTED COD

This recipe does not produce bacalao, which is dried salt cod; it's more like bacalao verde, which is still moist. It has a good flavour, though, and you can use it instead of bacalao if you can't get hold of the real thing. Whole anchovies and filleted sardines can be salted in just the same way, but you must place a weight on top of them.

1kg cod fillet
1.25kg rock salt or very coarse sea salt

Cut up the cod fillets into pieces of your own choice, or leave whole. In a ceramic or stainless-steel dish, put a 1cm layer of rock salt and lay the fillets on top. Cover with the remaining salt and place in the fridge for 1–2 weeks. When you are ready to use the cod, wash off the salt and soak for a couple of hours in cold water.

BOQUERONES EN VINAGRE
MARINATED ANCHOVIES

1kg very fresh anchovies
4 garlic cloves, very finely chopped
2 tablespoons finely chopped fresh flat-leaf parsley
8 tablespoons good-quality white wine vinegar (see page 287)
4 tablespoons olive oil
fine sea salt

Fillet or butterfly the anchovies and arrange a quarter of them in one layer on a plate. Sprinkle over a quarter of the chopped garlic and parsley, followed by the vinegar, olive oil and a good pinch of salt. Continue until you have four layers. Place in the fridge and leave overnight. (They will keep for 1 week.) Eat on a buttered piece of toasted ciabatta with a salted anchovy – what the Spanish call a matrimonio (marriage) – or as you like.

KHLII

MOROCCAN PRESERVED MEAT

Walk through the medinas of Morocco and you will see buckets with ominous dark meat peering through white fat. This is khlii – marinated beef that is dried in the sun, then submerged in rendered fat to last indefinitely. We ate it only once in Morocco, as we waited for someone to load some tiles we had bought on to the camper-van. The khlii had been quickly fried with scrambled egg for breakfast, a fry-up Fez style. Importers found it impossible to bring over the real thing, so we developed our own, which unlike the original, you might be pleased to know, does not involve rendering large amounts of lamb fat from the tails of rare sheep. Our khlii is very easy, and although we use it predominantly with a green bean salad (see page 110), it is a fantastically useful snack to have around as it lasts for weeks.

Serves 4

> 250g beef brisket or lamb shanks, off the bone and trimmed of fat

MARINADE

> 2 tablespoons finely grated onion
>
> 3 teaspoons coriander seeds, ground
>
> 3 teaspoons cumin seeds, ground
>
> 4 garlic cloves, crushed to a very smooth paste with salt
>
> $^1/_2$ teaspoon hot paprika
>
> 1 tablespoon water
>
> 2 teaspoons fine sea salt

Preheat the oven to the very lowest it can go. Slice the meat across the grain (that means widthways rather than lengthways) into medallions 1cm thick, then pound with a mallet or rolling pin until 3mm thick. Mix all the marinade ingredients in a bowl, then spread evenly all over the lamb. The meat does not need to marinate for long (an hour or two) as it is so thin, but you can leave it longer if you wish. Spread out each piece of meat on a large baking tray or two and place in the very low oven for 3–4 hours. Turn each piece of lamb three times during this period so that it all dries evenly. When ready, the khlii should be very leathery, but not so dry as to be brittle. It is now ready to be eaten, or stored in an airtight container in the fridge.

MERGUEZ

We went to Al Fna market in Marrakech one evening before dusk. As we sipped mint tea on a terrace overlooking the square, we marvelled at how exotic it all was: snake-charmers piping pythons out of their baskets, monkeys cavorting, water-sellers in traditional attire, acrobats tumbling, men beating drums. The noise was deafening and never let up. As it got dark, we decided to investigate the food stalls. Thick swirling clouds of brochette-scented smoke greeted us, and it was hard to ignore the cries of the merguez vendors touting for custom. In the end, we headed for the busiest stall with the most locals. We watched as the little spiced sausages sizzled and spat on the charcoal brazier. We were soon handed a plate, along with some finely chopped tomato seasoned with harissa and coriander, and some bread. They were good.

Makes approx. 20 thin sausages, each 20cm long

8 metres lamb's sausage casings (narrow sausage skins)

850g lamb shank or shoulder meat, boned and trimmed of skin and sinew

200g lamb kidney fat (beef suet is an acceptable substitute)

2 rounded tablespoons sweet paprika

$1/2$ teaspoon freshly ground black pepper

1 tablespoon crushed dried rosebuds

2 teaspoons rosewater

$3/4$ teaspoon ground cinnamon

2 tablespoons Harissa (see page 282) or $1^1/2$ tablespoons dried crushed chilli

1 teaspoon roughly ground fennel seeds

1 tablespoon crushed cumin seeds

1 small bunch (30–40g) fresh coriander, washed, stalks retained

5 whole garlic cloves, peeled

$2-2^1/2$ teaspoons fine sea salt

Soak the casings in cold water, and run through once or twice by putting the end of the casings over the cold tap. Combine all the other ingredients in a bowl, then put everything through a fine die on a mincer. Load the casing on to the nozzle of a sausage stuffer and form into links 20cm long and the thickness of your little finger. Grill the sausages over a high heat until just cooked through but blistered on the outside.

Alternatively, if you have no mincer and sausage stuffer, ask your butcher to mince the meat and fat. Chop the coriander and crush it to a paste with all the spices, garlic and salt in a mortar or small food processor. Knead the spices into the meat and fat, then, if your butcher is unable to make sausages, form the mixture into small patties, which can be grilled or pan-fried on a high heat.

FRESH CHEESE
(WITH RENNET)

One day we were sitting on the terrace watching an insect similar to a bluebottle busily making a home in the cane of the shaded part of the veranda when there was a loud knock on the door. 'Tengo queso fresco. Quieres?' (I have fresh cheese. Do you want one?) Some five minutes later, the woman returned with a beautiful fresh cheese and a bunch of radishes from her huerto (allotment). Just a couple of days old, the cheese was soft, creamy and mildly goaty, made from the milk of her goats that roam around the foothills of the mountains munching wild herbs and jangling their bells, letting the goatherd and his dog know where they are. This inspired us to make our own cheese, which is so easy to do, provided you have what the Spanish call cuajo (rennet). Animal rennet comes from an enzyme extracted from the stomach of calves and lambs. Vegetarian rennet, often made from crushed cardoon flowers, is sometimes used in Spain and Morocco. You can buy both types of rennet on the Internet (see page 315) or in some supermarkets. We made our first batch of cheese with a gift of some goat's milk that arrived in a Sunny Delight bottle.

Makes approx. 1kg cheese
> 2.4 litres full-fat organic milk, goat's or cow's
> $1/2$ teaspoon rennet

Gently heat the milk to 32°C/90°F, then stir in the rennet. Transfer to a stainless-steel or glass bowl, cover with clingfilm, and leave in a warm place for half an hour until the curd starts to separate from the whey, and the milk sets. Cut the curd into 3cm squares with a thin knife to help release more of the whey. Cover and leave in a warm place for another hour. When the cheese is firm enough to lift with a slotted spoon, carefully transfer to a colander set within a bowl. Refrigerate for at least 6 hours or until the curds and whey have fully separated and the cheese is firm. If you want to speed up the process, cut the curd into smaller cubes.

FRESH CHEESE

(WITHOUT RENNET)

Makes approx. 1kg cheese

     2.4 litres full-fat organic milk, goat's or cow's

     5 tablespoons lemon juice

     1 teaspoon salt

Wet the bottom of a large saucepan (see recipe below), then pour in the milk, lemon juice and salt. Place over a low flame and slowly heat to 80°C/176°F. Stir very gently if you think the milk is sticking, but it is best not to stir at all. Remove from the heat and leave for 15 minutes, by which time you should have small curds surrounded by clearish whey. Strain through a sieve and leave to drain overnight in a cool place or the fridge. This cheese will have a finer grained curd and be less velvety than one made with rennet. Eat as is, or wrap in a couple of muslin cloths and store in the fridge. Press the parcel under a weight if you prefer a slightly firmer cheese.

HOME-MADE YOGHURT

Our brilliant head chef, David Cook, taught us the trick of putting a little bit of water at the bottom of the saucepan before adding milk and bringing it to the boil, as this stops the milk from catching and burning.

Makes approx. 1kg

     50ml cold water, just to cover the bottom of the saucepan

     2 litres full-fat organic milk

     200-250ml double cream, depending on how creamy you want it

     150g live yoghurt

Place the water in a large saucepan, followed by the milk (make sure the pan is no more than two-thirds full). Bring to the boil, then simmer gently and reduce, stirring occasionally, by a third to a half, until the milk is off-white. Remove the pan from the heat and transfer the milk to a ceramic or stainless-steel bowl. Add the cream and stir well. Allow to cool. When you are able to hold your finger in the milk and count to ten, add the yoghurt and stir well. If the milk is too hot when the live yoghurt culture is added, the bacteria may be killed. If it is not hot enough, it will take a lot longer to set. Cover with clingfilm and leave to stand in a warm place, wrapped in a cloth, for about 8 hours or overnight until set. Yoghurt keeps in the fridge for at least 7-10 days.

LABNEH

Labneh is an eastern Mediterranean cheese made from strained yoghurt.

Makes approx. 1kg

    1 kg Home-made Yoghurt (see page 279), or Greek yoghurt

    1 teaspoon fine sea salt

Place the yoghurt in a mixing bowl, add the salt and stir well. The amount of salt you need will depend on the acidity of the yoghurt; use just enough so you can taste it. Line a bowl with muslin or a fine cloth and spoon the yoghurt into the centre. Draw up the corners of the cloth and tie together with string or an elastic band. Suspend over a suitable place, either a sink or bowl, and leave overnight, or longer if necessary. The thickness of the labneh depends on how long you strain it for. The consistency of a thick mayonnaise is a good guide. Keep in the fridge until ready to use, or spread on a plate, drizzle with olive oil and scoop up with warm flatbread (see page 36). Labneh can also be spiced with chopped green chilli, garlic, soaked and softened fenugreek seeds and black onion seeds.

PRESERVED LEMONS

Preserved lemons are a great feature of North African cooking, especially in Morocco. They have a strong, distinctive flavour used to give character to tagines (stews), sauces, fish dishes and salads. In Morocco they preserve a special variety of lemon, which is almost impossible to find in the UK, so at Moro we use unwaxed, organic lemons instead. Below are two ways to preserve lemons: the traditional method, which takes at least two months, and a quick way, which takes five days.

For 10 lemons

> 10 unwaxed, organic lemons, washed and drained
>
> 1kg coarse sea salt
>
> 3 cinnamon sticks, broken up roughly
>
> 1 tablespoon coriander seeds
>
> 1 tablespoon whole cumin seed
>
> 1 teaspoon black peppercorns
>
> 1 teaspoon cloves
>
> 5 small dried red chillies
>
> 5 bay leaves (preferably fresh)
>
> juice of 8 extra lemons

Make a cross in the top of each lemon and continue to cut until two-thirds the way down. Open out slightly, pushing some salt inside each one and press together again. In a large, sterilised preserving jar of about 1.5 litres, alternate the salt with the spices and the lemons so that everything is more or less evenly packed in the jar. Press down on the lemons to help extrude some of the juice. Pour on the extra lemon juice to cover completely. Close the jar and leave at room temperature for about 2 months, or until the skins are soft all the way through. When you are ready to use a lemon, remove it from the jar, rinse under cold water to remove any excess salt, pull out and discard the pulp, then chop the skin as desired. Preserved lemons are deceptive in their strength, so only the smallest amount will be necessary in most recipes: although it may seem like nothing, beware adding more. The lemons should keep for up to a year in the fridge.

Paula Wolfert, in her book 'Couscous and Other Good Food from Morocco' (HarperPerennial), gives a quick way to make preserved lemons: boil them whole in water with lots of salt and the same spices as above until the skins are soft. Place in a jar with the cooking liquid and spices and leave to cure for 5 days. They do not last very long, so you could cover them in olive oil instead of the cooking liquid and keep them in the fridge.

HARISSA

This is our recipe for the harissa that we make at Moro. Recently we have tasted a few variations of harissa, and particularly like ones with either 2 tablespoons finely chopped preserved lemon added to the recipe below, or 2 tablespoons ground rosebuds or rosewater.

Serves 6–8

> 250g long, fresh red chillies
>
> sea salt
>
> 3 heaped teaspoons caraway seeds, ground
>
> 3 heaped teaspoons cumin seeds, ground
>
> 1 teaspoon black cumin seeds, ground (optional)
>
> 4 garlic cloves
>
> 100g piquillo peppers, or roasted and peeled red bell pepper (see page 78)
>
> 1 dessertspoon tomato purée
>
> 1 dessertspoon red wine vinegar
>
> 2 level teaspoons smoked paprika
>
> 4 tablespoons olive oil

Prepare the chillies as described on page 88. Blend them with a pinch of salt, half of each of the spice seeds and the garlic cloves until smooth. It is important that the chillies are as pulverised as possible, with no little bits. Add the peppers, the rest of the spice seeds, the tomato purée and vinegar, and blend again until very smooth. Transfer to a mixing bowl. Now add the olive oil. (It is important to add the oil at this stage, for if you add it to the food processor, it will turn the harissa a creamy colour.) Sprinkle the paprika on top of the oil and stir in. Taste and season with more salt to balance out the vinegar. Harissa keeps well in the fridge, but be sure to cover it with a little olive oil to seal it from the air.

POMEGRANATE MOLASSES

This recipe is for those who can't find this luscious syrup to buy, or don't wish to have extra bottles cluttering up their cupboard. Pomegranate molasses gives a sweet and sour fruity character to many soups, sauces and stews, and can also be used as a cordial. When we make our own molasses in the restaurant we use pomegranates from Turkey or Iran, which are in season from late October through to January. These are larger and redder than those usually seen in UK shops, and their juice is slightly tarter, which is desirable when using it for savoury cooking. The final product has a particularly beautiful colour, and the flavour has greater freshness and fruit than the bought molasses. If you use Spanish, slightly paler pomegranates, a dash of lemon can be added at the end to redress the sweet-sour balance (although it will not have the wonderful colour and flavour of Iranian pomegranates). As a guideline, one pomegranate makes 1–2 tablespoons of molasses.

You need a non-reactive saucepan (not aluminium or cast iron) that is the right size for the amount of molasses you are making. A potato ricer (which looks like a giant garlic crusher) is the best way to juice a pomegranate, but you could use a mouli instead.

First, cut the fruit into quarters and turn inside out to remove the red seeds. Discard every scrap of the bitter yellow pith, as it can adversely affect the flavour and colour of the molasses. Push the seeds through the potato ricer and strain the juice.

Transfer the juice to your pan and reduce over a medium heat until it looks syrupy on the back of a spoon. Remember, if you have the juice of 2 fruits, you should be left with around 4 tablespoons of syrup. If you have the juice of 6 fruits, you should be left with about 12 tablespoons. Be careful not to let the liquid caramelise or boil dry (speaking from experience!). We keep our molasses in a covered ramekin in the fridge.

HOME-CURED OLIVES

The olive harvest takes place between December and January, and some Cypriot and Turkish shops sell fresh, uncured olived at this time. If you do follow this recipe, we think it unlikely that you will ever have tasted such good olives. We learnt this particular method of curing in the Alpujarras.

> 2kg ripe black olives
> fine sea salt
> olive oil, to finish

CURING MARINADE
> 1 litre water (or to cover)
> 500ml red wine vinegar
> several sprigs of thyme or rosemary
> 8 garlic cloves, skin on
> peel of 1 orange
> 1 tablespoon coriander seeds
> 2 teaspoons fennel seeds
> 1 teaspoon black peppercorns
> 1 dried red pepper, broken up, or a couple of dried small red chillies

Make one or two little slits down to the stone in each olive. To remove the bitterness, cover in a brine solution (1:9 fine sea salt to water) and leave to soak for 3–4 months, changing the brine every 2 weeks.

Drain the olives and place in one or more storage jars, then add the remaining ingredients, seasoning well with salt to balance the vinegar. Leave for at least 1 month.

When the olives have acquired enough flavour, drain off the marinade and cover with olive oil.

DRIED LIMES

Dry out limes in the coolest oven of an Aga (the plate-warming oven, not the one below the roasting oven) for a week or until dry and crisp. Alternatively, set the electric or gas oven to the very lowest possible temperature, and leave the limes inside for 8 hours or until dry and crisp.

VINEGAR

Some opened wines, if forgotten on a kitchen shelf, will turn liverish-brown and develop a sediment. This could be the beginning of a vinegar 'mère' (mother) or culture. It is a rare and magical thing, though, and you can't rely on it happening, so you will probably have to buy a mother (see page 315). If it does happen, pour it into a large ceramic jar and double the volume with wine. If it turns to vinegar after 2 weeks at room temperature, you know you are on to something.

You can invest in an earthenware vinegar jar (see page 315), which allows you to siphon off the vinegar without disturbing the mother. If your vinegar tastes very sour, add more wine; if it tastes very winey, give it some time. At home we use our vinegar 3 times a week and usually replace the volume every week or two with fresh wine. Ideally, stick to red or white wines. We stick to red wine at home, but sometimes we add a slug of port or sweet sherry for character. (Never too much of these fortified wines, though, as mother does not like too much alcohol!)

The other vinegars that we find most useful are as follows:

SWEET VINEGAR

As the name suggests, these vinegars are sweet, light and fruity. The ones we buy specify single grape varieties – moscatel, chardonnay, cabernet sauvignon (Forum) or Pedro Ximénez – which are widely available. If necessary, balsamic vinegar can be used as a substitute, or add a little sugar to a good-quality red wine vinegar.

SHERRY VINEGAR

Strong with lots of flavour and body, the best sherry vinegars say 'reserva' or 'vieja' on the label, denoting quality and age (we use Valdespino at Moro). It's always worth buying the best sherry vinegar you can afford.

STANDARD WINE VINEGARS

Use these when you don't want an additional flavour to be part of the dish, but you need a high acidity to add a kick, as in harissa.

PUDDINGS AND CAKES

A sign of getting older since the first Moro book appeared is our increasing need for a pudding to finish off the meal. Here is a selection of puddings, some eccentric, some classic. We hope you enjoy them.

JEREZ CREAM

This is our Spanish version of the Italian pudding pannacotta, but instead of grappa, we use a combination of Jerez brandy and sweet, raisiny Pedro Ximénez sherry.

Serves 8

$1^1/_2$ vanilla pods

140g caster sugar

70ml brandy, preferably Spanish

110ml Pedro Ximénez sherry

800ml double cream

rind of $1^1/_2$ oranges

3 gelatine leaves, softened for 5 minutes in cold water

100ml milk

TO SERVE

300g fresh raspberries or blueberries, or 3 eating/blood oranges, segmented

Split the vanilla pods in half lengthways and scrape out the seeds. Mix the seeds with the sugar, brandy and sherry and set aside.

Place 550ml of the double cream in a saucepan with the orange rind and vanilla pods and bring to the boil. Simmer over a low heat for 10 minutes. Meanwhile, squeeze the gelatine dry and warm with the milk in a small saucepan until completely dissolved. Strain the cream mixture into a large bowl, and stir in the gelatine-milk. Once that has incorporated, stir in the alcohol mixture. Chill over ice until cool but not set. Lightly whip up the remaining cream and fold it into the vanilla cream mixture. Using a ladle or a jug, transfer the creamy mixture to eight small bowls, then cover and chill in the fridge for at least 6 hours, preferably overnight, until the pudding sets. If you want to turn them out, warm each bowl in some hot water for a few seconds, then invert on to a plate. Serve with the fruit on top or on the side.

ARROZ CON LECHE
RICE PUDDING

It is amazing how little rice one needs for this pudding. The secret is the time involved: a long, slow bake allows the rice to swell to its full potential.

Serves 6–8

> 100g pudding rice
> 1.2 litres milk
> 130g caster sugar
> 2 x 4–5cm cinnamon sticks
> rind of 2 small oranges, peeled in large strips with a potato peeler
> 1 teaspoon ground cinnamon (optional)

Preheat the oven to 150°C/300°F/Gas 2.

Mix all the ingredients, apart from the cinnamon, in a glass or ceramic baking dish and bake for $2^1/_2$–3 hours, stirring once after 45 minutes, until just solidified. Allow to cool for 30 minutes before serving; alternatively, serve chilled. Sprinkle with the cinnamon, if you like.

KATE'S SHERRY TRIFLE

Our friend Kate renewed our passion for trifle. The combination of a nutty, medium-sweet oloroso or cream sherry that is sprinkled over sponge, home-made custard and raspberry jam, cream and toasted almonds is sublime. We usually make the lower half of the trifle the day before it's needed so that the flavours mature together, then put the cream and almonds on top on the day. We serve this in the restaurant only as a celebratory Christmas treat.

Serves 8

> 1 quantity Old-fashioned Trifle Sponge (see opposite)
> 75g ratafia (or amaretti) biscuits
> 200ml oloroso or cream sherry
> 250g good-quality seedless raspberry jam
> 300g raspberries (fresh or frozen)

1 quantity Custard (see overleaf)

350ml double cream

150g whole blanched almonds, toasted until golden

2 tablespoons icing sugar

To assemble the trifle, have ready a largish (glass) bowl, about 25cm in diameter, or, if you prefer, 8 individual glass bowls. Break up the sponge into large chunks and place in the bottom of the bowl, interspersing the pieces with the ratafia biscuits. Sprinkle with the sherry and let it sit for a few minutes to soak in. Heat the jam until melted, stir in the raspberries and barely warm them through. Spoon over the sponge, then pour the custard on top. Up to here, the trifle can be prepared a day or a few hours in advance.

Just before you are going to eat the trifle, whisk the cream until it is thick, then spoon on top of the custard. When the almonds are cool, chop roughly, toss with the icing sugar and sprinkle over the trifle. Enjoy!

OLD-FASHIONED TRIFLE SPONGE

2 eggs

110g caster sugar

45g plain flour

25g cornflour

1 teaspoon baking powder

Preheat the oven to 180°C/350°F/Gas 4.

Whisk the eggs lightly, then add the sugar and whisk for 20 minutes until very thick and pale. Sieve the flours with the baking powder and fold through the egg mixture. Pour into a buttered and floured 500g loaf tin on a baking sheet. Bake for 20–25 minutes on the middle shelf. If it browns too much, cover with baking parchment. Allow to cool on a wire rack before using.

CUSTARD

1 vanilla pod

100g caster sugar

1 tablespoon cornflour

4 egg yolks

2 eggs

420ml milk

300ml double cream

rind of $^2/_3$ lemon, in large, thin strips, without the pith

Halve the vanilla pod lengthways and scrape the seeds into a large bowl. Add the sugar and cornflour. Slowly whisk in the egg yolks and eggs until incorporated. Place the milk, cream, lemon rind and vanilla pod in a saucepan and simmer gently together for 5 minutes. Slowly strain the hot liquid into the egg mixture, whisking constantly. Return the custard to the pan, put over a medium to low heat, and whisk until thickened and just about to bubble. Remove the pan from the heat, pour the custard into a bowl and cool in iced water to room temperature. If the custard goes lumpy while you are cooking it, place the pan in iced water and whisk well.

DATES WITH COFFEE AND CARDAMOM

The classic Arab flavours of coffee and cardamom go particularly well with dates. Although this dessert takes a matter of minutes to put together, it is best made at least one day before needed to allow the dates to soak up the coffee.

Serves 4

400g dates, preferably Medjool

500ml strong black coffee (espresso strength)

1 teaspoon caster sugar

20 green cardamom pods, lightly crushed

1 cinnamon stick, broken in half

200–250g Labneh (see page 280), or Greek yoghurt

Stone the dates carefully to keep their shape, and place in a bowl. Heat the coffee with the sugar and cardamom until just before it begins to boil, then pour over the dates. Leave to infuse with the cinnamon in the fridge overnight or for up to 2 days. Serve chilled with labneh or yoghurt.

PISTACHIO AND ALMOND TART WITH ORANGE AND CARDAMOM

We have been struggling on and off for a few months, without success, to make a good nut tart for the book. Enter Jacob, one of our former chefs who has returned for a few months. Being the talented young man that he is, he immediately set about experimenting and came up with this recipe. The tart is simply a rich, aromatic pistachio paste baked on to the crumbliest butter pastry. The only tricky bit is finding blanched pistachios. The easiest route is to get nibbed pistachios (which always have the best colour) from an Iranian shop (see pages 314–15); the harder route is to blanch and peel the pistachios yourself. Otherwise, supermarkets sell shelled, unsalted pistachios for baking, although the colour is not as vibrant.

Serves 12

PASTRY CASE

> 225g plain flour
>
> $^1/_2$ teaspoon fine salt
>
> 50g caster sugar
>
> 12 green cardamom pods, black seeds only, ground to a powder
>
> 250g butter
>
> 1 egg yolk

FILLING

> 200g blanched almonds
>
> 300g blanched pistachios
>
> 250g caster sugar
>
> 15 green cardamom pods, black seeds only, ground to a powder ($^1/_4$ teaspoon)
>
> 150ml orange juice
>
> 4 egg yolks
>
> finely grated zest of 1 medium orange

GLAZE

> 1 egg yolk
>
> 2 tablespoons milk or cream

First make the pastry case. Combine the dry ingredients in a food processor with the butter, and pulse until only small lumps of butter remain. Add the egg yolk and process for 20 seconds more, then turn out into a bowl and bring together by hand.

Form the pastry into a flat disc 1–2cm thick, and refrigerate until chilled, at least half an hour. Roll out on a cool, floured work surface to a rough circle 4–5mm thick – don't worry if it cracks a little – and use to line a 24cm tart tin right up to the rim. Prick the base and freeze (this can all be done well in advance).

Preheat the oven to 180°C/350°F/Gas 4.

To cook, take the still-frozen base and line with baking parchment, fill with baking beans and bake in the preheated oven for 20 minutes, until the pastry has set. Then remove the beans and parchment and continue to bake until the pastry is an even, light gold colour.

While the pastry shell is cooling, make the filling. Put the nuts, sugar, and cardamom in a food processor and grind until very, very fine. When ready, the nuts will have begun to release their oil and cake together. Slowly add the orange juice to make a very thick, smooth paste – let the machine run for a while, and stop only when you're happy with the consistency or fear the motor will overheat. Let the paste cool for a few minutes, as it will have become quite warm during the blending process. Finally, add the egg yolks and orange zest and process until incorporated.

Spread the filling into the shell and smooth with a wet spatula; it should be thick and sticky, so be careful not to break your pastry. Bake at the same temperature as above for 10–15 minutes to dry the surface, then brush on the glaze (made by mixing the egg yolk and milk or cream). Continue to bake for a further 10 minutes, or until golden.

FLAN DE NARANJA

ORANGE FLAN

Flan is the crème caramel of Spain. We are fond of flan, though it can be too sweet, which is why we prefer one made with orange. This recipe is adapted from 'The Spanish Kitchen' by Nicholas Butcher (Macmillan).

Serves 4

> 6 large organic or free-range egg yolks
>
> 60g caster sugar
>
> 300ml freshly squeezed orange juice, unstrained (make sure you use
>   delicious oranges!)

Preheat the oven to 120°C/250°F/Gas $^1/_2$.

Whisk the egg yolks with the sugar until thick, light and fluffy. Gradually add the orange juice, whisking all the time, making sure you scrape all the whisked egg yolk from the sides and bottom of the bowl. Pour into four ramekins and place them in a bain-marie: make sure the water in the bain-marie is cold to start with and comes up to the level of the top of the orange/egg mixture. Bake for $1^1/_2$ hours. The top will become a nice caramel colour and the flan, which only just sets, will be deliciously creamy and orangey with a clean flavour. Refrigerate before serving.

CHOCOLATE, CHESTNUT AND ALMOND CAKE

We especially like the organic chestnuts from Sierra Rica, supplied by Brindisa (see page 314).

Serves 8–10

> 180g butter, plus extra for greasing
>
> flour, for dusting
>
> 200g vacuum-packed chestnuts
>
> milk, for soaking
>
> 180g sugar
>
> 180g whole blanched almonds, medium ground in a food processor
>
> 200g chocolate containing 70% cocoa solids, such as Valrhona or Green and Black's, roughly chopped
>
> 5 large eggs, separated

Preheat the oven to 160°C/325°F/Gas 3. Take a 20cm spring-form pan, line the bottom with greaseproof paper, and butter and flour the inside.

Place the chestnuts in a saucepan, cover with milk and simmer gently for about 5–10 minutes until soft, then drain, cool and chop roughly.

While the chestnuts are softening, beat the butter with 140g of the sugar in a mixer until very light, pale and fluffy. Then add the egg yolks, one by one, and transfer to a bowl. Stir in the chopped almonds, chocolate and chestnuts. Whip up the whites until foamy, add the remaining sugar and whip until just firm. Gently fold the whites into the nut mixture in two additions. Put the mixture into the prepared tin and bake in the oven for 50 minutes. To check if it is ready, give the tin a gentle shake: if the filling is still wobbly, it needs more cooking.

ORANGE AND DATE SALAD
WITH ROSEWATER

This salad is a traditional and refreshing end to any meal. The additional sprinkling of rosewater makes it exotic and fragrant.

Serves 4

> 4 large juicy oranges (or 5–6 blood oranges in the winter)
>
> 8–12 dates (in season), preferably Medjool, stoned and broken up roughly or quartered lengthways
>
> a generous sprinkling of rosewater (about 2–3 tablespoons)
>
> a handful of small fresh mint leaves
>
> a fine dusting of icing sugar
>
> $^1/_2$ teaspoon ground cinnamon
>
> a small handful of dried rose petals (optional)

With a sharp knife, cut the rind off each orange, leaving no bitter yellow pith. Slice each orange into rounds, discard any seeds and arrange on a plate. Scatter the dates over the orange, then sprinkle the rosewater on top. Scatter with mint leaves, then dust with icing sugar and cinnamon. Finish with a few rose petals.

MAGDALENAS

A beautiful maiden named Magdalena, who lived on the route to Santiago, is said to have given these little cakes to passing pilgrims. This is our version of them.

Makes approx. 18–24

> 125g butter, plus extra for greasing
>
> 125g caster sugar
>
> 2 eggs
>
> finely grated zest of $^1/_2$ lemon
>
> 50g plain yoghurt
>
> 125g plain flour
>
> 1 teaspoon baking powder
>
> 100g pine nuts
>
> 100g raisins, soaked in 100ml Pedro Ximénez sherry for 1 hour
>
> granulated sugar for the top, to give it crunch

Preheat the oven to 200°C/400°F/Gas 6. Grease 2 muffin tins or madeleine moulds.

In a processor, cream the butter and sugar very well for about 5–10 minutes, stopping the machine occasionally to scrape the butter and sugar back into the centre of the bowl. When pale, light and fluffy, slowly mix in the eggs, one at a time, along with the lemon zest and yoghurt. Transfer to a bowl and fold in the flour and baking powder. When they are mixed in, add the pine nuts, raisins and sherry. Spoon into the prepared tins or moulds, sprinkle with granulated sugar, and bake in the oven for 10–15 minutes until golden brown. Remove and cool on a rack.

SEVILLE ORANGE ICE-CREAM

This is a fantastic orange ice-cream made with bitter Seville oranges that are in season around the middle of December. In Andalucía, these orange trees line the streets of many towns. We like to serve the ice-cream in hollowed-out oranges, just as we used to get it on the beach in France as kids. As Seville oranges have such a short season, using half sweet orange juice and half lemon juice (to taste) is a good alternative.

Serves 8 (makes just over 1 litre)
> 1 vanilla pod
> 220g caster sugar (to taste)
> finely grated zest of 2 Seville oranges
> 7 egg yolks
> 300ml milk
> 600ml double cream
> 1 x 5cm cinnamon stick
> 200–250ml Seville orange juice (to taste)

Halve the vanilla pod and scrape the seeds into a large bowl. Add the sugar, orange zest and egg yolks, and whisk until pale and fluffy. Place the milk, cream, vanilla pod and cinnamon in a saucepan and simmer gently together for 5 minutes. Slowly strain the hot liquid into the egg mixture, whisking constantly. Return the mixture to the pan, put over a medium to low heat and whisk until thickened (do not allow it to boil). Remove from the heat, pour into a bowl and place over iced water to cool. As the mixture cools, add the orange juice, and taste to make sure you have the right balance between orange and sugar. Churn in an ice-cream machine.

TURRÓN AND COFFEE ICE-CREAM

A delicious home-made coffee ice-cream is given a Spanish twist with turrón (Spanish nougat), preferably one with almonds in it.

Serves 8 (makes just over 1 litre)

> 1 vanilla pod
> 150g caster sugar
> 7 egg yolks
> 300ml milk
> 600ml double cream
> 2 tablespoons freshly ground coffee
> 2 small handfuls whole coffee beans
> 1 x 5cm cinnamon stick
> instant coffee to taste (about 3–5 tablespoons)
> 200g almond turrón, cut into small pieces

Halve the vanilla pod and scrape the seeds into a large bowl. Add the sugar and egg yolks, and whisk until pale and fluffy. Place the milk, cream, vanilla pod, ground coffee, coffee beans and cinnamon in a saucepan and simmer gently together for 5 minutes. Slowly strain the hot liquid through a colander into the egg mixture, whisking constantly. Return the mixture to the pan and put over a medium to low heat, add the instant coffee to taste and whisk until thickened (do not allow it to boil). Churn in an ice-cream machine. Once it is frozen, fold in the chopped turrón and put in the freezer for around an hour to firm up.

BLOOD ORANGE AND ROSEWATER SORBET

Oranges and rosewater are a traditional combination in Morocco, and sometimes for breakfast we have freshly squeezed orange juice with a few splashes of rosewater mixed in. This heavenly scented sorbet is along the same lines.

Serves 6

        200g caster sugar

        100–150ml rosewater, to taste

        600ml blood orange juice

        finely grated zest of $^1/_2$ blood orange

        a squeeze of lemon

Place the sugar and rosewater in a small saucepan over a low heat until the sugar has dissolved. Simmer for a couple of minutes until a thin syrup has formed. Allow to cool. Add the syrup to the orange juice along with the zest and a squeeze of lemon, to taste. Churn in an ice-cream machine, or place in a freezer, stirring the sorbet by hand every half-hour for the first 2 hours to prevent crystallisation. This is wonderfully refreshing, and delicious with crispy biscuits.

YOGHURT ICE-CREAM

The yoghurt makes this slightly sharper than ordinary ice-cream If you make a large batch for a party, you could offer an assortment of toppings for people to choose from. We give several ideas below and opposite.

Serves 4–6

      3 large egg whites

      200g caster sugar

      750g Greek yoghurt

Mix the egg whites with the sugar and heat over a low flame or in a bain-marie, stirring constantly, until steaming hot but not boiling (around 80°C/176°F). Transfer to a bowl and whisk for 10–15 minutes until you have a cool, stiff and fluffy meringue texture. Still whisking, add the yoghurt and continue to whisk until incorporated, then transfer to an ice-cream machine and churn until frozen.

POACHED CHERRIES AND CRUSHED SWEET ALMONDS

      400g cherries

      rind of 1 lemon

      50g caster sugar (to taste, depending on the sweetness of the

         cherries and your palate)

      lemon juice, if necessary

      $^1/_2$ quantity Crushed Sweet Almonds (see page 216)

Stone the cherries, keeping them whole if possible, and put them in a saucepan with the lemon rind and caster sugar. Add enough water to come halfway up the cherries, then bring to a simmer and cook for 5 minutes, or until the liquid has reduced to about 6 tablespoons. Taste for sweetness, adding more sugar or a squeeze of lemon as necessary. Remove the lemon rind and chill the cherries before using. Serve the ice-cream in small bowls with the cherries spooned around and almonds scattered on top.

SOUR CHERRY SYRUP WITH PISTACHIO AND POMEGRANATE

8 tablespoons sour cherry syrup (from an Iranian shop, see page 314), or
 Pomegranate Molasses (see page 284)
seeds of 2 pomegranates
150g nibbed pistachios (from an Iranian shop, see page 314), or chopped
 raw pistachios

Serve ice-cream in individual bowls with this syrup poured around it and the seeds
and nuts scattered over the top.

PINE NUTS WITH APRICOTS AND MINT

150g pine nuts
250g semi-dried or dried apricots
20 stems fresh mint, tips and small leaves only (use the remaining big
 leaves and stalks for fresh mint tea)

Toast the pine nuts in a 180°C/350°F/Gas 4 oven until golden, and cool before using.
Coarsely chop the apricots and scatter with the pine nuts and mint over the ice-cream.

WALNUTS AND HONEY

200g shelled walnuts
8 tablespoons orange-blossom honey (or any other runny honey)

Blanch the walnuts in plenty of unsalted boiling water, then drain and dry out in a
cool oven (140°C/275°F/Gas 1), being careful not to let them brown. Cool and serve
scattered over the ice-cream, with the honey drizzled over everything.

PRUNE ICE-CREAM WITH OLOROSO SHERRY

120g prunes, stoned

100ml sweet oloroso sherry

1 vanilla pod

7 egg yolks

120g caster sugar

600ml double cream

300ml milk

1 x 5cm cinnamon stick

150g whole blanched almonds, lightly roasted, then roughly chopped

Roughly chop each prune into about 6 pieces and soak in the oloroso sherry. Halve the vanilla pod lengthways, scrape out the seeds and place them with the egg yolks and sugar in a large bowl. Put the pod in a medium saucepan with the cream, milk and cinnamon, and bring to a gentle simmer over a medium to low heat. Leave simmering for 5–10 minutes. While the cream is heating, use an electric whisk to beat the egg yolks until thick, light and fluffy. Still whisking, slowly pour the hot cream through a sieve into the yolks. Return the whole mixture to the pan, place over a medium to low heat and stir continually until the mixture thickens (do not allow it to boil). Chill over ice, covered with clingfilm, before churning in an ice-cream machine. When the ice-cream is made, fold in the soaked prunes and sherry, and put in the freezer for at least an hour to firm up. Serve with the almonds scattered over.

ANISE BISCUITS

One of our favourite breakfasts in Spain is a strong café con leche (milky coffee) with Innes Rosales anise biscuits from Seville. The following recipe is for a simple tuile biscuit containing whole anise seeds, but you could use 100g roughly chopped unsalted pistachios instead. These biscuits make a perfect accompaniment to any ice-cream or sorbet.

Makes approx. 40 biscuits

> 170g butter
> 170g caster sugar
> 170g plain flour
> 3 tablespoons finely ground almonds
> 1 rounded tablespoon anise seeds
> 1 tablespoon brandy
> 3 egg whites
> 150g flaked almonds
> 150g granulated sugar

Preheat the oven to 160°C/325°F/Gas 3.

Cream the butter and caster sugar together until light and fluffy, then beat in the flour, ground almonds and anise seeds. Still beating, slowly add the brandy and egg whites until evenly incorporated. This mixture can be used immediately, or made up to 2 days in advance if kept refrigerated.

Line an aluminium baking sheet with baking parchment, and dollop heaped teaspoons of the dough on the tray at 10cm intervals. Drop the dough from a great height (1 metre or just under) so that it splats out, or use the back of your spoon to flatten the biscuits slightly into discs about 3cm across if you're worried you might not be able to aim accurately. Sprinkle liberally with the flaked almonds and granulated sugar. Bake for 20 minutes in the preheated oven until evenly golden and crisp. (For biscuits with a crunchy edge and softer centre, bake for around 7 minutes at 200°C/400°F/Gas 6 until brown at the edges with a pale yellow-gold middle.)

APPENDIX

The following information is our personal point of view – an insight into what informs the choices we make when buying food for the home and restaurant.

ORGANIC AND WHAT IT MEANS TO US

At Moro we use two English organic growers who always have priority while their produce is in season. Yes, organic food is better for you, and yes, it probably should taste better as well, yet there are other important factors in choosing to go organic.

At this point, we tend to get partisan in our argument. If you buy British organic produce, you are supporting local nature and rural employment. Without the use of blanket pesticides and monocrops, insects and wild plants re-colonise areas depleted by conventional farming, and birds and small mammals soon follow. Organic agriculture tends to use older varieties of crop plants, chosen for their superior taste and quality, as well as their natural resistance to pests and disease. These varieties tend to give one-third lower yield to the farmer, as well as being difficult to store and transport. On average, for every person employed on a conventional, intensive farm, three would be required for organic farming.

Many perceive organic produce to be overpriced, but the added costs to the farmer more than justify the price being asked; and the added benefits to our countryside (as well as to ourselves) surely justify paying it. We don't buy organic flour – or any other organic produce – just for organic's sake: we make sure it comes from Britain to help support rural life and land in this country.

CHICKEN

Chickens can be victims of bad diet, conditions and chemicals. At Moro most of our chickens come from a farm in Cornwall, where they are bred and raised organically and free range. We also buy French blackleg chickens, which have good feed and welfare conditions.

LAMB

Lamb is, relatively speaking, a safe meat. At Moro we try to use only British lamb, and get most of our supplies direct from two Scottish estates. Not only do the farmers get a reasonable price, but we can monitor the quality closely (we know what breed it is and how long it has been hung for, and can have it butchered exactly as we want). It is always preferable if your butcher or supermarket can state exactly where the meat has come from, so read the labels.

PORK

Like chicken, most pork production leaves much to be desired, whether buying from a local butcher or a supermarket. It is important there is some sort of traceability and that the animal has been reared in better than average conditions (small or local farms, free range and/or organic). The pork we buy at Moro is a variety called Middle White. It is less lean than the predominantly used long white, and therefore has a better flavour and is less dry. We buy from two different farms that are not organic, but rear responsibly on a small scale.

BEEF

Most beef for sale in this country comes from Herefords (milk cows). Their meat is very lean and therefore pretty tasteless. The breeds traditionally used for beef include Dexter, Aberdeen Angus and Long Horn. Again, the breed is important, but it has to go hand in hand with some sort of knowledge or guarantee that it has been well reared. At Moro we buy Long Horn directly from a farm in Herefordshire.

FISH

Just as we are being told that fish is really good for us, we are also told that the stocks of most species are seriously in decline because of indiscriminate trawling in virtually every part of the world. Our main supplier fishes off the coast of Essex using mainly lines rather than nets. This is a more sustainable way of fishing, and also means that the fish reach us in better condition.

PRAWNS

It is not that easy to source good, fresh prawns in Britain. Those still in their shells definitely have the best flavour, and the two varieties most available are North Atlantic/Greenland prawns, which are usually sold cooked and frozen, or the larger, slightly inferior raw tiger prawns. North Atlantic prawns can be used straight away as they are already cooked, but if heating them through, always add at the end so that they retain their juiciness. Tiger prawns need a little longer to cook, but not much – just until they go pink. Of course, if you can find fresh prawns, all the better. Small brown shrimps are delicious, and Scottish langoustines, though expensive, are wonderful.

The shells of prawns make an unbelievable difference to the flavour of stocks for paellas, pilavs or soups. Keep in the fridge or refreeze them.

VEGETABLES

The first spring vegetables we buy are broad beans from Turkey, Jordan or Spain in late February, early March. We buy only in season, starting in the Mediterranean and finishing in Britain. We believe that better varietals grown in season with a more natural style of agriculture have a superior flavour and texture. Fruits and vegetables need to be grown in a climate and environment that suits them, not the farmer; most soft fruits need sun and heat, which is why tomatoes force-grown in England or Holland before July or after September are so tasteless. See our list opposite for optimum buying times.

VEGETABLES, FRUIT AND THEIR SEASONS

Italics = Mediterranean dates

Artichokes, globe: *November–April*
Artichokes, Jerusalem: October–December
Asparagus: *March–April*; May–mid June
Aubergines: *May–September*
Beans, broad: *mid-March/April–May*; May/June–July
Beans, green: August–September
Beans, runner: August–September
Beetroot (small with leaves): May–August

Blackberries: August–September
Cabbage, white: November–March
Carrots: April/May–July/August
Cauliflower: February–early May and late June–November
Celery: October–April
Chard: summer and spring
Chestnuts: October–November
Chicory: October–May
Courgettes: *May–July*; August–September
Fennel: *November–January*
Garlic leaves, wild: March–April
Grapes: *September–November*

Leeks: October–March
Lemons: *December–February*
Mangoes (Alfonso from Pakistan): *May–June*
Morels: April–May
Mushrooms, wild: August/September–November
Oranges (Seville & blood): *December– February*
Parsnips: October–March
Peas: *mid March–April*; August
Peppers: *July/August*
Pomegranates: *October–January*
Potatoes, new: June–August
Pumpkin/squash: September–November

Quinces: *September–November;* October, November
Radishes: June–August
Raspberries: July–September
Spinach: mid March–July/August
Spring greens: February–April
Sprouting broccoli: *February–April*; March–April
Strawberries: August–September
Sweetcorn: *June–July*; August–September
Tomatoes: *April–July*; July–September
Turnips (small with leaves): *April–June*; December–March

BASIC STOCKS

Chicken stock
Makes approx. 1½-2 litres

1 large chicken carcass with giblets, leg bones and wings if possible
1 large carrot, chopped in half length ways
1 large onion, skin on, halved
1 head garlic, cut in half horizontally
2 sticks celery
3 bay leaves
1 teaspoon whole black peppercorns
2 sprigs flat-leaf parsley
a few fennel seeds (optional)
sea salt and black pepper

To make a light chicken stock:
Place all the ingredients in a large saucepan or stockpot and cover with cold water (about 4 litres). Bring to the boil, then turn down the heat to a gentle simmer, skimming off any scum. Simmer for 1½–2 hours until the stock has reduced by roughly half and acquired a good smell and colour. Do not boil the stock too fast as this can make it go cloudy. Strain through a chinois or fine mesh sieve and allow to cool completely. Skim the fat from the top with a ladle, or freeze the stock and simply peel off the solidified fat.

To make a dark chicken stock:
Split the carcass in half and put on a large roasting tray along with the giblets, wings and legs. Also put the carrot and onion, cut-sides-down, on the tray. Roast at 220°C/425°F/Gas 7 for 1 hour, until well browned, then deglaze the roasting tray with a little water. Tip the roasted chicken and vegetables into a large saucepan, scraping their juices in too. Add the remaining ingredients, and follow the directions for light chicken stock.

Fish stock
Makes approx. 2 litres

head (without gills) and bones of
    1 large white fish (turbot, seabass, brill or cod – about 1.5kg)
1 tablespoon olive oil
20 frozen or fresh prawns, shells on
1 carrot
1 medium onion, skin on, halved
1 head garlic, cut in half horizontally
2 sticks celery
2 tomatoes, halved, or ½ x 400g tin whole plum tomatoes
½ fennel bulb, quartered, or 1 teaspoon whole fennel seeds
3 bay leaves
1 teaspoon whole black peppercorns
2 sprigs flat-leaf parsley

Give the head and bones a good wash under cold water until the water more or less runs clear. Put a large saucepan over a medium heat and fry the prawns in the oil until they smell sweet, like grilled seafood. Add the fish head and bones along with all the other ingredients. Generously cover with cold water (3-4 litres). Bring to the boil, then turn down the heat to a gentle simmer, skimming off any scum. Simmer for 15-20 minutes, no longer, otherwise the stock will not taste fresh. Strain through a chinois or fine-mesh sieve. Taste and reduce a bit more to intensify the flavour if it tastes a little watery.

Vegetable stock
Makes approx. 2 litres

2 heads garlic, cut in half horizontally
3 sticks celery
1 large onion, halved
1 medium leek, washed
1 large carrot, halved
2 tomatoes, halved
5 slices dried ceps or 5 medium chestnut mushrooms
3 bay leaves
5 sprigs thyme
5 sprigs parsley
1 dried ñoras pepper, seeds removed (optional, for Spanish recipes only)
½ head fennel or 1 teaspoon fennel seeds
1 teaspoon whole black peppercorns

Put all the ingredients in a large saucepan and cover generously with water (about 3 litres). Bring to the boil over a high heat, then reduce the heat to low so it's barely bubbling. Cook for 1-1½ hours, then strain through a fine-meshed sieve.

SUPPLIERS

The following addresses all have a good general selection of ingredients, and many also sell specialist items. Some will order things not in stock, so always ask.
For full details please log on to our website, www.moro.co.uk

LONDON

T. Adamou & Sons, W4 (Cypriot Greek)
020 8994 0752
Alsur, N4 (Spanish products)
020 8374 3544
contact: Hannah
Archie, W4 (Lebanese)
020 7229 2275
La Belle Boucherie, NW1 (Middle Eastern)
020 7258 0230
Brindisa (wholesale)
020 8772 1600
(www.brindisa.com)
Brindisa retail:
Brindisa at Exmouth Market, EC1
020 7713 1666
Brindisa at Borough Market, SE1
020 7407 1036
Damas Gate, W12 (Middle Eastern)
020 8743 5116
East Dulwich Deli, SE22
020 8693 2525
Extravaganza, E2
020 7613 0303
Fortnum & Mason, W1
020 7734 8040
R. Garcia and Sons, W11 (Spanish)
020 7221 6119
Green Valley, W1 (Lebanese)
020 7402 7385
Harvey Nichols, SW1
Fifth Floor Food Market
020 7235 5000
Jeroboams, W11
020 7727 9359
Khayam Supermarket, W1 (Iranian/Persian)
Tel: 020 7258 3910
Lebanese Food Centre, W3
020 8740 7365
Lisboa Delicatessen, W10 (Portuguese – good for salt cod)
020 8969 1052

MacFarlane's, SW4
020 8673 5373
Le Maroc, W10 (Moroccan)
020 8968 9783
Le Marrakech, W10 (Moroccan)
020 8964 8307
Andreas Michli & Son, N4 (Cypriot)
020 8802 0188
Mortimer & Bennett, W4
Tel: 020 8995 4145
Nomades Moroccan Recipes Ltd, SW9
020 7733 3722
Persepolis, SE15 (Iranian)
020 7639 8007
Reza Patisserie, W8 (Iranian/Persian)
020 7603 0924 (mail order)
Rias Altas, NW8 (Spanish)
020 7262 4340
Sayell Foods Ltd, N1
020 7256 1080
www.sayellfoods.co.uk
Selfridges Food Hall, W1
08708 377377
(general enquiries for all stores)
Sorour, SW15 (Iranian/Persian)
020 8974 5955
The Spice Shop, W11
020 7221 4448
www.thespiceshop.co.uk
Super Bahar, W8 (Iranian/Persian)
020 7603 5083
Turkish Food Centres
TFC Dalston, E8
020 7254 6754
TFC Leytonstone, E11
020 8558 8149
TFC Harringay, N4
020 8340 4547
TFC Lewisham, SE13
020 8318 0436
TFC Croydon
020 8681 7631

Vallebona, SW19 (cured fish roe/bottarga)
020 8944 5665
Villandry, W1
020 7631 3131
Yasar Halim, N4 (Turkish)
020 8340 8090
Yasar Halim, N13 (Turkish)
020 8882 0397
Yasar Halim, W12 (Turkish)
020 8740 9477
Zen, W2 (Lebanese)
020 7792 2058

REST OF ENGLAND

AVON
Olive Garden Delicatessen
(especially Spanish)
Tel: 01275 341222

BIRMINGHAM
Harvey Nichols
0121 616 6000
House of Fraser
08701 607225
Selfridges
08708 377377
(general enquiries for all stores)

BRISTOL
Chandos Deli
(several branches; good Spanish selection)
0117 973 5222
www.chandosdeli.com
Fresh and Wild
(Spices, harissa, pulses)
0117 910 5930
Spice Route (Persian/Middle Eastern)
0117 904 0040

CAMBRIDGE
The Cambridge Cheese Company
01223 328 672

CHESHIRE
DeFine Food and Wine
01606 882101

CORNWALL
Café Citron
01872 274144
Entre Amigos
01752 603007
www.entreamigos.co.uk

DEVON
Effings
01803 863435
Riverford Farm Shop
01803 762 523

EAST SUSSEX
The Cheese Shop
(Spanish and Moroccan)
01273 601129
Trencherman & Turner
01323 737535
(also mail order)

GLOUCESTER-SHIRE
Maby's Food and Wine
(wide range of Brindisa products, plus some Moroccan)
01451 870071

HEREFORDSHIRE
Ceci Paolo
The New Cook's Emporium
01531 632976
Hay Wholefoods & Deli
01497 820708

KENT
Williams & Brown Delicatessen
Whitstable (mainly Spanish ingredients)
01227 274507

LEEDS
Harvey Nichols Food Market
0113 204 8888

Maumoniat International
Supermarket (limited
Spanish & Middle
Eastern supplies)
0113 276 1515

LINCOLNSHIRE
Simpole Clarke
01780 480646 (also
mail order)
www.simpole-clarke.com

LIVERPOOL
Matta (good range of
Middle Eastern produce)
0151 709 3031
Number Seven Deli
0151 709 9633

MANCHESTER
Harvey Nichols
0161 828 8888
Love Saves the Day
Delicatessen
0161 834 2266
Selfridges Food Hall
08708 377377
(general enquiries for
all stores)

NORTH
YORKSHIRE
Arcimboldo's (good
Spanish selection)
01423 508760
Roberts & Speight
01482 870717

SHROPSHIRE
Appleyards Delicatessen
01743 240180

SUFFOLK
Bailey's
01502 710609

NORTHERN
IRELAND

BELFAST
Asia Supermarket
(some Moroccan items)
0289 032 6396
The Olive Tree (some
Spanish ingredients)
0289 064 8898

SCOTLAND

EDINBURGH
Dionika Ltd
0131 556 3890
Harvey Nichols
0131 524 8388
Lupe pintos
0131 228 6241
Valvona & Crolla
0131 556 6066 (also
mail order)
www.valvonacrolla.co.uk

GLASGOW
Andreas (Greek/Cypriot)
0141 576 5031
Heart Buchanan
0141 334 7626
Lupe pintos
0141 334 5444
I. J. Mellis (fabulous
cheese but also a few
Spanish ingredients)
0141 339 8998
Scherezade
(Middle Eastern)
0141 334 2121

WALES

CARDIFF
Continental Deli
(Arab ingredients)
029 2045 2540

ARGAN OIL
www.wildwoodgroves.com

COUSCOUSSIERS
Available from Le Maroc
and Le Marrakech (see
page 314)

FARMERS'
MARKETS
London
020 7359
1936www.lfm.org.uk
Nationwide
Send an SAE for list to:
National Association of
Farmers' Markets
PO Box 575
Southampton SO15 7BZ

MORTARS &
PESTLES
John Julian Design
www.johnjuliandesign.
com
020 7249 6969

OLIVES &
PRESERVED
LEMONS
The Fresh Olive
Company of Provence
020 8453 1918 (mail
order)

ORGANIC
VEGETABLES
For deliveries to your
door, enquire at:
Soil Association
0117 314 5000
Organics Direct
www.organicsdirect.com

PAELLA PANS
www.the paellacompany.
com

RENNET
Westons
01273 846504
www.westonshealth.co.
uk
Ascott Smallholding
Supplies
(rennet, sausage
casings, mincers and
stuffers, yoghurt cultures
0845 130 6285
www.ascott-shop.co.uk

SUPERMARKETS
Sainsbury's
Special selection range
includes smoked
paprika, cabernet sauvi-
gnon vinegar, sherry
vinegar, paella rice, saffron, dried mushrooms,
membrillo, pomegranate
molasses and more.
Waitrose
Dried peppers and
piquillo peppers.

VINEGAR JARS
Richard Dare, NW1
020 7722 9428

VINEGAR
MOTHERS
Defalcos
Although based in
Houston, Texas, this
company will ship over-
seas by post (slow) or
courier (expensive).
(713) 668-9440
www.defalcos.com

INDEX

acili biber (Turkish pepper paste) 189

Ajo caliente 119

al ajillo method, variations on 207

Alcachofas y guisantes con oloroso 126–7

Almejas con habichuelas 80

anchovies
garum (olive sauce) 191
Grilled red pepper and anchovy salad 97
Marinated anchovies, home-made 272
Paprika and anchovy butter 189
Sea bass with anchovies and tomato and pepper sauce 182

Anise biscuits 311

Anise bread 34–5

apples, Morcilla with caramelised apple 102

apricots, Pine nuts with apricots and mint 309

argan oil 38, 60

arroces 250

Arroz a la marinera 254–5

Arroz con leche 292

Arroz de conejo 11–14

artichokes
Artichoke and potato salad with harissa 156–7
Artichokes and peas with oloroso sherry 126–7
scrambled eggs variations 141–2
Sweetbreads with artichokes, cardamom and preserved lemon 116–17
Turkish poached sweet and sour leeks 130–1
Vegetable paella with artichokes and piquillo peppers 252–3

asparagus
Asparagus with two sauces 124–5
Scrambled eggs with prawns and asparagus 141–2
Scrambled eggs with wild garlic and asparagus 20

aubergines
Aubergines with oregano and pine nuts 238
Chicken fattee with rice, crisp-bread and yoghurt 210–12
Courgette and aubergine salad with charmoula 160–1
Fried 210, 212
Fried aubergines with honey 236
Grilled aubergine salad 159–60

avocado, Cured mullet roe with avocado and dill 92

Bacalao frito 98–9

beans 55
Broad bean salad 163
Clams with white beans and saffron 80
Cuttlefish with broad beans and mint 83
Dried pea soup with cumin and argan oil 60

fava 60

Fennel, potato and white bean soup 17

Khlii with green bean salad 110

Lamb stew with white beans and coriander 221

Morels with butter beans, toma-toes and sweet herbs 123–4

Paella with chicken and prawns 250–1

Peas with ham 101

scrambled eggs variations 141–2

Turkish poached sweet and sour leeks 130–1

Turkish village soup with bread and caraway 62

White bean, chorizo and parsley soup 56

beef
Beef tagine with prunes 225
Beef with horseradish and sherry vinegar sauce 205–6
Calf's liver with oloroso sherry, pine nuts and raisins 115–16
Grilled sirloin steaks 205
guide to cooking 205–6
Moroccan preserved meat (khlii), home-made 272
Oxtail with rioja and chorizo 219–21
production methods and choices 312
Roast rib of beef on the bone 205–6
Spiced beef salad with fenugreek and hummus 104–5
Sweetbreads with artichokes, cardamom and preserved lemon 116–17

beetroot
Beetroot and potato salad with mint and spring onion 246
Warm beetroot in yoghurt 245

Berenjenas fritas 236

Bessara 60

Besugo al horno 174

Boquerones en vinagre 272

bottarga (cured grey mullet roe), Cured mullet roe with avocado and dill 92

breads and flatbreads
Anatolian stuffed flatbread 44–6
Anise bread 34–5
Barley bread 264
Basic flatbread 36
breadmaking 30
Chorizo rolls 48
Crispbread triangles 135
Empanadillas 49–50
Feta salad with anise bread, tomatoes and oregano 136
Flatbread baked in ashes 38
Flatbread with lamb, pine nuts and pomegranates 42–3
Gözleme 44–6
Molletes 31
Moroccan bread salad with grilled green peppers and tomatoes 128–9

Quick flatbread 36–7

Rustic Moroccan bread 33–4

Seed bread 32–3

Spinach with walnuts 244

Stuffed breads 44–50

Thick gazpacho 55

Turkish pizza with tomato, lamb and allspice 41–2

Turkish village soup with bread and caraway 62

Warm tomato, bread and garlic purée 119

Wet bread 31

Buey con rábano picante 205–6

bulgur (cracked wheat)
Tomato bulgur 262
Walnut and red pepper bulgur 262–3
Winter Tabbouleh 148

cabbage
Braised cabbage, panceta and chestnuts 233
Greens 19
Spring cabbage with capers, but-ter and paprika 234
Turkish poached sweet and sour leeks 130–1
Turkish village soup with bread and caraway 62
White cabbage, mint and car-away salad 156

cakes
Almond cake 27
Chocolate, chestnut and almond cake 299
Magdalenas 300–2
Old-fashioned trifle sponge 293
Pistachio and almond tart with orange and cardamom 296–7

Calamar a la parrilla 84–8

Caldo de pescado 57–8

Carne en salsa de almendras 26

carrots
Carrot purée with caraway and feta 135
Carrot salad with orange-blos-som water 162
Lentils with chorizo 267

cauliflower
Cauliflower and coriander soup 68
Cauliflower salad with tomato and cumin 161
Chickpea, cauliflower and pre-served lemon salad 153
Turkish poached sweet and sour leeks 130–1
Winter Tabbouleh 148

Celery and preserved lemon salad 166

Cerdo con membrillo 203–4

chard
Chard salad with preserved lemon and olives 163–4
Harira with chard, tomatoes and oregano 63
Lamb stew with white beans and coriander 221

charmoula 87
charmoula marinade 160–1
Courgette and aubergine salad with charmoula 160–1

cheese
Carrot purée with caraway and feta 135
Chicory salad with picos blue cheese, walnuts and Pedro Ximénez dressing 139
Courgette fritters with feta and dill 138–9
Feta salad with anise bread, tomatoes and oregano 136
Fresh home-made 278, 279
Home-made labneh (strained yoghurt cheese) 280
Winter leaves with frisée, fresh cheese, pomegranates and walnuts 14–15

chestnuts
Braised cabbage, panceta and chestnuts 233
Chocolate, chestnut and almond cake 299

chicken and other birds
Chicken and cardamom dumplings 64
Chicken braised with pine nuts, raisins and saffron 207
Chicken dumpling broth 64
Chicken fattee with rice, crisp-bread and yoghurt 210–12
chicken production methods and choices 312
Chicken stock 313
Livers with oloroso sherry, pine nuts and raisins 115–16
Paella with chicken and prawns 250–1
Partridge with oloroso sherry 218
Quail stuffed with couscous and almonds 214–16
Quail with grapes and ginger 217
Rabbit (or chicken) rice with almonds and rosemary 11–14
Roast chicken stuffed with sage and labneh 213
Roast chicken with preserved lemon 208

chickpeas
Chickpea purée 198
Chickpea, cauliflower and pre-served lemon salad 153
Chickpeas and rice 260–1
Chickpeas with pomegranate molasses 268
Harira with chard, tomatoes and oregano 63
Hummus 105
Lamb with chickpea purée and hot mint sauce 197–9
Moorish chickpea and spinach soup 59
Spiced beef salad with fenugreek and hummus 104–5
Warm pumpkin and chickpea salad with tahini 242

chicory

Chicory salad with picos blue cheese, walnuts and Pedro Ximénez dressing 139
Winter Tabbouleh 148
chilli flakes 45, 46
chilli paste, Zhoug 88
Chocos con habas 83
chorizo (Spanish paprika sausage) 100
Chorizo rolls 48
Hot chorizo salad with fino sherry 100–1
Lentils with chorizo 267
Oxtail with rioja and chorizo 219–21
White bean, chorizo and parsley soup 56
Cigalas con oloroso 77
Col con castañas 233
Coles con alcaparras 234
Collejas 19
Cordero al horno con tomillo 23–4
Cordero al romero y miel 196
Cordero con garbanzos y salsa de hierbabuena 197–9
courgettes
Courgette and aubergine salad with charmoula 160–1
Courgette fritters with feta and dill 138–9
couscous
Couscous stuffing 214
Quail stuffed with couscous and almonds 214–16

dates
Dates with coffee and cardamom 294
Orange and date salad with rosewater 300
Parsnip, yoghurt and date salad 151
desserts see puddings

eggs
Custard 294
Grilled red pepper and anchovy salad 97
Moroccan eggs with tomatoes and cumin 143
Orange flan 298
scrambled eggs (cooking technique) 141
scrambled eggs variations 141–2
Scrambled eggs with prawns and asparagus 141–2
Scrambled eggs with wild garlic and asparagus 20
Empanadillas 49–50
Ensalada de anchoas 97
Ensalada de chorizo 100–1
Ensalada de cogollos al ajillo 147
Ensalada de hinojo 150
Ensalada de patatas con oregano 22–3
Ensalada de setas 129–30
Ensaladilla rusa 120
Espárragos con dos salsas 124–5
Espinacas con nueces 244

fennel 16
Fennel, potato and orange salad

150
Fennel, potato and white bean soup 17
Fish stew with anís, fennel, saffron and almonds 173
Lentils with fennel and nettles 18
Slow-cooked fennel with dill 240
Winter Tabbouleh 148
fideos (Spanish pasta), Seafood pasta 255–6
Fiduea 255–6
fish see also seafood
(note: substitutes can be made for many of the fish in the recipes)
Baked bream with potatoes and tomatoes 174
cod, Home-salted 272
Cured mullet roe with avocado and dill 92
Deep-fried salt cod in saffron batter 98–9
Deep-fried sardine balls 186–8
Empanadilla sardine stuffing 50
Fish stew with anís, fennel, saffron and almonds 173
Fish stock 313
Galician fish soup with clams and prawns 57–8
garlic and bay marinade 178
Ginger and cardamom fish 181
ginger and cardamom marinade 181
Grilled red pepper and anchovy salad 97
Grilled sardines wrapped in vine leaves with tahini sauce 90
Hake with hot paprika dressing 179–81
Hake with lemon and bay 178–9
Home-salted cod 272
Marinated anchovies, home-made 272
Piquillo peppers stuffed with salt cod 94–5
pomegranate marinade 184
Roast skate with sherry sauce and crispy capers 170–1
Salt cod, orange and potato salad 96
Salt cod, scrambled eggs variations 141–2
Salt cod, tomato and olive salad 25
sauces for 189–91 see also individual recipes
Sea bass with anchovies and tomato and pepper sauce 182
Swordfish with pomegranate molasses 184
Wet fish rice 254–5
Flan de naranja 298
flatbreads see breads and flatbreads
fruit, seasons for 313

Gambas al ajillo 76
Gambas y setas 73
garum (olive sauce) 191
Gözleme 44–6
Greens 19
Guisantes con jamón 101
ham see jamón serrano

Harira with chard, tomatoes and oregano 63
harissa
Artichoke and potato salad with harissa 156–7
Harissa dressing 157
Home-made 282
Mussels with harissa 79
Pan-fried squid and prawns with harissa 89
Higado con oloroso 115–16
hummus, Spiced beef salad with fenugreek and hummus 104–5

ice-cream see puddings

jamón serrano (cured ham) 55
Jamón serrano and parsley sauce 125
Peas with ham 101
scrambled eggs variations 141–2

khlii (spiced, dried meat)
Home-made 275
Khlii with green bean salad 110
kirmizi biber (Turkish chilli flakes) 45, 46

labneh (strained yoghurt cheese) 213, 280
Lahmacun 41–2
lamb
Flatbread with lamb, pine nuts and pomegranates 42–3
guide to cooking 194
Harira with chard, tomatoes and oregano 63
home-made sausages 276
Lamb mechoui with cumin and paprika salt 200
Lamb steamed with preserved lemon and cumin 222
Lamb stew with white beans and coriander 221
Lamb tagine with peas and tomatoes 226
Lamb with chickpea purée and hot mint sauce 197–9
Liver with oloroso sherry, pine nuts and raisins 115–16
marinade with garlic, thyme and red wine vinegar 197
Moroccan preserved meat (khlii), home-made 272
Potato cakes stuffed with minced lamb and pine nuts 113–14
production methods and choices 312
Roast lamb with honey and rosemary 196
Roast lamb with tomatoes, potatoes and thyme 23–4
Sweetbreads with artichokes, cardamom and preserved lemon 116–17
Turkish pizza with tomato, lamb and allspice 41–2
Turkish ravioli with spiced lamb and yoghurt 106–8
leeks
Leeks with yoghurt 239
Turkish poached sweet and sour

leeks 130–1
lemon (preserved)
Celery and preserved lemon salad 166
Chard salad with preserved lemon and olives 163–4
Chickpea, cauliflower and preserved lemon salad 153
Home-made 281
Lamb steamed with preserved lemon and cumin 222
Preserved lemon and olive sauce 191
Roast chicken with preserved lemon 208
Roast red pepper, preserved lemon and caper salad 154
Sweetbreads with artichokes, cardamom and preserved lemon 116–17
Lentejas 267
Lentejas con andrajos e hinojo 18
lentils
Harira with chard, tomatoes and oregano 63
Lentils and rice 260–1
Lentils with chorizo 267
Lentils with fennel and nettles 18
Syrian lentil purée 266
limes (dried) 64, 286
Lomo con vinagre de jerez 202–3
Lubina con anchoas 182

Manti 106–8
mayonnaise 120
Saffron Alioli (garlic mayonnaise) 86–7
meat see beef; chicken and other birds; fish; lamb; pork; rabbit
Merguez 276
Merluza a la gallega 179–81
Merluza con limón 178–9
morcilla (Spanish blood sausage) 100
Lentils with chorizo 267
Morcilla with caramelised apple 102
Morcilla con manzana 102
Muhummra 189–90
mushrooms
Morels with butter beans, tomatoes and sweet herbs 123–4
Mushroom salad with sherry vinegar and oregano 129–30
Prawns and oyster mushrooms with manzanilla sherry 73
scrambled eggs variations 141–2
Vegetable paella with artichokes and piquillo peppers 252–3
Mutumma 221

onions
Crispy caramelised onions 261
Saffron potatoes 231
oranges
Blood orange and rosewater sorbet 306
Fennel, potato and orange salad 150
Orange and date salad with rosewater 300

Orange flan 298
Pistachio and almond tart with orange and cardamom 296–7
Quail with grapes and ginger 217
Salt cod, orange and potato salad 96
Seville orange ice-cream 302
organic produce, production methods and choices 312

paella 14
Paella with chicken and prawns 250–1
Rabbit rice with almonds and rosemary 11–14
Vegetable paella with artichokes and piquillo peppers 252–3
panceta, Braised cabbage, panceta and chestnuts 233
paprika
Hake with hot paprika dressing 179–81
Lamb mechoui with cumin and paprika salt 200
Lamb stew with white beans and coriander 221
Paprika and anchovy butter 189
Spring cabbage with capers, butter and paprika 234
Parsnip, yoghurt and date salad 151
Pastel de almendras 27
Patatas aliñadas 232
Patatas con azafran 231
peas
Artichokes and peas with oloroso sherry 126–7
Dried pea soup with cumin and argan oil 60
Lamb tagine with peas and tomatoes 226
Pea soup with yoghurt and mint 67
Peas with ham 101
Russian salad 120
scrambled eggs variations 141–2
peppers (fresh, green)
Moroccan bread salad with grilled green peppers and tomatoes 128–9
Paella with chicken and prawns 250–1
Prawns marinated in yoghurt and spices with wheat berries 78–9
Seafood pasta 255–6
Seafood salad 74–5
Turkish chopped salad 132
Warm potato salad with red onion and sweet vinegar 232
Wet fish rice 254–5
peppers (fresh, red)
Roast red pepper, preserved lemon and caper salad 154
Sea bass with anchovies and tomato and pepper sauce 182
Tomato and red pepper sauce 182
Turkish chopped salad 132
Walnut and red pepper bulgur 262–3
peppers (ñoras, dried) 24
Lentils with chorizo 267

Saffron potatoes 231
Salt cod, tomato and olive salad 25
Seafood pasta 255–6
Slow-cooked fennel with dill (variation) 240
Wet fish rice 254–5
peppers (piquillo)
Gem lettuce with crispy garlic 147
Grilled red pepper and anchovy salad 97
Hot chorizo salad with fino sherry 100–1
Muhummra 189–90
Piquillo peppers stuffed with salt cod 94–5
Piquillo sauce 94, 95
Sea bass with anchovies and tomato and pepper sauce 182
Tomato and red pepper sauce 182
Vegetable paella with artichokes and piquillo peppers 252–3
Perdiz con oloroso 218
pilavs 250
Pine nut, raisin and dill pilav 259
Tomato bulgur 262
Walnut and red pepper bulgur 262–3
Pimientos de piquillo rellenos con bacalao 94–5
pine nuts
Aubergines with oregano and pine nuts 238
Calf's liver with oloroso sherry, pine nuts and raisins 115–16
Chicken braised with pine nuts, raisins and saffron 207
Flatbread with lamb, pine nuts and pomegranates 42–3
Pine nut, raisin and dill pilav 259
Pine nut tarator 190
Pine nuts with apricots and mint 309
Potato cakes stuffed with minced lamb and pine nuts 113–14
pizza, Turkish pizza with tomato, lamb and allspice 41–2
Pollo al ajillo con piñones y pasas 207
Pomegranate Molasses 43
Home-made 284
pomegranates
Chickpeas with pomegranate molasses 268
Flatbread with lamb, pine nuts and pomegranates 42–3
Muhummra 189–90
Pomegranate molasses dressing 148
Pomegranate sauce 88
Sour cherry syrup with pistachio and pomegranate 309
Swordfish with pomegranate molasses 184
Tomato, walnut and pomegranate molasses salad 151
Winter leaves with frisée, fresh cheese, pomegranates and walnuts 14–15
Winter Tabbouleh 148

pork see also chorizo; jamón serrano (cured ham); morcilla
Empanadilla pork stuffing 50
Pork in almond sauce 26
Pork loin roasted with sherry and sherry vinegar 202–3
production methods and choices 312
Roast pork with quince purée 203–4
Potaje de pescado con anís 173
potatoes
Artichoke and potato salad with harissa 156–7
Baked bream with potatoes and tomatoes 174
Beetroot and potato salad with mint and spring onion 246
Fennel, potato and orange salad 150
Fennel, potato and white bean soup 17
Gözleme potato stuffing 46
Hake with hot paprika dressing 179–81
Piquillo peppers stuffed with salt cod 94–5
Potato cakes stuffed with minced lamb and pine nuts 113–14
Potato salad with oregano 22–3
Roast lamb with tomatoes, potatoes and thyme 23–4
Russian salad 120
Saffron potatoes 231
Salt cod, orange and potato salad 96
scrambled eggs variations 141–2
Warm potato salad with red onion and sweet vinegar 232
puddings
Blood orange and rosewater sorbet 306
Custard 294
Dates with coffee and cardamom 294
Jerez cream 290
Kate's sherry trifle 292–4
Orange flan 298
Prune ice-cream with oloroso sherry 310
Rice pudding 292
Seville orange ice-cream 302
Turrón and coffee ice-cream 304
Yoghurt ice-cream and toppings 308–9
pumpkin
Pumpkin salad 164
Warm pumpkin and chickpea salad with tahini 242

Rabbit rice with almonds and rosemary 11–14
Rabo de toro con rioja 219–21
Radish salad with orange-blossom water 166
Raya con salsa de jerez 170–1
Remojón 96
Revuelto de ajo porro y espárragos 20
Revueltos 141–2
rice see also paella
Chicken fattee with rice, crisp-

bread and yoghurt 210–12
Galician fish soup with clams and prawns 57–8
Lentils and rice 260–1
Pine nut, raisin and dill pilav 259
Rice pudding 292
Wet fish rice 254–5

saffron
Chickpeas with pomegranate molasses 268
Clams with white beans and saffron 80
Deep-fried salt cod in saffron batter 98–9
Fish stew with anís, fennel, saffron and almonds 173
Saffron Alioli (garlic mayonnaise) 86–7
Saffron potatoes 231
Saffron, tahini and yoghurt soup 69
Spinach with walnuts 244
salad dressings 74
dressing with zaatar 153
Harissa dressing 157
Pedro Ximénez dressing 139
Pomegranate molasses dressing 148
Sweet vinegar dressing 232
salads
Artichoke and potato salad with harissa 156–7
Beetroot and potato salad with mint and spring onion 246
Broad bean salad 163
Carrot salad with orange-blossom water 162
Cauliflower salad with tomato and cumin 161
Celery and preserved lemon salad 166
Chard salad with preserved lemon and olives 163–4
Chickpea, cauliflower and preserved lemon salad 153
Chicory salad with picos blue cheese, walnuts and Pedro Ximénez dressing 139
cooked Moroccan salads 159–66
Courgette and aubergine salad with charmoula 160–1
Courgette fritters with feta and dill 138–9
Cured mullet roe with avocado and dill 92
Fennel, potato and orange salad 150
Feta salad with anise bread, tomatoes and oregano 136
Gem lettuce with crispy garlic 147
Grilled aubergine salad 159–60
Grilled red pepper and anchovy salad 97
Hot chorizo salad with fino sherry 100–1
Khlii with green bean salad 110
Moroccan bread salad with grilled green peppers and tomatoes 128–9

Mushroom salad with sherry vinegar and oregano 129–30
Orange and date salad with rose-water 300
Parsnip, yoghurt and date salad 151
Potato salad with oregano 22–3
Pumpkin salad 164
Radish salad with orange-blossom water 166
Roast red pepper, preserved lemon and caper salad 154
Russian salad 120
Salt cod, orange and potato salad 96
Salt cod, tomato and olive salad 25
Seafood salad 74–5
Spanish 146
Spiced beef salad with fenugreek and hummus 104–5
Tomato, walnut and pomegranate molasses salad 151
Turkish chopped salad 132
Warm potato salad with red onion and sweet vinegar 232
Warm pumpkin and chickpea salad with tahini 242
White cabbage, mint and caraway salad 156
Winter leaves with frisée, fresh cheese, pomegranates and walnuts 14–15
Winter Tabbouleh 148
Salmorejo 55
Salpicón de marisco 74–5
sauces
Almond and sherry vinegar sauce 125
Black ink sauce 86
Charmoula (marinade) 87
Chickpea purée 198
garum (olive sauce) 191
Horseradish and sherry vinegar sauce 206
Hot mint sauce 198–9
Hot paprika and oil dressing 179–81
Jamón serrano and parsley sauce 125
Muhummra 189–90
Paprika and anchovy butter 189
Pine nut tarator 190
Piquillo sauce 94, 95
Pomegranate sauce 88
Preserved lemon and olive sauce 191
Quince purée 203, 204
Saffron Alioli (garlic mayonnaise) 86–7
Salmorejo (variation) 55
Sherry sauce 170
Tahini sauce 242
Tomato and red pepper sauce 182
Tomato sauce 210, 212
Tomato sauce with cumin 186–8
Zhoug (green chilli paste) 88
seafood see also fish
Black ink sauce 86
Clams with white beans and saffron 80

Cuttlefish with broad beans and mint 83
Fish stew with anís, fennel, saffron and almonds 173
Galician fish soup with clams and prawns 57–8
Garlic prawns with white wine and chilli 76
Grilled squid and sauces 84–8
Langoustines with oloroso sherry 77
Mussels with harissa 79
Paella with chicken and prawns 250–1
Pan-fried squid and prawns with harissa 89
Prawns and oyster mushrooms with manzanilla sherry 73
Prawns marinated in yoghurt and spices with wheat berries 78–9
prawns, production methods and choices 312
Scallops with breadcrumbs 176
Scrambled eggs with prawns and asparagus 141–2
Seafood pasta 255–6
Seafood salad 74–5
Wet fish rice 254–5
Sopa de garbanzos 59
Sopa de habichuelas 56
Sopa de hinojo 17
soups 54–69
Cauliflower and coriander soup 68
Chicken dumpling broth 64
Dried pea soup with cumin and argan oil 60
Fennel, potato and white bean soup 17
Galician fish soup with clams and prawns 57–8
Harira with chard, tomatoes and oregano 63
Moorish chickpea and spinach soup 59
Moroccan bessara 60
Moroccan harira 60, 63
Pea soup with yoghurt and mint 67
Saffron, tahini and yoghurt soup 69
Thick gazpacho 55
Turkish village soup with bread and caraway 62
White bean, chorizo and parsley soup 56
yoghurt soups 66–9
spinach
Chard salad with preserved lemon and olives 163–4
Gözleme spinach stuffing 46
Moorish chickpea and spinach soup 59
Spinach with walnuts 244
spring greens
Braised cabbage, panceta and chestnuts 233
Spring cabbage with capers, butter and paprika 234
squash, Pumpkin salad 164
stews 218

Beef tagine with prunes 225
Lamb steamed with preserved lemon and cumin 222
Lamb stew with white beans and coriander 221
Lamb tagine with peas and tomatoes 226
Oxtail with rioja and chorizo 219–21
sumac 45, 46

tagines 218 see also stews
tahini (sesame seed paste) 242
Tangia 222
tarator (Turkish garlicky nut sauce) 190
Tascaburras 25
tocino (pig fat), Lentils with chorizo 267
tomatoes
Baked bream with potatoes and tomatoes 174
Cauliflower salad with tomato and cumin 161
Chicken fattee with rice, crispbread and yoghurt 210–12
dried 24
Feta salad with anise bread, tomatoes and oregano 136
Grilled aubergine salad 159–60
Harira with chard, tomatoes and oregano 63
Lamb tagine with peas and tomatoes 226
Morels with butter beans, tomatoes and sweet herbs 123–4
Moroccan bread salad with grilled green peppers and tomatoes 128–9
Moroccan eggs with tomatoes and cumin 143
Roast lamb with tomatoes, potatoes and thyme 23–4
Salt cod, tomato and olive salad 25
Sea bass with anchovies and tomato and pepper sauce 182
Seafood salad 74–5
Sweet tomato jam 165
Thick gazpacho 55
Tomato and red pepper sauce 182
Tomato bulgur 262
Tomato sauce 210, 212
Tomato sauce with cumin 186–8
Tomato, walnut and pomegranate molasses salad 151
Turkish chopped salad 132
Turkish pizza with tomato, lamb and allspice 41–2
Turkish village soup with bread and caraway 62
Warm tomato, bread and garlic purée 119
turrón (Spanish nougat), Turrón and coffee ice-cream 304

vegetables 230–46 see also individual vegetables
production methods and choices 312
seasons for 313

Vegetable paella with artichokes and piquillo peppers 252–3
Vegetable stock 313
Verduras de Murcia 238
Vieiras con migas 176
vinegars 287

walnuts
Chicory salad with picos blue cheese, walnuts and Pedro Ximénez dressing 139
Muhummra 189–90
Spinach with walnuts 244
Tomato, walnut and pomegranate molasses salad 151
Walnut and red pepper bulgur 262–3
Walnuts and honey 309
Winter leaves with frisée, fresh cheese, pomegranates and walnuts 14–15
Winter Tabbouleh 148

yoghurt 66
Cauliflower and coriander soup 68
Chicken fattee with rice, crispbread and yoghurt 210–12
Dates with coffee and cardamom 294
home-made 279
labneh (strained yoghurt cheese) 280
Leeks with yoghurt 239
Parsnip, yoghurt and date salad 151
Pea soup with yoghurt and mint 67
Prawns marinated in yoghurt and spices with wheat berries 78–9
Saffron, tahini and yoghurt soup 69
Turkish ravioli with spiced lamb and yoghurt 106–8
Warm beetroot in yoghurt 245
Yoghurt ice-cream and toppings 308–9
yoghurt marinade 78

zaatar flavouring 153
Zhoug (green chilli paste) 88

For Eve

Thanks to...

SPAIN: Wendy and Alejandro Tamborero at Hotel Berchules (00 34 958769000), Peter Barbier and Laura Hook, Josefa Castillo, Hilde Creve, our neighbours Maria and Adoración, and Anton Volckaert (walk guide: 00 34 958768140), Michael Jacobs, Lidia and Milagros Flores, Chris Cooke, Monika Lavery

MORO: our partner and dear friend Mark Sainsbury, managers Danny McSorley, Claire Spellman and Sean Key, all our chefs, especially David Cook and Megan Jones, and all staff past and present at Moro

OUR WONDERFUL TESTERS, ESPECIALLY: Lisa Armour Brown, Jacob Kenedy and David Cook; also Megan Jones, Lucy Boyd, Natalie Smith and Frank O'Hanlon

DESIGN AND EDITORIAL: designer Caz Hildebrand (who is brilliant); editors Fiona MacIntyre, Lesley McOwan, Trish Burgess, Susan Fleming, Sarah Barlow and Imogen Fortes; agent Pat Kavanagh for her continued support; Mark Hutchinson for all his help with PR;

PRODUCTION: production manager Katherine Hockley

Claudia Roden and Paula Wolfert for continual inspiration; also Rose Gray and Engin Akyn

PHOTOGRAPHY: many many thanks to Simon Wheeler and Toby Glanville, and for locations to Tony and Sabrina Fry in Carmona, to Teddy and Carinthia Clarke for Dar Farnatchi, and to Steven Skinner for Riad Edward in Marrakech; also Khalid L'âaouannt and Ashuma

FAMILY, ESPECIALLY: Sarah Clarke, Celly Clark, Teddy and Carinthia Clarke, Tony and Sabrina Fry, and the team that help look after Luke and Eve: Silvana, Florrie and Joe Evans, George and Doreen Renshaw and Sarah Clarke

Moro, 34–36 Exmouth Market, London EC1.

T. 020 7833 8336 www.moro.co.uk